DIVINE
TURBULENCE

NAVIGATING THE AMORPHOUS WINDS OF LIFE

GARY LEE PRICE
MASTER SCULPTOR
WITH BRIDGET COOK-BURCH

Divine Turbulence
Navigating the Amorphous Winds of Life

Inspired Legacy Publishing is a division of (DBA) Inspired Legacy, LLC
PO Box 900816
Sandy, UT 84090-0816

ISBN 979-89860638-05 (paperback)
ISBN 979-89860638-12 (hardcover)

Visit us on line at www.GaryLeePrice.com
Printed in the United States of America.

What People Are Saying

"Gary's book is a reminder that no matter the circumstances, we can always choose how we respond.'"
—Alexander Vesely, MA, grandson of Viktor Frankl, Head of the Viktor Frankl Media Archives in Vienna, Co-founder of the Viktor Frankl Institute of America

"Gary is a world-class sculptor and artist who has made this journey for the good of us all."
—Dr. Nancy O'Reilly, Psy D., Founder and CEO of Women Connect4Good

"Gary lays himself out vulnerably, in a life that transforms pain into promise, and heartache into heartfelt inspiration."
—Jay Abraham, Founder & CEO of The Abraham Group, Inc

"This book bridges the chasm between the East Coast and the West Coast, bringing life to the dream of a man destined to breathe character into the very thinking of mankind. Viktor Frankl had the dream, Gary Lee Price had the answer."
—Gerald R. Molen, Film Producer, Academy Award Winner/Best Picture for Schindler's List

"His beautifully told story will leave you speechless, teary-eyed, and in awe of how his spirit could not be broken. I highly recommend this well-written memoir, which is worthy of the big screen."
—Dr. Connie Mariano, Rear Admiral, Former White House Doctor

"What perfect timing for this book! It illustrates the liberating power of responsibility and choice even when confronted with the worst that life has to offer."
—Brett Harward, Author, The 5 Laws That Determine All of Life's Outcomes

"This memoir carries its reader through the crucifixion of innocence to the soul's ascension; from extraordinary childhood violence, trauma, and abuse, to the medicine of divine human compassion, hope, forgiveness and the call to social justice."

    —Piper Dellums, Director, Filmmaker, Writer and Victims Advocate

"I was spellbound by this book. This is not a story you read very often, as its messages and inspiration transform you with every page you turn . . . and live."

    —Jack Berkman, CEO and President of Berkman Strategic Communications

Dedication

Never in my life have I been in such an inner quandary: Yes, No, Yes, No. YES!

First birthing, and then ultimately deciding to release this book to the public, has been difficult, to say the very least. My thought processes finally settled on a hope and a prayer. The prayer is that if this book saves one little kid out there in the world somewhere, then the pain and suffering that I went through will all be worth it. My greatest hope? That we all will become more aware and respectful of each other on our mortal, and mutual journey. Every child deserves a beautiful, peaceful, loving childhood - period!

I dedicate this memoir to my mother, Betty Jo, and the beautiful life she gifted me with. Our time together was short, Mom, but we've both done good!

—Gary

Contents

A Letter to My Readers

If you were to believe experts in the field of psychiatric disorders, what I experienced as a buoyant little boy of six means that I would have PTSD at best. At worst, they would say such tragedy could have triggered within me anything from suicidal depression and anxiety to borderline schizophrenic pathology or a sociopathic disorder.

Surviving a murder-suicide only to be thrown into the confines of a dark, secret, and predatory world at a young age—and held captive there, should have killed me off mentally.

And yet . . . something saved my mind, my heart, and my soul.

The term "amorphous" in sculpting means literally "without form" or lacking shape. Much of my young life felt amorphous, devoid of meaningful form. Yet, amidst all the senseless destruction and violence around my little self, there came an energy of *creation*: sketching, drawing, coloring and painting . . . things we determine in our society as simply art and some even deem unnecessary.

This ability to create something bigger and grander than myself, however, invoked in me an imagination and a greater vision, along with guidance and inspiration from a wellspring deep within me. It brought me much-needed hope and light. It thawed the growing coldness. Developing these visionary skills and abilities laid the foundation for me to create a better life than the one I knew. Finally, and certainly equally important, my journey through the wild squalls and tempests to become a renowned sculptor took time and practice . . .

Lots and lots of practice.

Much has been said about Michelangelo's *David* because it is so magnificent—though not as magnificent as the sculptor himself, the living and breathing creator that he was. We are each a creator. In fact, we can each master the unknown and unformed outside of us by *first* facing the amorphous within us.

We must be willing to look deep into our darkness that we might recognize our light. When we embrace both shadow and light, we hold in our hands a palette containing a full spectrum of gorgeous colors and the substance from which to form our choices and our character.

Like the block of marble from which the artist birthed the *David*, many opportunities come to us without form. They are meant for *us* to do the forming. We begin through our thoughts, and those thoughts become our actions. We must first sculpt our thoughts and let our behaviors follow. Every time, every choice; it matters.

The winds of life buffet us and blow us about. They can knock us down. It happens to everyone at some point. It happens to some more than others. And, yet, it is in the rising and shakily standing our ground that those same winds can sculpt us, etching us grain by grain, into something smoother and far more eloquent than we ever imagined.

Yes, I went through hell at a young age. Would I allow my circumstances to make me better or bitter, victim or victor? Would I allow my brokenness to be an excuse to hurt others in the way I had been so battered? Or did there exist the possibility that I could use what happened, molding it and transforming it into something of such breathtaking beauty that it could inspire and empower me, and maybe, eventually, others?

I can now acknowledge that in my darkest days, the heavens blew winds of choice upon choice, even when it seemed I had none. Yes, I was watched over. Though I was perhaps not rescued physically, I was never alone . . . even when I felt so isolated and abandoned. Even then, I was connected to the Great Spirit, who continued to provoke the muse inside of me.

Out of all this, one great question arose: *What would I do with what I had been given?*

I did not know that there was a gift in the hardness, the challenges, the difficulties. I did not know that in our darkness lie the seeds to our greatest glory. It not only became my responsibility but ultimately my greatest destiny, to explore the mystery and learn to navigate . . . *divine turbulence.*

Double Jeopardy

"Death is the dropping of the flower that the fruit may swell."
—Henry Ward Beecher

In Benjamin Franklin Village, one of the dense military housing complexes at the U.S. Army base in Mannheim-Heidelberg, my family might as well have been living in a fishbowl. We were surrounded by those who could hear the peals of laughter from my baby brother Billy. Unfortunately, they could also hear my mother and stepfather's fights as easily as I could in the next room.

Mom and Ted didn't fight every day—just often enough to make me uncomfortable, especially when drinking red wine and other horrible-smelling stuff.

I knew my mom was beautiful, but I was too little to notice that men stared in fascination wherever she went. The neighbors said she and Ted were a handsome sight together, and Ted always softened when she dressed all pretty, her attention focused on him. She was at her most dolled up when they went out dancing with other couples from the base, one of their favorite pastimes. It was 1961, a time when Elvis Presley, Chubby Checker, Bobby Lewis, Patsy Cline, the Edsels, the Marcels, and Roy Orbison were all the rage.

Mom looked forward to their nights out each week. Despite the gossip I sometimes overheard about my parents' squabbles, people spoke of Ted as charming and seemed to like him. He had a ready smile, but to me, he seemed almost shy until he tipped back those couple of beers with his buddies. It only took one or two and he became exceptionally playful. He'd order me over to him, give me a hug, and tickle me before turning me loose, laughing as he messed up the dark curls on my head. I had more hair than he did because even though mine was short, his dark hair was military scarce, cropped close to the scalp like all the other men here.

As funny as he was when he drank, I liked my stepdad best when he was sober. I smiled when he and Mom held each other and kissed. He often made my mother laugh, which I liked, especially when it reached her eyes.

I liked it when my mom was happy, and she seemed as happy with Ted as I had ever seen her.

But not this afternoon. Something was wrong.

Mom tried to carry on like normal. While my baby brother napped, she set aside her white bone-china plates. Carefully, she folded back the pristine, ivory-colored linen tablecloth far enough to let me color to my heart's content—well, at least until dinner. Taking a few minutes as she did each afternoon, she pulled me up onto her lap. Today, Mom showed me how to mix the primary colors of red, blue, and yellow to make additional color palettes of purples, oranges, and browns. My mouth fell open in surprise. Suddenly I had a small array of colors at my fingertips! Each waxy scratch of a crayon over another filled me with awe and wonder.

It was here in this small kitchen where Mom constantly shared with me the gift of imagination. We sketched and colored, bringing forms to life. We made the dog look so real he could bark and the sky so blue it begged for a cloud. Recently, Mom had introduced me to ballpoint pens, and I was fascinated with the precise way I could now draw lines, especially with the use of a ruler.

I continued mixing colors, enthralled by this new magic, as my mother scooted me off her lap and began pacing the linoleum floor. Kneeling on my chair for added height, I hunched over sheet after sheet of paper as my mother bustled about the kitchen.

At one point, I looked up to see her wringing her hands and pushing her stylish, dark curls from her furrowed brow as she paced, glancing nervously out the window. I stared at her for a moment, noticing how escaping wisps of dark hair framed a face that was enchanting even before she powdered her nose and freshened her lipstick. As the early August sun began setting in a golden sky, I didn't need a clock to recognize the shadows growing in the tall, military apartment complex—and in her eyes.

I didn't understand what was wrong. I just knew that something had to be. I was used to my mother's rising anxiousness in the late afternoons, but usually, it was mixed with excitement. This was the time of day Ted was due to arrive home from his work on base, just minutes away by car. Mom would make sure everything was spick-and-span and have something delicious cooking in the oven or on the stovetop.

My stillness broke Mom's pacing. She gathered herself and stepped closer to inspect my work. "Well done, Gary!" she cried, and snatching one of the melded-color pictures I had finished, she proudly put it on the fridge with a bright yellow magnet, joining a myriad of my other drawings.

Outside, I could hear neighbors chatting in English as the troops finished up their day at work and headed back to relax at their barracks and apartments. The Village was a city within the city, where ten thousand Americans lived and worked. Resting on two hundred acres between the Funari and Sullivan Barracks, Benjamin Franklin housed about two thousand homes, kindergartens, schools, playgrounds, a clinic, a movie theater, a church, a hotel, businesses, clubs, and sporting facilities.

Just ten years before I was born, U.S. forces had wrested the region from the Third Reich. Although we resided in what was then West Germany, most of our neighbors hailed from the States. Mom said it only felt like a foreign country when we headed twenty minutes away into the heart of the historic city of Heidelberg, nestled in the mountains. That is when she would open the world to me, through an adventure of senses that included the awe-inspiring sights, smells, and tastes of Germany.

"Gary," she would encourage, her emerald eyes sparkling, "Greet the storekeepers with *guten tag*! It means hello, or good day." She always smoothed my dark, unruly curls out of my eyes so I could see. "All right, my little man," she would remind me when shopkeepers let me have a taste of their sweets or breads or hot chocolate. "Say *danke schön*. It means thank you."

Everything was a feast along the cobblestone streets and sweet shops. I plugged my nose at the pungent odor inside the butcher's shop but loved the sensuous, buttery smells of the bakeries. My ears captured the rapid, guttural-sounding language, and my eyes devoured the architecture, a blend of old and new. On our way home, Mom and I always picked one aspect of the day's quest to capture on paper. It became our chronicle of adventure. She looked at one of these drawings now, my interpretation of the *Alte Brücke*, or Old Bridge.

Still, I didn't think she was seeing its arches crossing the wide Neckar River, which I colored in blue. She seemed very far away.

Suddenly, Billy's cry erupted from the bedroom he and I shared.

"Pumpkin's up!" Mom gave me a wink before striding down the hall. Seconds later, she emerged with the baby on her hip and tender, singsong noises in her throat. My little brother's dark hair stuck straight up on one side, his face still red and puckered from sleep. I made a face at him, and he grinned at me, turning his head toward me as Mom marched back to the stove. She checked on something stewing that smelled delicious.

Tonight, Mom was preparing to go out with Ted, so the delicious dinner was all for me and the baby. Satisfied, she turned and placed Billy in his highchair and nestled him right up to the table.

Billy's inquisitive, chubby fingers grasped for my colorful papers, but I was too fast. "Oh no, you don't!" I giggled. An expert now at saving my artwork from the baby, I quickly swooshed my papers out of his reach. He began to protest until Mom gave him a hard biscuit to chew on. Within moments he was soothed, slobber drooling down the sides of the biscuit.

Officially, Billy was my stepbrother as he came from Mom and my stepfather, but to me, he was just my little brother. A growing toddler, Billy was starting to walk and talk. He laughed most when I played with him. He cried when he took a tumble, which was all the time.

"Uhh . . . Gawy! Uhh!" Billy grinned, pointing. He wanted me to show him my artwork. He especially liked animals, so I selected one with two colors of purpling sky and two colors of sun over a green landscape and grazing horse.

"Gary, put your crayons away and wash your hands." I could hear the anxiousness in Mom's voice as she glanced out the window again.

I grumbled, but only because of the battle between my heart and my stomach. I wanted to keep coloring! Yet I was hungry enough to eat the horse I had just drawn. I carefully placed the nubs of crayons into the small cardboard box with my growing stack of artwork and raced off to wash my hands.

As I scurried back toward the kitchen, ready to sit down, my stepdad opened the front door to our apartment. Just outside the door, I could see the light filtering into the alcove where the front doors of the apartments across from us stood. Ted slowly shut the door, smiling as my mother greeted him with a return smile and a lingering kiss.

With Ted home, Mom fed and bathed Billy and me, and I played with my military frogmen, the baking soda inside making them rise with the bubbles. We were ready for the sitter, and as my mother gave her instruction, I was proud of being a lot older and that I could stay up a whole half hour longer than Billy.

Before she grabbed her wrap, my mother tipped back her glass holding the deep, red liquid I was never allowed to have. It made her breath smell warm and fruity when she lighted little kisses on my cheek. She tightly hugged me goodbye and strolled out the door Ted held open for her.

I just hoped it would be one of their good nights.

Late that night, I was fast asleep in bed when I was awakened without warning, my mother shaking me.

"I need your help, Gary!" she whispered frantically. Sleepily, I took her hand as she led me out of the bedroom so as not to wake Billy.

On our way down the small, hardwood hallway, I glanced into my mom's bedroom, lit from overhead. I stopped short, even though Mom was still tugging on my arm. My eyes were riveted to the bed, where the mattress was nearly half off the box springs, as if an earthquake had knocked it loose!

Alarm bells started going off in my head, especially at my mother's shaking hands as she led me into the living room. She perched on the big mohair chair and stood my little body right across from her, keeping my arm around her neck as she looked me straight in the eyes.

"Your stepdad and I have been in an argument," she whispered, her eyes wild and urgent. "It was bad, Gary Lee. It was really bad. He told me to dance with another man, and when I did, he became so very angry! I don't know what to do, little guy. What should I do?"

At first I didn't know what to say. I felt a huge weight of responsibility. I stood there dumbfounded, watching her wring her hands. We heard a noise outside our door, and she jumped, but it was just some people walking by, laughing and talking. Immediately, Mom snapped her attention back to me, the fear in her eyes even more evident.

"Go lock the front door!" I ordered, my heart pounding, not even thinking about Ted having keys. "Go lock it, Mom, and make sure it's good and locked. And no matter what, don't let him in."

When she came back from doing that, I finally noticed by the lamplight that Mom's normally perfect hair was riotously askew, and her lipstick was smeared across one section of her jaw. Dark mascara dripped from the corners of her eyes. I looked more closely as it seemed like one cheek was bruised, but I didn't know if it was makeup. I just wanted to wrap my arms around her and protect her. Instead, I felt my mother squeeze me tight as she took a steadying breath. Finally, she reassured me that everything would be okay before she took me back into the bedroom I shared with the baby.

I glanced at her worriedly as she tucked me into bed. I hoped she would heed my warning and not let Ted back into the apartment. I knew once the alcohol wore off, he'd be back to his regular self.

Willing my wildly beating heart to still, I reassured myself with the knowledge that they got in disagreements like this all the time. Just last week when I was headed out to meet my buddy from kindergarten to play a game, I overheard the woman from downstairs talking about my parents. "Ted was at Betty again last night. He is always jealous of any man even looking at her! And that Betty . . . well, she is always trying to prove to him that she's devoted and that he has nothing to be jealous about."

They bicker, I thought, cuddling back into my blankets. *They bicker, and they always get over it. In a few days, it will be fine again. It always is.*

Once, just once, I had felt the measure of Ted's wrath. I'd said the word *damn* outside when I thought it was just me and my friends. Instead of giggling, their faces turned pale with shock. I looked up into the eyes of Ted. I was in trouble despite the fact it was everyday language for our fathers. My stepdad ordered me into the apartment where I dropped my drawers and he proceeded to use his khaki army belt on my backside.

After that day, I certainly did "watch my language." Even as the neighborhood ringleader, I no longer just blurted out what I wanted to say to my army of cohorts. I also noticed how, after a fight, Mom minded her p's and q's as well. *It will be all right,* I said to myself again.

Finally, after long moments of silence, I fell asleep.

Sometime later, I shot up out of bed.

What had I heard? *Was that a scream?*

Startled, I raced out of the bedroom into the hallway, my pajamaed feet skidding on the floor. How long had it been since Mom had put me back to bed?

My heart froze when I saw that the front door was open. It was supposed to be locked! Out of the corner of my eye, I saw movement from the direction of the kitchen and heard another sound, like the crashing of the silverware drawer. However, my attention was riveted to the form slumped across the foyer in front of our neighbor's door. I ran out.

There was my mother, lying on her back in an expanding pool of blood. I felt immediately sick at the sight.

Desperately, I bent over and looked into her beautiful green eyes. Why were they bloodshot? She was staring at me, but quite suddenly there was an ebb: no emotion showed in her gaze. I wanted to reach down and comfort her and hold her, but the blood scared me. I just couldn't. She still looked right into my eyes, but there was no conversation. The blood continued pooling under her, getting bigger and bigger.

"Mom!" I shrieked. "Mom! Mommy! Get up! Get UP, Mom! MOMMY!" I kept screaming, distraught. *She has to get up. She just has to*! Something was terribly wrong. I didn't dare move, but I knew I needed to help her get up so we could fix what was bleeding, like she did for me when I skinned my knees.

I didn't notice when our neighbor's door opened tentatively. I didn't feel the cooling night breeze or take in anything around me. I was still crying for my mom to get up. Hands yanked on me, pulling me away from the blood, taking me from my mother. I struggled a little and had to glance behind me, but adults had surrounded her, so I could not see her. Finally, adult voices around me calmed me down.

"It's going to be okay, Gary."

"Shh, little one," said another voice. "It's going to be all right. You'll see."

Those words were whispered over and over, somehow comforting me, though my heartbeat still hammered in my chest.

"But . . . Mom?" I asked, my eyes wide.

"It's going to be okay," they said. "People have come to help." The sounds of running footsteps mixed with tense but muted tones of people calling out to each other. They seemed as far away as the sirens in the distance. Still, Ted didn't come and get me to take me home. A few minutes later and I was whisked into an unfamiliar little bed with pink sheets. Only a short while after, my sleeping baby brother was placed beside me. Now I couldn't fidget, and I *had* to be quiet or Billy would wake up. I knew how unhappy my parents would be if I woke the baby.

Resigned, I just watched everything around me with wide eyes. I was in a girl's room, but the light was too dim to focus on pictures or posters on the wall. A couple who was friends with my parents joined the group and looked in on me. They too whispered that everything was going to be okay. They left the tiny lamp in the room on for me, and not for a moment was I left alone, even with Billy.

"It's going to be okay," they all kept saying, stroking my hair and forehead.

"Your mom is at the hospital," one woman finally said quietly. "You'll see her later."

The hospital. Oh, good. I remembered talking about the hospital in my kindergarten class. *The hospital is where they help people. Mom really will be okay.*

Many Mourn Double Death in Germany
Hailey Times, Idaho, August 10, 1961
Tragedy came into the life of Mr. And Mrs. John Reeder of Hailey

on Monday afternoon with sudden and crushing force when they were informed by the U.S. Defense Department that their son S/Sgt George Theodore (Ted) Reeder, 26, and his wife Betty Jo, 28, were both killed by gunfire as the result of a calamitous argument Sunday night at their family home in West Germany, some four miles from Mannheim. Press reports stated that Ted Reeder had fired three shots from a pistol into his wife's back as she attempted to escape from their home: then the Hailey young man used the pistol to end his own life.

S/Sgt. Ted Reeder was stationed at Mannheim, Germany with Company C. First Battle Group of the 18th Infantry. And sharing the couple's home were Garvey (sic) L. Price, six-year-old stepson of Reeder; and their year-old baby son William T. Reeder.

Both little boys are being cared for by nearby servicemen's families at the present: but the youngsters orphaned with such stunning swiftness are to be brought to Hailey and very likely make their home with Mr. and Mrs. John Reeder.

Ted Reeder was born at Hailey on March 2, 1935 and graduated from Hailey high school with the class of 1953. During his high school career, he was a varsity player on the Wolverine football team for two seasons, active in student drama and a member of the Thespian club.

He joined the local national guard unit when he was 17 years old and still in school. And after getting his high school diploma in May of 1953 he enlisted in the regular army a few months later. He was assigned to overseas duty in 1954 and served 15 months on foreign soil before being discharged. Ted spent one summer at the family home, then decided to re-enlist and has been advancing steadily in rank as a regular Army serviceman.

The marriage of Ted Reeder and Betty Jo Price was solemnized in a ceremony performed Jan 25, 1959 in Seattle. Shortly after their marriage, the couple and young Garvey L. Price moved to Germany to make their home.

Mrs. Betty Jo Reeder was a native of Oklahoma and was born in the Sooner state on July 20, 1933. She became a resident of San

Francisco at an early age, and her schooling and nurses training were in a Catholic school in the Bay area. Both Betty Jo and her husband were of the Catholic faith. . . . No word has been received as of Thursday morning on funeral plans or whether the McGoldrick Funeral Home is to receive the bodies of both victims or only the remains of Ted Reeder.

Unwanted Adventure

"It cannot be seen, cannot be felt,
Cannot be heard, cannot be smelt,
It lies behind stars and under hills,
And empty holes it fills,
It comes first and follows after,
Ends life, kills laughter."
—*J.R.R. Tolkien, The Hobbit*

I jolted awake, gasping as the plane touched down. The loud roar of the engine had kept me asleep during much of the flight. Startled, I now looked into the kind eyes of Sergeant Gay.

"Are you ready?" the uniformed man winked as the plane came to a final stop. "Let's use your big muscles to grab the luggage." I had only met this stranger in his dress uniform and his wife, right before they escorted us on the two long flights, first across the ocean to the Eastern Seaboard, then on the final flight out west. As his wife held a squirming Billy, Sergeant Gay let me help him lower our two small cases to the aisle. I felt important. Inside were the only clothes and toys Billy and I brought with us. Fortunately for us, my mother's dear friend Fran Klassen, who'd let us stay with her for a few days after Mom and Ted's big fight, let me pick our favorite outfits and the toys I knew Billy liked best.

I'd been grateful for Fran's kindness, but I couldn't help but wonder, *Where is Mom?* I hadn't been taken to any hospital to see her. Ted never came to get us either. Confused, I latched on to the one thing I had been told that gave me hope: Mom was being cared for in the hospital and I would see her soon.

Within minutes of touchdown, I was peering up into the wrinkled faces of people I barely recognized—Ted's mom and dad, Grandma and

Grandpa Reeder. They thanked Sergeant Gay and his wife before whisking Billy and me up and away.

On the long and mountainous drive to Billy's grandparents' home in Idaho, I noticed their faces were pinched. They were nearly silent the whole way, rarely speaking between themselves. I found myself longing for their words. Just like at Fran's, I wanted, needed, an explanation, tired of police and adults who wouldn't share anything with me.

We passed a cemetery in the afternoon sun, and Grandma Reeder turned her back to it and stared in the other direction. Both my grandparents seemed hunched over and heavy, their faces etched with something I couldn't name but somehow felt.

Compared to our apartment in Germany, the Reeders' home was spacious, with beautiful views of the Idaho mountains around it. With a pang, it reminded me, a little, of Heidelberg's mountains and rivers. We settled in a little, but within a day, I felt stifled, tired of being shut up tight in the house. With few toys, it was hard for Billy and me not to touch anything despite strict orders.

Still, Grandma Reeder doted on us from her cast-iron stove in the kitchen. We were well-fed over the next few days. Food quickly became synonymous with comfort and assuaged my boredom. I welcomed whatever she gave me.

On a bright morning within days of our arrival, I sat playing on my rump on the floor of the small living room with Billy. When I rolled a ball to him, he would try to roll it back in a fit of giggles. I'd spent the last few days ignoring the adults coming and going. Just like at Fran's house, too many shot me glances that made me uncomfortable. A few tried very hard to talk with me. I knew they were being kind, but I wasn't sure what to say or how to act. I hoped no more would come today.

Disappointed, I glanced up as a knock sounded at the door. When Grandma opened it, a tall, lanky man entered. I purposely glanced away and focused on Billy. Without a word, the man slowly and carefully got down on his haunches so he was at eye level with me as I stood to be polite.

I peered into his eyes, and then I knew.

Wayne, I remembered. *Oh, my gosh, it's my dad!*

The whole world suddenly went away as I walked slowly into my father's now outstretched and waiting arms. It would be decades before I knew the full truth of what had happened, but it didn't matter at that moment. I couldn't find Mom, but as Dad's arms enfolded me, a part of me felt that maybe I had come home.

"We'd better get going, Gary Lee," Dad quietly apologized a few minutes later. "We have a long way to go before dark. Montpelier is in Idaho but 240 miles away, and it will take us awhile in my baby." He chuckled dryly, pointing through the living room window to the '57 Ford Fairlane parked at the curb.

My eyes went wide. It was stunning! Two-toned pale yellow and white with long tailfins, it looked straight out of a science-fiction movie. It was cool. In that moment, a memory washed over me: the smell of green, green grass and my father's throaty laugh. . . the sensation of him picking me up and twirling me around and around in a series of my giggles, then clutching me tightly to him in a hug. Momentary joy washed over me. But leaving? I looked over at Billy and had to go pick him up.

"Can't we take him?" I asked for the third time. All three adults shook their heads but offered no explanation. As I clutched my little brother to me, I felt pain pricking at my eyes. Billy was to stay with Grandma and Grandpa Reeder in the house where Ted grew up. I was to go with my father.

I suddenly didn't want to leave my brother. I was also scared, not knowing a soul in Montpelier except my dad. I began feeling numb.

"Goodbye, Billy," I finally whispered in my squirming brother's ear. I set him down as carefully as I could. "You be a good boy."

"Gawy bubba. Gawy bubba," babbled Billy.

"Yes, I am your brother. Gary will always be your brother," I promised him fiercely. Just then, Dad quickly stepped up to take something from Grandma Reeder. It was my little suitcase. I didn't even know she'd packed it! I felt suddenly unanchored again as we all walked out to Dad's car. Everyone seemed to know what was going on except me and Billy.

Dad strode to the Fairlane, hefted my small suitcase into the back, and secured it. Shutting the heavy trunk, he shook my grandparents' hands and turned on his heel without a word. Grandpa Reeder just stood there. My grandmother gave me a squeeze on the shoulder.

"Climb up there now, Gary. You listen to your father and be a good boy."

Be a good boy. Just like what I'd told Billy.

The purr of the car's powerful motor abruptly captured my attention. The interior of the car was classy, with silver piping around seats that were surprisingly hot in the mid-August sun. As soon as I climbed in and Grandma shut the door, I noticed the car smelled of gasoline and cigarettes. The aroma was oddly comforting; I was hit with a melancholy ache for my mother, who smoked. Swallowing hard, I waved goodbye to Billy.

Dad remained still and quiet as we drove through the small-town streets of Hailey. I felt like I had to hold on tight as he sped around corners. The engine did not sound anything like the *chug* of Mom and Ted's new dark-blue Volkswagen in Germany. No, this was different, and it felt powerful. I loved the purr of Dad's Fairlane even before he pushed the accelerator to join traffic on a two-lane highway. Having settled at a steady speed except on steep hills, my father finally glanced over at me, his eyes sad but kind.

"I've never been much of a talker," Dad said, his voice apologetic. In fact, he didn't say much more as we rolled along. Occasionally he smoked a cigarette, flicking the ashes into the full ashtray built into the dashboard. Stopping for gas a second time, he let me get a can of pop to go along with the handmade tuna-and-egg salad sandwiches he said his wife had made for us to eat while we drove.

Miles of railroad tracks wound beside us as we drove parallel to them on the highway. As we rounded one hill, we came upon a long freight train. I tried to count the innumerable cars as Mom had taught me. *Seventeen, eighteen, nineteen . . .* Dad noticed me craning my neck to get a better look.

"You like that train, Gary? Well, guess what? I work for one of the largest railroads in the entire United States! You'll be able to see some of it. We have nearly four hundred engines and seventy thousand cars."

I stopped counting and stared at my dad. These were the most words that had come out of his mouth the whole drive thus far, his voice passionate and his face alight.

He nodded at me and continued. "I'm a telegrapher," Dad said proudly. I didn't know what that meant, so he explained that he did many things, like counting engines and rail cars and managing traffic when two or more trains traveled on the same track.

"See, I tell them which one is the *superior* train and which one is the *inferior* train—the one that has to pull over on a side piece of track so the superior train can pass. My job is making sure that everyone and everything arrives safely at the train station."

He flicked his cigarette again. "My job is important," he added gravely. "Without what I do, trains could crash into each other, and, believe me, that's not a pretty sight."

My eyes went wide, and I shook my head, thinking of the destruction two full-speed engines crashing head-on might wreak. As I sat there, picturing it, a deep and sudden sense of foreboding passed over me.

Under the hot afternoon sky lay miles of scorched grass and desert plains, along with golden fields of wheat and alfalfa. We drove through tree-dotted hills and a couple of mountain passes before we pulled into the small town of Montpelier.

I stared and stared all around me as we slowed. On the main street of this small, Idaho town, colorful red and yellow brick buildings lined up like sentinels. I noticed most of them were two-story, although a few were a bit taller. The town was a mixture of small homes, very small homes, prominent businesses, and a lot of farmlands.

Still, I was fascinated; every block was different. We passed a sprawling, yellowish brick building with some playground equipment. "That's AJ Winters Elementary School," Dad explained. "You will be joining the first-grade class there on Monday."

My heart abruptly panged in bewilderment, and I suddenly missed my school friends in Germany. *I am going to attend school here?* The slow car ride suddenly felt like it was going all too fast.

"You're going to like it, Gary Lee," said my father, "and you'll like

Nellie and Craig too. Nellie is my new wife. We've been married for a couple of years now. And then there's Craig. He is Nellie's son, and he lives with us. He's excited to have a little brother."

I had no idea who Nellie and Craig were. I had never even seen pictures. It felt so strange to just be meeting someone I was going to live with. *How long will I be here?* I had gone from place to place, and I still didn't understand why Billy couldn't be with me. Wasn't family supposed to stay together?

Again, my mother was never mentioned, just this Nellie and Craig.

Despite my feelings of anxiety, I started to get excited at the prospect of having an older brother. I loved Billy, but he couldn't do a lot yet. An older brother? Despite myself, I felt a lifting of my heart. An older brother could be fun!

We both went quiet again, and I just took everything in, my eyelids glued open. Montpelier was surrounded by mountains, too, but these weren't nearly as tall or as close as the mountains in Hailey. I was sad to see there were not as many trees, either. The hillsides and mountains were much drier, mostly covered in dirt, boulders, and scraggly sage. At least there were trees lining the streets of certain neighborhoods. I was relieved to see their beauty—that fragrant, living green I loved to color in Germany.

Just then, Dad pointed up to a large white *M* clearly etched upon the mountainside. The letter was so huge, like a guardian over the whole town; it took my breath away. "This way you can always know you are home, Gary." There was tenderness in his voice until he cleared it, explaining that many local towns had letters built into the mountainside, representing the name of the city or high school.

I nodded. *Too bad it's not a G.*

We pulled around a corner and abruptly stopped on Main Street in front of a two-story, redbrick building nestled right next to what Dad said was the only pool hall in town. Before we even emerged from the speedster, I could smell french fries, and it made my stomach growl. There was a large sign marking the "Kit Kat Café," and I hoped he was taking me there to eat. Once we got out, however, Dad avoided the glass door to the restaurant and instead hauled my suitcase inside and up a narrow flight of stairs to the top floor. I tiptoed in after my father, realizing this must be where I would be living.

The main area was filled with a small kitchen—much smaller than my kitchen in Germany. Still, it was adjacent to the dining room table and living room area with its big, overstuffed chairs. It gave the ambiance of being nice and open despite how tiny it was.

The first thing I noticed was how much of the town I could see from the corner front windows. The street was filled with more of the red and yellow brick buildings, but farther out, neighborhoods, barns, and other signs of a more rural life intertwined with the edges of the small city. Dad told me neither he nor Nellie owned the café below. But Nellie had once cooked there, so she knew the owners well.

"It's an affordable apartment while Nellie and I are saving for our own home." He shrugged in explanation. He came and stood beside me, looking out at the deepening evening sky. "I figure there's less than a thousand people here, but it's a good town, Gary. Folks care about each other here."

As if on cue, two people rounded the corner from the hallway. One was a blonde woman with friendly eyes and a kind smile. *Nellie*, I remembered. She made a sound and came over to hug me. In a fraction of a second, I could tell how extraordinarily strong she was before she held me at arm's length. She looked me in the eyes as if she were searching for something, but just as I started to look away, she brightened.

"We're glad you are here, Gary Lee. I bet you're hungry! You two missed dinner. Craig and I saved you some. Why don't you wash your hands, and we'll get something in your tummy? Then we'll show you where you will be sleeping."

I nodded, but I wasn't paying attention. Instead, I was gawking at the other person in the room. He was a boy, all right, but nowhere close to my age. Lean and wiry, Craig was taller than Nellie by a foot—and at least a couple of feet taller than I was! He looked to be preteen, with dark, close-cropped hair that made his cheekbones even more prominent in his handsome face. He was dressed nicely in Levi's and a long-sleeved, button-down western shirt that brought out his brown eyes. Those eyes seemed friendly enough and were alight with curiosity. As we ate homecooked food, I found myself alight with my own curiosity. Nellie told me about herself. She was gentle, although her voice was rough from cigarettes.

"Wayne and I both work night shifts, so you're going to have to get used to us not being around a lot after dinner," she said almost apologetically. "We both took tonight off, but we work every night except Sundays and Mondays. That means we will be sleeping during the day while you're at school. You'll be fine, though," she added quickly as my eyes widened. " Craig will be home with you every night, and he'll walk you to school on your first day."

Unlike my mom, Nellie seemed a little tattered around the seams. Although her hair was carefully coiffed, both she and Wayne were much more casually dressed than my mom and Ted ever were. From the time she warmed up dinner, she had a cigarette in her hand. She called herself a "smokestack," and I was genuinely surprised to see how many times she lit up during our little conversation alone. My mother never smoked that much!

Craig was nice and asked me a lot of questions about Germany. I answered as best I could. Everyone here also seemed to tread lightly around the subject of my mom and Ted.

After dinner, Nellie showed me where I would be sleeping. She talked a lot more than Dad and chatted amicably with me about my new school while I bathed.

"I checked, and Mrs. Anderson will be your first-grade teacher. She's related to your dad and lives just a few blocks away. She's really nice, and she's excited to have you in class." The more she talked about the school, the more it seemed like Montpelier was like our fishbowl complex at the Mannheim army base, except even smaller. Everyone seemed to know just about everyone else.

At the thought, I suddenly felt it hard to breathe as the accumulated anxiety rose in my chest. Just a few days before, I had been in Germany. There was my parents' fight, then staying at Fran's, then Grandma and

Grandpa Reeder's, and now I would be going to a new school in just two days. It made my head spin.

"I looked through your clothes, and I think they'll be fine for school," Nellie assured me. "But when we can afford it, we're going to have to buy you a pair of blue jeans so you can play with your friends in the schoolyard." She looked up at Dad, who watched from the hallway as he nodded. I tried to concentrate on what she was saying, but I couldn't keep my eyes open. I nearly drifted off to sleep in the bath before Nellie pulled me out, helped me don clean underwear and pajamas, and tucked me into bed.

"Good night, Gary," she said softly.

"Good night," I answered sleepily, and remembered no more.

By the next night, however, I was not okay. Nellie and Dad had left for work. I kept fighting to go to sleep, listening to the soft snoring of the only other body within the boxed walls of the small apartment, once he'd finally gone to bed late into the night. I kept wishing for my heart to still and my brain to stop whirling. It was dark—too dark, and I whipped my head around like a trembling mouse in a den of wolves.

I had never admitted it to my mother or my friends, but I'd been afraid of the dark in Germany. Here, the pitch-black corners and unfamiliar shadows seemed to writhe and twist menacingly, especially whenever a lonely car would pass, headlights illuminating the windows and bounding along the walls. The longer I stayed awake, the more panicked I became. The shadows seemed to taunt me.

I ached for my mother. I missed her every single day, but tonight with my whole life's breath, I wanted to bury my face in her neck and for her to wrap her warm arms around me and take me out of this place. I wanted to hear her voice as she sang and danced to the radio and watch her eyes sparkle with laughter. I wanted her to take me into town and teach me more German words. I wanted her to set me on her lap to paint and draw and color and glue, her hands always guiding mine to the next step. Oh, how I wanted her to be guiding me now! It had only been a week or so since I had last seen her, but it felt like forever.

A tear spilled down my cheek and joined the others in the wetness of my pillow. I felt lost and ungrounded. Even the smells of this place were abrasive and unfamiliar.

Mommy, I miss you!

Where are you?

Why don't you come for me?

Into the Fire

"If you truly believe love conquers all, try to give a kiss to a rattlesnake."
—*Erik Tanghe*

Over the next several weeks, time lost its relevance. Many relatives swept in and out, showering me with unwanted attention, with more whispered comments in the corners. Most of these relatives were on my dad's side. Nellie's aunt came by, as well as her sister, who had a pinched look to her face. I did enjoy seeing Grandma and Grandpa Price from Gooding, Idaho, because their warmth and kindness were somewhat familiar and cozy to me. They radiated gentleness, like my dad.

My new brother, Craig, had seemed to welcome all the new attention to our family at first, along with the sweets and toys that came with the company. But once or twice, I could not help but notice a sour twist in his smile. I did not understand why. I just wanted people to go away, especially when I could not find my mom among the crowds of faces. Every time the doorbell rang, my heart filled with hope, only to be dashed again.

My feet felt slippery and tenuous. School began to be the only thing that felt solid. Although first grade at AJ Winters Elementary was certainly different from the school on the military base in Germany, the familiar, everyday routine was something I could count on. Mrs. Anderson's classroom was warm and inviting, and I especially liked how kind she was. Her broad smile and the twinkling eyes behind her cat-eye spectacles greeted me every morning and after every recess. It made a difference. I was, frankly, overwhelmed by the newness of everything and found it nearly impossible to concentrate in class.

Fortunately, when the bell rang during recess, I had free time. Once, I would have roughhoused with the boys outside, probably as the ringleader, and enrolled them in my superhero games. Now, I sought permission to quietly play with colorful wood blocks, Lincoln Logs, and Tinker

Toys. I had enjoyed these in Germany, but now I became absorbed in them—in fact, nearly obsessed with them. Anything I could feel, any tactile surface beneath my fingers, consoled me. It was as if I *needed* this.

In fact, when I could not be building, erecting, drawing, or coloring, I would find myself panicking slightly. Just like in the night, disturbing images would materialize in my mind. I had to fight the screaming in my head, the crashing of what sounded like silverware, even as our nice teacher instructed us on how to add numbers and explained simple sentence structure. As I fought the trembling in my little body, I would grip the solidness of the pencil and, white-knuckled, draw something on paper that eased my shaking and took me into another world.

When I got home from school, I was okay until after dinner, when Dad and Nellie left and the darkness came. The sun was setting earlier as fall set in fast. While the aroma of french fries from the café below during the day made my tummy growl, at night, the apartment reeked of old fryer grease mixed with cigarettes. It made me nauseated.

I mostly saw Nellie in the early mornings, arriving home from work, ready to collapse just as Craig and I prepared for school, then later in the evenings as she cooked dinner for the family before she and Dad left for their night jobs a few miles away. Craig and I were under strict orders during the day to let them sleep when they were home. Kind but firm, they threatened we were never to wake them unless we were losing an eye or a limb.

Nellie was obviously a hard worker. She had muscles where most women seemed soft. Although so different from my mother, I was grateful when she cooked for us, and I appreciated her occasional hugs. My biggest comfort at home and school was food. The smell of the cafeteria cooking at the elementary school made me look forward to lunch, especially the homemade, fluffy white rolls and once a week, the special cinnamon rolls for dessert.

Nothing, however, matched the glorious breakfast at the Kit Kat Café. Craig and I would go downstairs to eat before he left for fifth grade and I for first. We were allowed to have almost anything we wanted: pancakes, waffles, eggs, bacon, and french toast. I looked forward to it every morning, especially being with Craig.

Hanging out with my new stepbrother was cool, and I liked the feeling of having an older sibling. I missed Billy, but I remembered he cried a lot. Plus, his toys were not to my big-kid standards. Craig had a brilliant mind and was incredibly imaginative and creative. Over these first few weeks above the Kit Kat, he made life so fun I forgot everything else when he played with me. This also meant that no matter what, I desperately wanted to please him.

Sometimes I did not know how to act or what to say, so I just followed him around, grateful when he included me in some of his activities. Craig enjoyed so many of the things I loved! He was always building something, setting up elaborate Erector Sets and sketching and painting intricate model cars and airplanes. I watched everything he did in complete fascination.

One of Craig's particular hobbies was setting up complex battles with one-inch, colored, plastic Roman soldiers and their enemies. A brilliant strategist to my six-year-old mind, he placed them in ways I had never even thought of, creating barricades with Lincoln Logs and having dips in the dirt where he would have soldiers drag off their wounded and dead.

Craig made it clear that his items were "hands off!" unless he gave me special permission. I did not dare touch anything in case he took away the privilege. I noticed that the more comfortable he got with me, the more he liked to show me things. It took me by surprise but began to fill the gaping, dark hole in my heart. I was eager and grateful.

For the first handful of weeks above the Kit Kat, I felt safe with my step-brother. If anyone in town asked now, I just called him my brother, and I was proud of it. At home, life had fallen into a rhythm. When my dad and Nellie had Sundays and Mondays off, they would go out for a night on the town. Their ritual was to go to the bar to drink and dance until the music stopped. Then they would drink coffee with friends until the wee hours of the morning. They were used to staying up all night anyway.

Each work morning, Nellie arrived home around six before heading straight to bed. Dad arrived a little later, making sure Craig and I got breakfast and were off to school before he joined her.

As the chill of late September's air rushed in one morning, it fol-lowed a customer into the Kit Kat Café. Despite the fact I wore a jacket, I shivered. I was sitting across from Craig in our favorite booth downstairs. We had been eating an enormous helping of breakfast before rushing off to school every day. Our large, vinyl-covered booth was in the corner where we could have privacy and goof off without reprimand.

The café, far past its prime, still boasted a very long counter with a row of twirling seats. Both seats and booths filled up fast due to Kit Kat's popularity with the locals for morning breakfast and coffee. This morning, I glanced up at Craig and momentarily froze as I noticed that same sour twist in his smile. I didn't know what it meant. It made me nervous as he set down his fork and stared at me as I ate.

"Fat little bugger, aren't you?" he asked.

I looked up, shocked. No one had ever called me fat before. In fact, I did not remember ever being called names except when grouped with other boys at school and the girls proclaimed we had "cooties". Now I glanced down at myself and thought about what the other kids in my first-grade class looked like.

I'm not fat, am I? And I'm not a bugger!

"I think we'll have to put you on a diet," said Craig, a malicious grin on his face. "You can eat whatever you want here in the mornings, but you have to give me your lunch money."

Instinctively, I reached to place my hand over the two dollars Dad had pinned inside my jacket pocket so I would remember to give it to my teacher. Craig knew it was there. He had watched his stepfather pin it there himself that morning for me. At thirty cents a day, it was meant to feed me for almost a week and a half.

"No," I said flatly, my hand still patting the money bulge. I did not like his joke. Then I went back to pouring syrup on my pancakes.

A sudden sharp kick met my shins under the table. In a panic, I tried not to spill the syrup all over the table or choke on the mouthful of buttery pancake I was in the process of swallowing. My face screwed up in pain, and tears bit at my eyes.

"What . . . did you say to me?" Craig asked, his tone low and threatening.

"No!" I began to protest again when I felt another swift kick to the same spot on my shin. This time it was even harder—a *lot* harder.

"OW—" I began to howl before Craig's hands swiftly reached over the table. One came down hard over my mouth, and the other hand grasped my head to keep it in place.

"Shh!" he ordered, holding me until I stopped squirming. He looked around furtively before continuing. "You don't ever tell me no," he glowered with a startling meanness in his eyes I had never seen before. "I know what happened in Germany, and you have no one here to protect you, not even Wayne, because he works all the time and is expecting *me* to watch *you*."

I gulped but said nothing.

"You think what happened to your mom was rough?" he growled. "It's nothing compared to what *I* can do to you."

Suddenly I felt faint. *He knows about Ted and Mom arguing? Does he know about her getting hurt?* I swallowed hard. *Oh, my gosh! Does he know about her lying in a pool of blood?* I hadn't said anything to him or Nellie or even Dad about that, but I still hadn't been able to erase the images from my mind. I suddenly turned cold and began to shiver, feeling absent from my own body in the booth.

"You're *my* little brother," Craig snarled quietly, "and *I'm* the leader. *I'm* the boss. You don't ever tell me no. Get it? NEVER!" He drew the last word out with an ugly hiss.

I nodded, and he let go of my mouth and my head, but not before wrenching it to the side with a menacing crack.

"Never no," I pleaded, coughing, and reached down to clutch my shin. I could feel the swelling knob through the rough, too-big Wrangler's Nellie said I would grow into. *Never say no.*

Craig had made it clear. We were two engines on the same track. He was the superior train, and I was the inferior. I had to pull over and wait for him to pass or there would be trouble—a horrific crash. His word was law.

"That's right," he said a little more gently. "Now, give me your lunch money." He extended his hand, palm outstretched over my uneaten pancake. "You'll thank me for it later when the girls don't call you *fatty*."

I didn't hesitate this time, although my hands shook and I fumbled a little as I unpinned the money from inside my jacket. Reluctantly, I handed it to him. My throbbing shin demanded it.

One morning at the end of the month before school started for the day, I was surprised to see Nellie still awake to greet us after we changed out of our pajamas. Craig and I were preparing to go downstairs to the café for breakfast when she stopped us. "Boys," she said, her tone hesitant and somber. "I need to talk to you. We can no longer afford to have you two eat breakfast at the Kit Kat."

My face likely mirrored the shock on Craig's.

No Kit Kat Café? That's the only reason I can make it through the day!

"I promise to keep you stocked up on all kinds of your favorite cold cereals," she added. "I'm sorry. It's just too expensive. You're going to have to make do."

I was crushed. Behind Nellie and from across the room, Craig shot me a look of hatred worse than his twisted smile. My eyes plummeted to the ground, along with my heart. By the time we'd made it only a block from home, Craig screamed that I was the burden he had been telling me I was. His parents could not afford breakfast at the café anymore because of *me*.

I walked on eggshells that afternoon, and the next, but it didn't help. Craig refused to play or let me use any of his supplies. He also refused to let me have anything to eat after school despite having no lunch. He punched me just for trying to sneak a bite.

After school, I began racing home. I had just three or four minutes to arrive first, quickly sneak some food, and squirrel it away or shove it in my mouth when I pretended to go to the bathroom. That Friday, I rushed home as soon as the final bell rang. I never even heard Craig's tiptoes on the squeaky wooden stairs. When he entered the kitchen, I gasped, then shut my lips. We had to be quiet to not wake our parents, but I was caught red-handed, one fist still clutching a handful of Captain Crunch. The other held the pouch I had made with the front of my oversized flannel shirt by lifting the bottom hem past my belly, two fast handfuls of cereal stashed inside it.

I stood frozen. My eyes went wide as Craig approached.

"I warned you," he whispered menacingly. "No eating!" He ripped the box away from me with one hand and punched me in the stomach with the other. The impact made a grinding noise against the makeshift pocket where the cereal was hoarded next to my stomach. The cereal didn't protect me. I doubled over, unable to breathe or cry out. When I collapsed to the floor, I became an easy target for the sharp tip of his cowboy boots.

"You want crunch?" he cried low and terrorizing. "I'll give you crunch!" With that, he drew back like a crazed soccer champion, then kicked the pocket of cereal at my belly *hard*. It didn't matter that our parents slept only thirty feet away behind the door. The hard crisps of the cereal were pulverized into sugar dust, my stomach was on fire, and still he didn't stop.

I couldn't protect myself. And I still couldn't breathe.

My eyes started to bulge. My face must've turned purple because Craig suddenly bent down beside me.

"Breathe, Gary!" he hissed, his tone different now. "Breathe, damn it!" I was shocked to see that his face was suddenly wet.

"I'm sorry, Gary!" he cried in a hoarse whisper, and now he was sobbing harder because I still couldn't breathe. "Gary, I'm so sorry. I won't do it again, I promise. You just made me so mad! Don't steal food again, don't make me mad, and I won't have to hurt you, okay?"

I nodded but was about to pass out. I thought I might die. I lay curled in a ball, confused by his sudden apology. Almost tenderly, he brushed my hair out of my wet eyes, then leapt up to grab a bowl from the cupboard. He poured a large bowl of cereal and placed it in front of me on the floor. Grabbing milk and a spoon, he plunked the spoon inside the bowl, frantically gesturing.

"Eat!" he commanded. "You can have as much cereal as you want tonight. I'll tell Mom I ate it all."

I was bewildered. Even if I could talk, I didn't know what to say. For my brother to go from torture to tenderness made me curl up inside to protect myself against his two wildly contrasting sides. It took me a few minutes, but, finally, air squeaked more easily through my lungs. Eventually I sat up. I ate his proffered peace offering. He even played games with me that night, so I said nothing to Nellie or Dad. Anything to keep "mean Craig" at bay.

That night, Craig's words kept echoing in my brain. While I had missed most of what the family said at the dinner table that evening, I had learned a fact that would forever change the course of my life.

Never say no. Never say no. Never say no.

Turbulence in the Desert

"A truly creative man is motivated by the desire to achieve,
not by the desire to beat others.
—Ayn Rand

In 1958, Crayola had come out with their signature box of crayons with sixty-four colors and a built-in sharpener. No longer were young artists relegated to a box of just eight or twelve colors; there was now a full array of the world's most vibrant and beautiful hues! By 1961, I was delighted to learn that the crayons had become a regular item at King's Variety Store in Montpelier. Crazy-happy, I beheld the different shades of reds, blues, purples, greens, oranges, and even browns to match how my mind's eye saw the world. Finally, there was a color—and a name—to capture what I wanted when I drew.

I didn't know that colors were called pigments; I just knew different people had varied tones to their skin, hair, and eyes. Even an idiot could see that trees held different hues of green, that sunlight played on shadow, and that nature's colors changed magically with the seasons. Compared to Germany, we lived in a desert, but the Crayola box magically contained close to what I thought was every color in the world.

And, boy, did I know the reds and oranges!

There was the red of the kickball at school, with its ruddy complexion, nearly a muddy-pink tone. There was the cherry red of the city's main fire truck. There was the deep brick red of the Jewel Motel Café, where Nellie worked. There was the vibrant red-orange of the late-blooming poppies in our neighbor's yard that were seeing their last days.

And then . . . and then there was the particular red of my mother's lipstick.

I kept plucking that red out of the crayon box and putting it in my pocket to carry around with me. That bothered Craig. I had quickly learned that *everything* had to be in perfect order for Craig. It was a compulsion for him.

It didn't matter that I bought this box with my own allowance. I'd only been able to do so because Nellie had come into the store with us, or Craig would have taken it, just like he still did my lunch money and allowance when we were alone.

Craig commandeered the crayons whenever he wanted them, and he made me put Mom's red crayon back. I never forgot that its name was Sunset Orange. The unusual color had a rosier hue than orange, and the name made sense. Whenever we could, Mom and I had watched the evening sky together, especially in the winters when the sun went down before my bedtime. At the memories washing in, I secretly plucked the crayon back out of the box, put it in my pocket, and carried it as long as Craig allowed.

I didn't tell Dad, but school was becoming a problem. I struggled to concentrate on my reading. I fell well behind on my math. I couldn't seem to grasp the concepts, especially after lunchtime—with no lunch.

To pay attention to the teacher, I had to doodle when she talked. If the class was too rowdy, I got irritated that I couldn't concentrate. But it was when class became too quiet that I really struggled. That is when the screaming in my mind resumed.

I did not tell anyone. I wanted Mrs. Anderson to be proud of me. No way could I tell her what was happening inside me. I also could not tell her why my stomach growled so loudly or why I never joined the hot-lunch line. The smell of the yeast rolls baking in the cafeteria almost broke me, my hunger pangs so fierce I even had to stop playing with Lincoln Logs and Tinker Toys. Desperately needing something more active, I snuck out early to begin playing ball, no matter how cold. A couple of boys wolfed down their food to join me, so I wasn't all alone for long. The play helped me forget about my tummy ache until I entered the building again.

I decided I had the most wonderful teacher. Her full name was Mrs. Clarissa Anderson. Even though she was older, I thought she was beautiful. In addition to her kind face, she never let the kids talk about me in the classroom, even though my mommy wasn't there to volunteer . . . even though I felt different from all the kids. From the things my teacher whispered to me, she must have known about me having to move from Germany. Instead of holding anything against me, she seemed the kindest, most compassionate person I had ever met.

Mrs. Anderson started to recognize my interest and adeptness in art. During class assignments, I paid particular attention and made sure I did everything just so, with my own little additions. When all the kids were drawing stick figures, bunnies, or unrecognizable creatures for hunting season so popular in Montpelier, I sketched multicolored pheasants with plump feathers, ducks with trim green necks, and enough detail on the antlers of a deer to be able to tell it wasn't a horse—and to tell its age.

The beautiful thing was that Mrs. Anderson *noticed*. She didn't just say, "Well done, Gary" as she went around the room. She stopped and picked up my work with her teacher's eye and studied it. Then, just like this morning, she picked out the details she loved the most and praised me in front of everyone.

"Class," she said, "Look at the detail on Gary's bullfrog. Can't you see that he fits right into the forest and the pond? Couldn't you imagine him slipping into the water? And understand how he makes such a great, big noise?"

As she pointed things out, people began to copy my work. That was new! It was nice to be renowned for *something* in the classroom. It made going to school each day better. I committed to doing my best to catch up to the other students despite my hunger every afternoon and the visions that still plagued me.

A month later, in November, Nellie brought home a Sears Christmas catalog. Craig snatched it out of her hands. He raced off into the easy chair and began excitedly flipping through pages.

"Christmas is coming up soon, Gary," Nellie explained.

"Yup," agreed Dad proudly. He was dressed in a crisp shirt for work at the UPR&R Train Depot and smelled of Aqua Velva. "Santa doesn't come here, but this year, Nellie and I want you to pick something too. We order in advance to be here before Christmas."

I glanced over at Craig, who was savoring his time with the catalog. I was excited to pick my own toy or art kit, too, but I was resigned that I would have to wait. Finally, he called me over, and we started going through it together, dog-earing pages of cool items we both liked. Craig kept trying to pressure me to like the items he liked most.

The mood in the apartment was almost festive until dinnertime, when we ate together. My stepbrother started talking animatedly about the catalog again.

"Now, Craig," replied Nellie's gravelly voice, almost as an afterthought. "You know Wayne and I work very hard, but we have a lot of bills to pay off. In the past, you've been able to select a forty-dollar item for Christmas, but we have *two* of you this year. You are limited to one twenty-dollar item, each."

A cold chill fell upon the room. Craig got up, grabbed his jacket, and stormed out. Nothing was said as Nellie, Dad, and I cleaned the kitchen. Craig was still in a dark mood when he came back in time for his mom and my dad to leave for work.

As soon as Dad's headlights drifted away down the street below, Craig turned from the window. The look on his face frightened me so much I couldn't follow my instincts to flee. He walked over, grabbed my shoulder, and sucker-punched me, hard, in the gut.

"Mine!" he screamed, his voice filled with a hollowed-out rage directed right at me. "Everything you are taking is mine, do you hear me? You think you can walk into our lives and steal all my stuff away? You're worthless! You hear me, Gary? *It's mine.*" His eyes burrowed into me with disgust. "And now whatever is yours will be mine anyway, and no one can say anything about it."

He socked me in the gut again, and I knew I shouldn't drop to the floor, but my body collapsed. Craig ferociously began kicking my stomach and even my privates as I lay on the ground, writhing in pain. Naturally, I curled into a protective ball. When he couldn't get a clear shot to my stomach or groin, Craig walked around to the back of my head, heedless of my pleas or my tears. He kicked and kicked and kicked. I didn't think he would ever stop until I died.

Abruptly, it was over. He cast me one more scathing glance before he walked away and started working on his plastic car model. There was no tearful apology this time. No Captain Crunch do-overs. When I could, I dragged myself to my bed to lie down. My knuckles were bloody, my privates and stomach ached, and the back of my head felt like it would explode, even under my thick, black curls. I cried myself to sleep, feeling the crayon in my pocket and wishing desperately for my mother.

I avoided Craig for the next three days. I would have avoided him forever, but I felt bereft and constantly craved affection. Craig would sometimes give it, and when he did, I would bask in it until he cruelly took it away.

Nellie seemed to sense my yearning for affection. She started treating me more warmly. At first it was wonderful in my desperation. But then she took it too far.

"Gary, come here and let's read a book," she said one afternoon after she had woken up a little early. She seemed to be feeling more tender than usual. Craig glared at me but said nothing as she gathered me to nestle in close as we read. When we finished reading the primer, she looked at me.

"I want you to call me Mom," she said suddenly.

"But you're not my mom," I said flatly and looked away from her, my eyes to the floor. Nellie was Craig's mom, and she also had an older daughter named Emma who didn't live with her anymore.

How can I call Nellie 'Mom'? My mom is coming home from the hospital anytime now. On TV shows, a person could be in the hospital for a long time if they were dreadfully sick or hurt badly—just like my mom—but they always came home.

"But I'm your *new* mom," Nellie said, and her voice suddenly had some steel in it.

"I don't need a new mom," I said and got up to play in a corner. I didn't want Nellie unhappy with me, but I wouldn't look at her. *She shouldn't ask! I have a mom!*

All of a sudden, Craig's voice came to me from the other side of the couch.

"Gary, do you want to play Roman soldiers with me?" he asked. His voice actually seemed chipper.

Why does he want to play now? Confused but not stupid enough to decline, I rushed over and began helping with his mandatory, intricate setup. Craig's battles held my rapt attention for the rest of the evening.

Deep in the night, however, Craig shook me roughly from my slumber. He had a new plan. I wasn't sure, but I thought it was sparked by Nellie's reaction to my refusal to call her Mom. That's when my stepbrother ordered me to start being rude and belligerent to Dad and Nellie.

I just blinked at him, not saying anything. How could I do what he was asking?

"Did you hear me?" Craig bellowed. "Do what I say, or I'll beat the shit out of you until you do. Get it, Gary? You will be rude and mean and nasty to the folks."

I now nodded vigorously, scared and relieved when he left me alone. I pulled the blankets over my head, my heart thudding wildly. It took hours to fall back to sleep.

At our small breakfast table the next morning, Dad and I were chatting when suddenly I felt a sharp kick to my shins under the table. I started to cry out when I caught Craig's glare from behind the cereal box. His look read, "Or else."

I turned my face away immediately from Dad and ignored him until the cheap clock chimed.

"Hurry and finish your cereal, please, Gary," Dad said.

"Nope," I mumbled. "I don't need to."

"What?" Dad looked at me quizzically. I had never talked back.

Silence. Another kick. I grimaced.

"No," I repeated. "I don't have to do anything you say. You're not my dad anymore. And my mom will come get me soon. I don't have to listen to anything you say. You're stupid."

Craig nodded slightly and this time smiled at me from behind the cereal box. I sat there stubbornly for a moment while my dad just stared at me. Then I grabbed another quick bite and jumped up to avoid Craig's next kick. I hurriedly ate the last bite before washing out my bowl, since I wouldn't have any more food until dinner.

When I arrived home after school, I was astonished that Craig greeted me with a grin. "Good work this morning," he said proudly, as if he really was my boss. "Keep it up, and I'll let you help me build my next model."

Part of me wanted to scream at him, but another part was afraid of what he would do if I did. Also, he *had* promised I could help him with his model. My little six-year-old fingers itched to work on the models with him. If all I had to do was make a game of it . . . Keeping Craig happy meant staying safe. I liked Nice Craig, not Mean Craig, and he made it clear it was up to me who showed up.

Therefore, my acting out continued. Things at home with Nellie and Dad quickly became intense. The more belligerent I acted toward them, the more Craig played with me. It was an easy choice. I only had to put up with Dad's and Nellie's anger for a couple of hours a day, and they never beat me.

At least at school I could escape the drama. I could not wait to go and be away from Craig.

My stepbrother must have sensed my relief as I ran off from him each day. Soon, Craig stole that from me, too.

"I want you to do exactly what you're doing to Mom and Wayne to your teacher now," he said one day after I arrived home from school, happy despite being hungry.

I stared at my stepbrother in shock and horror.

"No way!" I protested. "Mrs. Anderson is *nice*. I can't do that to her. I like her!"

Craig tortured me that night. He kept me up all night, striking blows to my body the second I fell asleep. I was terrified and so tired. He let me know more was coming if I didn't act up in class like I was doing at home.

I trembled all the way to school from lack of sleep and fear. I wanted to cry as I acted like a jerk to Mrs. Anderson in front of the whole class. The look on her face shattered my heart into hundreds of pieces. In exasperation, Mrs. Anderson sent me to Mr. Winters, the principal, who spanked me hard with a yardstick. It was brutal and humiliating to now have the threat of beatings at home and at school. I was sent back to his office nearly every day to follow.

The next two months were pure agony, as I was being berated for my behavior wherever I went. "What is *wrong* with you, Gary?" every teacher, administrator, and parent cried. I couldn't fix what was wrong. Craig had absolute control over my life.

Finally, Dad and Nellie were brought to the elementary office again. I was beyond in trouble, and I knew it. I wrung my hands under the desk, putting on the belligerent face Craig had taught me to. I had to pretend to be a hard, Roman soldier who was being tortured by the enemy. I had to act tough and pretend nothing was getting through my armor. I knew that if I didn't, my stepbrother would kill me.

That night after dinner, Nellie and Dad spoke to each other in low tones. The tense conversation went on for a long time. Neither went to work that night. Craig seemed to enjoy a home-cooked meal and not having to do any dishes, I noticed, as he happily painted one of his models in the corner. The smell of the acrid paint was making me nauseated. I felt something was about to happen.

"Gary, we need to talk to you," Dad said. "Please come over here."

I shot a glance back at Craig.

"No!" I said belligerently and folded my arms over my chest.

"Gary," demanded Dad sharply. "Now!"

My feet moved despite me, and I came over to where they sat. They both had concerned looks on their faces.

"Gary, you can't keep acting the way you have been," said Nellie bluntly.

"Sure I can." I had to be brave. *Soldier under torture. I won't break.*

"Gary," Dad continued, and the steel was back in his voice. "Don't talk to Nellie that way—or me. I mean it. We can't put up with this! We brought you into our home, clothed you, fed you. We enrolled you in school so you could learn something and improve your life. But we don't have the patience for this behavior any longer."

Then Dad's face softened, and he was silent until I looked up into his misty eyes. "We know you've had a hard life. You keep talking about your mom. Son, your mommy was killed in Germany. She's never coming home. She can't. She's gone for good. You'll have to get used to the idea. Ted's gone, too, so you're all alone now."

I already felt nauseated, but at his words of my mom, I thought I would retch right there.

No . . . No! This can't be. My face must have blanched white because Dad took me into his arms.

"But you have us. You have us, Gary, honey. You're not alone. I shouldn't have said it that way. But if you keep acting this way, we're going to have to send you up to be with your stepdad's parents, the Reeders. We won't have a choice. The principal at your school is about to kick you out. Your teacher is at her wits' end . . . and so are we."

He pushed me gently from him so he could look me in the eyes. "We know you've been hurt, but you have to make a choice. Keep acting this way and you'll have to leave. Settle down, treat everyone with respect, and you can stay with us."

I looked across the room to Craig. He looked stricken. I could tell he hadn't realized it would go so far. My stepbrother suddenly could not meet my eyes.

I felt desperate. I did not want to leave. It made me shudder, the thought of living with the Reeders. I was happy to be with my dad. *But . . . to never have Mommy again?* The thought made me feel like I was drowning; my life preserver was gone.

You have Mrs. Anderson, I reminded myself. *You have your painting and drawing. And you have Dad and Nellie.*

"I'll be good," I said in a tiny voice, although my heart was breaking. "I promise, I'll be good."

Dad and Nellie began to cry and then laugh, and then they hugged me tight. Dad nervously cleared his throat and set me loose. Craig wouldn't look at me as I went to bed.

I didn't care.

I kept my promise to Dad this time, and my ability to stay in Montpelier. Beginning the next day, school immediately got better. If not exactly a star student in academics, I quickly earned As in citizenship and art. I was so relieved that it only took a couple of days for Mrs. Anderson and me to get back to the way our relationship was before. At home, I was so relieved that things got better with Dad and Nellie too. My shins even began to heal without the daily beatings under the table.

When the cold winter thawed into spring and warmth filled the air, Dad and Nellie took Craig and me on an early-morning fishing trip up Montpelier Canyon. I was so excited to go! The icy waters melting off the mountains splashed into the beautiful river filled with fish. I was in awe of it all. The biggest plus was that whenever we were with Dad and Nellie, I was safe. Craig couldn't hurt me.

On our way home, we took a small detour into the sagebrush-and-sand desert. Our folks brought out a surprise from the trunk. It was a red kite. And not just any red kite.

I sucked in my breath. I would know that color anywhere.

Sunset orange! It's Mommy's red-orange!

Craig grabbed the kite and ran off, stripping off the packaging as he ran, littering the desert. I took off after him, the matching sunset red-orange crayon still in my pocket. My stepbrother struggled to get the kite up into the air at first. Finally, he tossed some sand to see which way the desert wind would blow it. Satisfied, he had me hold the kite and throw it up in the air while he ran in the opposite direction. A gust of warm wind caught it, and it puffed out like a blowfish before beginning to drift lazily, high in the sky.

The sunset red-orange of the kite was a gorgeous, stark contrast to the deepening desert azure sky. There was something majestic and lovely about it. I watched it for a long while, mesmerized by the sand-colored desert and the old, taupe tumbleweeds amongst the brighter green baby-sage ones.

Craig showed me he could make swirls with the kite in the sky. Finally, he taught me how to do it and let me do one or two beautiful figure-eight curves. Nellie and Dad clapped and cheered me on. For a moment, I was lost in a memory of an adventure with Mom. Her sweet, radiant smile reached her eyes, matching the curve of her sunset-red lips, as we went into the city to purchase a kite from a German shop with the promise of a day out on the army's field with friends. A day that had never come.

Craig snatched the string of the kite back out of my hands.

"My turn," he jeered, even though he'd already had it for most of the time before me. *Why is it when I don't want something, he gets bored, but if it is something I want, he has to hog it?* Nellie and Dad had gone back to their conversation and weren't paying any attention.

Suddenly, an angry gust of wind picked up the kite, and the string began to whip off the stick faster than Craig could hold it.

"Ouch!" he cried. "It's burning me!"

The string abruptly came to an end and was whisked out of Craig's grasp, just like that. Together we raced after it while the kite went farther up into the sky . . . farther away.

Craig kept chasing, but I stopped just to watch it as the horizon transformed into deeper hues in the evening sky. I drew in my breath as it floated up through different layers of color, the sky finally turning a last vibrant shade of burning red, like the crayon in my pocket, and my mother's lips, now in the heavens.

Goodbye, Mommy. I love you. I love you forever.

Shame and Censure

"You don't stare the devil in the eyes
and come out without some of his sin."
—Nina G. Jones

As the weather warmed into summer, Dad and Nellie made an exciting announcement. Our family would be moving from our tiny studio apartment above the Kit Kat Café to a little house of our own. Although I would miss some of the lively scents and sounds of the café below and the pool hall next door, we had our own house with a parlor, kitchen, and three bedrooms. Best of all, we had our own backyard, with the hope of neighbor kids to play with! I longed for the easy camaraderie I'd experienced with friends in the past.

I also secretly hoped that with more room, I could sometimes get away from Craig. Maybe Nellie could even stay home now. She was feeling more like a mother to me. She nurtured me when she could. I appreciated any small moment of kindness.

On the week we moved, Nellie's little sister came to help for a few hours. She didn't say much to me but complained a lot about everything, including the heat. It was stifling upstairs, making everyone cranky. Then she said something that shocked me.

"You're not pretty anymore, Nellie," she remarked callously. "You look like a man!" To add insult to injury, she flipped her hair back in a way that spoke volumes about how pretty she thought *she* was.

I felt a fire within me, and part of me hoped Nellie would deck her. Instead, she turned to face her sister. "If you had to work as hard as I do," she snapped bitterly, "you would look like a man too. And now that we have a house payment, I'll have to work even harder." Her glare said the conversation was over.

My hopes were dashed, realizing she couldn't stay at home. She already worked harder than any woman I knew. Sure, she was a little rough around the edges, but she was lovely in her own way, plus bright, and quick to speak her mind.

As I looked at her sister's unkind face, I made up my mind.

"Hey, *Mom*," I said with deliberate emphasis, moving in to give her a hug. "What can I do to help? Is there anything I can pack for you? You sure look pretty today."

Momentarily astonished, it wasn't lost on Nellie that I had listened to their conversation. Beaming at me, she hugged me back and gave me an assignment.

I called her Mom from that day forward. It felt nice to say that word aloud again. *Mom*. It had a different meaning, of course. Somehow, I recognized even at age seven that my stepmother was limited in her capacity to love but that she would give all she was capable of giving. For that, I was deeply grateful.

The only thing that bothered me about my new mom was how her son Craig could do no wrong. Sometimes I wondered how much she truly knew about him. He kept so many secrets from her and Dad. Some of those secrets I wore on my body. I was most often covered with cuts, abrasions, and bruises of all colors. He kept most of them where people couldn't see. As much as I had hoped for a new life, I wondered how many more secrets would be kept at the new house.

Despite Craig's often brutal care, his passion was contagious. He was over the moon about the new house and made big promises to me. There were going to be real benefits to having a larger place of our own and little, if any, supervision. Craig began making plans and sharing bits of them with me.

Early the next morning before it got too hot, Craig and I were tasked with taking the ironing board several blocks down and over to our new home, along with a myriad of odds and ends. As we each grabbed a side of the bulky, heavy steel ironing board to take down the steep stairs, Craig carefully placed his fox stole with the fancy clasp on it. Purchased from a second-hand store, the fur was soft and touchable but creepy to me that it was a dead thing.

"Gary, do you realize how cool moving is?" Craig asked. "I asked Mom, and each one of us will get our own art drawer to ourselves—*although you cannot ever touch mine.* Got it, idiot?" he asked, giving me the eye.

"I promise," I said. Then I grasped the ironing board tight as we bumbled our way out the apartment door. Craig made me go first, walking backward down the steep building stairs. After the first step, he began taunting me, pushing a little too fast for my stubby legs to carry me to the next step. Three times I almost fell in sheer terror, even as he pulled up short so I wouldn't. Worse, he was grinning.

"What I'm most excited for," my stepbrother continued breezily, ignoring my terror as we burst out into the morning sunshine, "is that we can *build* things! Did you know we can build our own racetracks outside, and now that we have enough room, we can build train tracks and a whole village in our house! Won't that be cool?"

Despite trying to catch my breath, I became immediately caught up in the unmistakable excitement in Craig's eyes. I often felt mystified how he could have me afraid for my life at one moment and then suddenly excited, not wanting to be left out of his marvelous plans.

Despite my learned mistrust, I also loved how Craig's mind worked. He was always thinking and scheming, building things in his mind first and then in reality. Soon he would be attending seventh grade and never too humble to tell me he was so much more advanced than I was. One of my brother's brilliant ideas was for us to share a room so we could use the other bedroom to build a large and elaborate train set, complete with stepped terrain and multiple tracks. As cool as it sounded, his dreams seemed over-the-top.

Two weeks after we moved in, Craig walked with me over to the King's Variety Store. The redbrick building with the massive yellow sign was a treasure trove of toys and all kinds of things not found elsewhere—especially in that small town.

Craig got me all excited about the new tracks we had just built for some tiny electric cars we were racing against each other. The size of Matchbox™ cars, most of my friends from school secretly carried one or two in their pockets to play with at recess. These were more expensive, with tiny electric motors. Craig and I spent hundreds of hours putting the tracks together in elaborate raceways. Using junk from our new yard and stuff we found in local fields, we made jumps and curves on an extremely fine racetrack boasting multiple levels.

We were having a ball with Craig's beat-up little cars, enticing some of the neighborhood boys to see what we were up to. But today, Craig said, we were headed to get *new* electric cars so we could finally, *really* test how well our new tracks worked. All the way as we walked, he explained how the brand-new cars would have slick, fast-moving wheels and how they were exactly what was needed to test out our fine workmanship.

"Our new racetrack deserves no less!" he exclaimed, and I agreed.

Before we pushed open the glass doors of King's, however, Craig stopped me.

"The thing is, Gary, I don't have any money," he admitted in a low voice. "You know I already spent my allowance this week on two more tracks."

I did know. He'd used his *and* my allowance both! As always, whatever was Craig's priority always had to be mine too. "Okay," I said, my face falling in disappointment. Then confusion set in. "So, why did we walk all the way here if we can't buy the cars?"

"You don't need money to get something here," Craig said. He pointed a thumb inside. "They have all the money they need. They won't miss an electric car or two."

No way! I blanched, and my heart crashed to the pit of my stomach. *Oh, gosh, I hope he's not thinking what I think he is.*

"Just watch," Craig stated flatly as he nudged me harshly into the store. Then he took me over to look at the toys, especially the electric cars. We spent only a few minutes there, deciding what we liked, and then Craig sauntered casually up and down the other toy aisles as if musing over how to spend his hard-earned money. I didn't realize he was casing the area until we returned to the electric cars. Craig took another glance to make sure no one was watching and then shoved the selected box down his pants and covered the bulge with his shirt.

"Now it's your turn," he said, his voice still low, his face stern.

"But I don't want to!" I whispered wildly. My heart pounded out of my chest. I had never stolen anything in my life. That's when I saw Craig back his leg up. I knew that move all too well.

I stepped back quickly, avoided his kick, and looked around. No one was watching. I glanced at the abundance of toys and household items in what seemed like a huge store. *Surely the store owner is rich. Maybe Craig is right.* But I still hesitated. It didn't feel right.

Mommy had taught me a long time ago not to take other people's things, and Mrs. Anderson had reinforced how important it was for the whole class to honor other people's belongings no matter how much you liked them. Her clear, strong voice rang in my ears. "We don't *ever* take something that belongs to someone else. How would you feel if someone took something that was important to you?"

My head felt fuzzy. I already knew how that felt. *Why is it that so many things that are supposed to be wrong are okay if Craig does them? Or if I do them for Craig?*

I felt twisted up inside. I'd learned very quickly it wasn't safe to tattle on Craig. Dad overlooked anything I said like I was overreacting. Mom always seemed to listen, but after asking for his side, she *always* believed Craig over me. Worse, later, when they were gone, I would end up in the fetal position on the floor, unable to protect myself from his violence. Already in the new house it was worse because we were spread out, and Craig took advantage of every bit of space. He knew how loud or soft we had to be in every area of the house not to wake our folks up—so we could continue to do all the things *he* wanted.

I was tired of getting pummeled. In fact, I would do just about anything not to get beaten up again. So, with eyes wide and frightened in the middle of the toy aisle at King's, I grabbed an electric car in its box and shoved it down my short pants. Then I pulled my button-down shirt over it. My new mom had been in the habit of giving me some of Craig's hand-me-downs or buying clothes extra big so I would grow into them. I had never appreciated that as much as I did now.

"Act normal," Craig snarled quietly, "or you're going to get us busted. Then I'll really be pissed."

I took barely a breath and walked closely behind him, trying to be normal. What was normal? When I looked around, it seemed like everyone else was "normal" and I was the only one I knew who was not.

So now, with a stolen electric car down my pants, I struggled all the way out the door and down the street. I thought for sure the cops would come to get me and put me in jail any minute. I kept listening for sirens.

Oh, my gosh, I stole!

Shame filled my chest. I felt it tighten around my heart like the grips we used to hold the high part of our racetracks to the buckets and plywood platforms. Somehow I felt like I had just betrayed my mom and Mrs. Anderson.

Unfortunately, once Craig saw that I could steal and get away with it, I became an integral tool in his weekly plans. At the grocery store, the variety store, the gas station, the animal feed store—wherever Craig had a fancy for something he didn't want to pay for, I was his pawn. Pretty soon, it became a weekly, if not daily, part of life.

Most of the time, I didn't get caught. After a while, a couple of stores began keeping a sharp eye on me, but Craig wasn't stupid. He made sure I could spend my allowance on something he wanted from the store so that we would gain their trust for a bit and then steal again the following few days. Or, better yet, spend some money each time we were stealing. It was diabolical.

Pretty soon, it didn't make my heart pound so hard when I stole. The hell I would catch from the store owners was nothing compared to what happened the two times I came home empty-handed.

Craig had a way of making everything all right when I delivered on the grab. In spite of my misgivings, I began to get excited about his plans. My stepbrother always made sure I benefited from what I lifted. It was all a game to him, and with Mom and Dad peacefully sleeping the days away before work, we were racing cars down tracks, getting the neighbors involved, and creating our backyard to be a wonderland. In the summer evenings with the folks at work, we could stay out as long as we wanted. When Craig rigged up some lighting, we wouldn't come in until the wee hours, dirty and grimy from building and racing.

The drag races were so much fun that the neighbors began coming out to watch—big folks as well as small. Over that summer, there were six or seven boys who competed with us. We began having a regular raceway there, and I loved it. It was fascinating learning to improve the motors and observing from all the kids what worked and what didn't. Craig's constant tinkering and exploration paid off, and we won a lot of races in a row with our new secret weapon—motors from gas model airplanes. They were much faster than gear-driven motors and cheap when Craig made me steal them.

The summer days flew by. Finally, our adventures were at an end, and Mom and Dad got us as physically prepared for school as they could afford, all the while exclaiming how happy they were that Craig took such good care of me.

As the weather became cold, my brother and I were forced to spend more time indoors, where we turned our attention to making our train set.

Starting small with the set Dad had given Craig for his birthday, we began meticulously planning and growing. One night, we even painted the linoleum to make the floor look like the background we wanted. We were proud—until our folks came home and saw it, their mouths open in shock.

Surprisingly, they didn't get upset. "It's the prettiest linoleum in the house!" exclaimed Mom, and so we continued being creative. As the weather grew bitter, each day after school, we painted roads, sprinkled sand to make those roads look textured, and made green grass. We had freedom to stay up for hours until I dragged myself to bed. My head often bobbed with exhaustion at school, worse, even, than from my nonexistent lunch.

Craig and I were both fascinated by trains, and Dad took it as a compliment because of his work at the train depot. He taught us a few things about trains, and everything else Craig figured out. My stepbrother and I continued to "share" allowances and swipes from the stores. I found the latter easier now that I wore a huge coat to mask my crimes. Therefore, the train set grew, and we dreamed of the day we could have strong transformers and engines.

Craig always showed me how things worked. He didn't just do something for me; he meticulously taught me how to do it—how to build it, how to mix it, how to paint it, how to glue it correctly, how to create it. I learned a great deal because of his precision in all he did. If I messed up, he made me do it over again, sometimes with a kick or a punch or a shove. What surprised me were the many times my stepbrother was kind as he taught me.

As my natural skills enhanced, I discovered how to transform my decent drawings into vibrant, dynamic, three-dimensional sketches that looked alive enough to jump off the page. I implemented a more scientific approach to mix colors—something I'd been fascinated with forever. The use of dark and light could take something from a symbol into recognizable form. Utilizing mixed hues along with delicate shading enhanced the critical importance of shadows, where I could now show more realistic size, depth, age, and emotion. My use of shadows now varied from the golden light of sunrise to stark high noon lengthening into late afternoon and dusk.

Day after day, Craig kept after me. While other kids were out playing in the snow, I was often set to the task of perfecting something, even foreground, background, and lighting. Pretty soon there was no limit to the drawings and watercolors that began to jump from my imagination to the page.

One day, a jousting game Craig and I were playing in the snow with the neighbors turned into a bigger battle. We essentially got slaughtered. Undaunted, Craig and I returned home that night, determined to make a showing the next day. He ripped apart an old crate. From the decrepit wood, we crafted swords and shields to do real battle with our enemies. My sword turned out pretty good, but my shield was worthless. Craig proved that with one jab of his sword.

"You idiot," Craig shouted angrily, giving me a shove. "That shield won't do shit for you! You've got to make it balanced and even. It's got to hold together, or one swipe with their swords will wipe you out. Warriors know better." He then proceeded to help me pull the pieces apart and taught me how to put them back together properly for strength and resilience.

It took me three times to get it balanced to Craig's expectations, but the balance did perform better than my previous creation.

As the games commenced, I pretended I really *was* living in medieval times. I was like an apprentice to a harsh but talented master. There was a lot of dark and a lot of light. I was being well-trained although disciplined severely. Deep inside, I held on to a tiny kernel of hidden truth and forbidden hope.

At some point, apprentices have to break away. I clutched at the thought like gulps of air. *Apprentices eventually become their own masters.*

The Whistle Is Blowing

"In captivity, one loses every way of acting over little details which satisfy the essentials of life. Everything has to be asked for: permission to go to the toilet, permission to ask a guard something . . . to brush your teeth, use toilet paper, everything is a negotiation."
—*Ingrid Betancourt*

One late Saturday midwinter morning, as all young boys' eyes glanced wistfully outside, I stared out the frosted window, wishing for a thaw in the below-zero windchill. No one was out.

We lived only thirty miles from Bear Lake, a stunning freshwater prism. Its azure blue made people's mouths pop wide open, just like it did mine every time I saw it. Craig told me that the brilliant turquoise was a color normally reserved for warm ocean bodies. For the past two months, however, the lake had been a dull and bitter gray, reflecting our overcast sky. It sent a chill through me when I saw it last, not knowing that a lake could hold such contrasts. I thought about that as I made designs in the frost on the glass, wishing for warmth and color . . . and freedom.

Craig suddenly popped through the door from downstairs, startling me. In our new house, we had a tiny, dark, dirt-floor basement I hated. With only one naked bulb for light, it was cold and dank. Still petrified of the dark, I never descended the steps except to grab potatoes or carrots for my mother when she was cooking. Although we'd lived in that house for six months, our parents never went down there except on occasion to store things.

I didn't mind the cool, earthy smell, but it was chock-full of cobwebs that stuck to my hair and freaked me out. What I hated was that at times when our folks were gone and Craig was mad, he locked me behind that basement door. I would sit in the pitch-black of the creaky wooden stairs and sob in stinging, tangible fear.

Today, however, Craig had a strange glint in his eyes, along with a rough smear of dirt down his neck and right forearm.

"You would never believe what I just found, Gary!" he whispered mysteriously. "It's our key to adventure. Now, get off your butt and come downstairs with me."

Well, at least he's not mad.

Reluctantly, I tiptoed down the stairs to avoid waking Dad and Mom. In a very dim corner of the basement, the one I knew pointed in the direction of the *M* up on the small mountainside, Craig pointed to a hole in the wall, and beyond that a tunnel through the dirt. With a broad smile, Craig shined his flashlight into what I could see must be a large cavern.

A cave? In our basement of all places? It must be the size of our living room!

Craig motioned for me to enter the tunnel. I hesitated. Like the basement when the bare bulb was off, it was pitch-dark. My body turned cold with alarm. I was frozen, unable to enter.

What if I get stuck? I thought, panicking. *What if the whole thing caves in and I get buried alive?* I'd never told Craig I was afraid of the dark. I would not! He exploited every weakness.

"C'mon, you fucking wuss," he snapped now, pushing a flashlight into my hand. Then he shoved me to my knees. Trembling a little, I shined my flashlight down the tunnel as I crawled and crawled, finally entering the cavernous room. It was silent and chilly but not nearly as cold as I expected.

Ugh, I thought as I slapped something off my cheek. *More cobwebs!*

But as soon as Craig shuffled in after me with another light, I couldn't help but notice other cool things about the cave room: there were pockets, niches, and holes in the brickwork that formed a kind of design in the dark.

"Won't Mom and Dad get upset with us being down here?"

"Quit being an idiot, Gary!" Craig said with an exasperated look. "The folks don't need to know. Plus, why would they ever even think to look for us down here? I can't hear either of them snoring, which means they can't hear us." He paused as he shined his flashlight around. "Just don't be a wimp or scream like a girl," he ordered. "I'll keep an eye out for time. We'll scoot back upstairs before they wake up for dinner, and they'll never know."

His light went back to revealing pockets of structures and holes in the crumbling wall. As much as I hated the dark, I begrudgingly admitted the cavern did hold massive potential for imaginative play.

"Can you see, Gary, where we can set up my Roman soldiers? We can have massive battles down here." His voice got dreamy and excited again. "And we won't have to clean them up every time like Mom insists. We can structure *ongoing* battles. Stories for days or weeks, maybe even months . . . just like real battles!"

Months? Being down in this dark hole for even an hour quietly terrified me. I could not, would not, imagine months.

Craig excitedly shared where we could set up the Roman figurines. As he went into detail and story, the trepidation of my surroundings melted a bit. I began to catch Craig's vision. It was hard not to; his imagination and passion were contagious.

"Gary, how many of our friends are dying to go outside to play in the dirt? And we have our own secret dirt fort!"

I knew he was right. As chilly as it was down here, it was so much warmer than being outside in the biting temps—by at least thirty degrees.

"And look over here," Craig said, moving the flashlight to another section. It was covered in cement. "See? It's perfect for a chemistry lab."

"Chemistry lab?"

"Yeah, man. That Gilbert chemistry set we got for Christmas! Mom and Dad said we couldn't do most of those experiments in the house," Craig began, chuckling mischievously. "Well, we aren't technically *in* the house, are we?"

For the rest of that day until Mom and Dad arose, Craig and I secretly transported certain toys and the chemistry set into the basement. After our parents left for work, we climbed into the blasted tunnel, transforming the cavern with every trip. Craig and I spent all our free time over the next several weeks building roads, digging ravines, establishing riverbeds, and even creating an underground lake to race mini sailboats. We even cut class to hang out in the cavern, and Mom and Dad never knew.

In the meantime, I shoplifted another chemistry set on behalf of Craig, and other items that would entertain us in our hideaway. The secret cavern would prove to be our indoor wonderland, filling many days and nights too cold to be outside. It also proved to be dangerous.

Away from prying eyes, Craig held absolute power over me. On his light days, full of enthusiasm and brilliant ideas, we spent hours in glorious battle or mixing colors and chemicals to see what they would do. We had picnics of sandwiches and water in our underground haven and brought old blankets to sit on so we wouldn't get as dirty. Not that we cared.

Like us, out of sight, out of mind.

After Christmas, however, I experienced a couple of Craig's dark days. Although he got just what he asked for, my stepbrother was bitterly disappointed he had to share the forty-dollar budget with me once again. After a short two days off for the holiday, our parents were back to work, and I found myself curled up in a ball on the floor, hopeless to deflect my brother's blows and kicks. Cringing in pain, I went to bed earlier than normal, hoping for a better day when I woke up.

In the morning, as Dad helped me clean up from breakfast, we got a knock at the door. It was David Trout, a kid from across the street. He was a couple of years older than me and a few years younger than Craig.

"I got a new train set for Christmas!" David cried. "Wanna see?"

Dad and I both nodded and went to grab our coats. I woke Craig up as I grabbed my boots from our bedroom. The three of us went over to the Trout's modest home to join the other curious kids and dads in the neighborhood.

My mouth dropped open at the sight. It was an O-Gauge train set, meaning that it was the largest collectible model toy train set in the world! I watched, mesmerized by each carefully designed engine passing by, carrying specialized cars and a caboose. Each car was about a foot long and made of heavy-gauge metal with special details of plastic and paint. The whole set was super slick! Dad and I were ecstatic for David.

I glanced over at Craig. Something was wrong. I recognized that sour look in my stepbrother's eyes and the set of his jaw. Uh-oh. Yeah, it was obvious. Craig was jealous.

"Did you see that?" Craig grumbled after we got home and Dad had gone to bed. "The transformer alone probably cost about $200!" I didn't have a real understanding of money, but I saw it had enough horses to simultaneously power four large engines around the large track, compared to our one.

Over the next few days at the slightest hint of an invitation, we raced over to David's house to join the others, ears and cheeks pink with cold. When we got done playing, David turned to the group.

"Hey, nobody can come tomorrow. We're leaving to visit family for New Years, but I promise when I get back, we'll play every day after school."

I was bummed. I loved that this older kid was paying attention to me and sometimes invited me over to play. David participated with us in drag races and stuff. I liked him because he was a genuinely nice guy.

The next day, I was cleaning up breakfast so our weary dad could go to sleep. Craig was up early, which was unusual during vacation. He even helped dry the dishes. I glanced at him, wondering if he had plans for our cave today. I could never have dreamed of what he had in store.

As soon as Dad's loud snores combined with Mom's, Craig walked over to me. The look in his eye filled me with dread.

"I don't know if you noticed," he began, "but the Trouts left early this morning with their suitcases tied to the top of their car. They've been gone for a few hours already. No one is going to be there for a long while. My guess is a couple of days at least."

"So?" I asked, not understanding what he meant.

"So now I want you to go nab that train set."

I just stared at Craig. *Surely he doesn't mean for me to steal our friend's new Christmas present.*

I wanted to scream, *NO! David is our friend.* But I just stood there, heart pounding and not speaking a word. I was still sore from Craig's beating over his scanty Christmas just days ago, my bruises purple and one scab still seeping under my shirt from his boots.

To avoid another pummeling in broad daylight, I found myself walking across the street with a cardboard box, trying to pretend I was just going to see my friend as I had been doing every day that week. Glancing around, I set the box on the front porch and ran down into the stairwell. Craig told me he'd noticed the Trouts had left their window unlocked.

I didn't know when he "happened" to notice that, so I sighed and pried open the unlocked window. Slipping inside, I peered around the dim interior before finding the light. Then, coming out to the front, I unlocked the door, grabbing the box I'd laid on the front porch moments earlier. It was just a regular brown cardboard box, with no markings on it. It should have screamed, "TRAIN!" because for the next few hours, I would carry every stinkin' piece of that train across the street. Transformer, cars, tracks, and everything else that easily came apart from that once-glorious O-Gauge train I kyped, one by one.

My face was ruddy and I was shivering—not just from the cold but the fear of getting caught. I jumped every time I left the house or a car slipped down our icy road, every time a neighbor let their dogs out or quickly ushered holiday visitors inside. The wind was biting to the point that few people were out. Every trip back across the street, Craig would quietly meet me at our door, eager for another piece to sequester in our secret cave. And every trip, instead of getting easier, made me want to throw up. Tears pricked at my eyes and froze on my lashes.

David, I'm so sorry.

Finally, I came in with the last piece. The freezing wind gusted through the neighborhood trees, making eerie sounds. I stood there for a minute, wondering what would happen when the Trouts got home and if I could go huddle up in my bed, away from the world, and never come out.

I knew better. Craig had already told me to come straight into the cave with the final item. He ignored my sullen glare as I entered, and soon the train engines whistled and whirled round and round. The sounds echoed in the room, but we'd learned by now that they'd never be heard upstairs.

We had already tested the dirt barrier for sound. It was nerve-wracking to me that Craig could yell at the top of his lungs and I couldn't hear him from our parents' bedroom at all! Even more nerve-wracking, however, was that from time to time, a bit of dirt fell from the ceiling, especially now with the roar of the train engines. My frequent nightmares would surely increase with visions of being buried alive.

As nauseated as I was, I had to admit the train was a breathtaking sight barreling up and down the hastily built tracks. It chugged up, down, and around our makeshift cavern, its headlamps shining eerily off the dirt-and-brick walls. Craig had built it nearly as intricately as we did the outside track from last summer that all the neighbors coveted as they'd joined us in play. Yet when the train turned off for the night, all I could think of was my friend David and how heartsick he would be when he got home. No one in our neighborhood had extra money. His parents must have saved for months, or years even, to get such an expensive set. David's family had joyfully shared that with us, and we had taken that joy away from them. Their family would probably never get another one.

When our folks got up the next evening to prepare dinner and get ready for work, Craig and I were carefully studying the manual from our chemistry set, quietly deciding on which experiments would work in our new lab. We decided we would purposely ignore our own train set for the next few days, showing the folks we were absorbed in other, more important priorities. Who had time to develop a cunning plan to steal a model train set, anyway?

As soon as the folks left for their respective jobs, Craig played on the train set all night, but after only an hour or so, I begged off, saying I was sick. It was true; the terrible ache in my gut had built up all day. It went away only when I finally escaped into sleep.

At the sound of Mom's arrival early the next morning, I gasped awake. I was suddenly afraid of getting caught—and severely punished for what we had done. My eyes went wide when I saw Craig's limp body spread across the top of his bed in yesterday's grimy, dirty clothes. I got up and quietly shut our door. Then I laid back in bed, my heart pounding loudly in my ears. The train was tucked safely away in our cave, where our folks couldn't even see it, much less get to it. Craig repeatedly told me we didn't have anything to be afraid of, that I was a wuss for worrying.

In my heart, though, I felt like it was only a matter of time before we were caught. *This can't go on forever, can it?* The only thing I knew about thieves was from watching television. The bad guys always got caught! Craig was enjoying the train, but *I* was the one who would get arrested.

I was the one who'd broken into the Trout's house. I was the one who'd brought it across the street. I was the one who would go to jail. And, strangely enough, at seven years old, it didn't even match my deepest fear, which was about to become a reality.

The Hole So Black

"Power tends to corrupt and absolute power corrupts absolutely."
—*Lord Acton*

When the Trouts arrived home from their holiday visit, they knew they had been robbed. What the police couldn't understand was why nothing else was missing. They asked around the neighborhood, but no one had seen a thing. I was relieved and confused. At home, Craig was the one who played with the O-Gauge when our parents were at work, keeping the ghostly train whistles going in the dark of our cavern every night with an obsessive fervor.

"You're too young, and it's too powerful. It would break the engines if they crashed," he explained, not taking his eyes off the tracks and controls. I didn't care. I didn't want to touch it. His eyes held an ugly glee. I'd lost even the tiniest bit of relish to play with David's stolen train set. Seeing him downcast was more than enough for me.

As January turned into February, every day we ventured down into the cavern, I would ask myself, *Will it be Mean Craig today? Or Nice Craig*? I never knew who was going downstairs and through that tunnel with me. Because Nice Craig could become Mean Craig in a blink, I was never safe. There was nowhere to go, and, now, nearly all day or night, there was no one to hear my screams. They echoed off the walls as loud as the train whistle when he maliciously beat me, methodically making marks my clothing and thick hair covered.

One night, however, Craig went too far. It was a Wednesday night after Dad and Mom left for the bar. Craig always made me cook him dinner on those nights. While he was eating his TV dinner and watching his favorite program, he had been sharpening a knife he had kyped from the feed and tackle store.

I, on the other hand, was taking advantage of his momentary lapse in observation, sneaking a piece of cheese while I pretended to begin cleaning up and putting the milk away. Under Craig's dominion, I went more often without food than with it. It had spread beyond the lack of school lunches and controlled snacks. At the table, even when Dad and Mom were present, my brother positioned himself so he could kick me under the table if he thought I was taking too much for my first serving or anytime I reached for seconds. It only increased my obsession with food. Therefore, when he wasn't watching, I hoarded bits of food to eat later.

"Hey," he ordered when the show ended. "Get over here, now."

I froze. Had he seen something? I quietly pushed the cheese farther into my pocket.

"I said get over here!"

I breathed in relief. *He just wants me to clean up after him as usual.* The moment I went to take the thin metal tray away, however, Craig told me to leave it. Then he directed me to stand in front of him with my arms stretched fully outward.

"I need to do an experiment," he said.

I shrugged with some hesitation. Craig was always doing experiments.

"Don't move," he added.

I looked at him quizzically but didn't dare defy him. In my T-shirt and jeans, I only came up to Craig's chest. Standing with my arms extended outward, Craig snatched something off the TV tray. Before I could react, he brought his knife blade down in a sharp motion, slicing my forearm. I looked at my arm in shock. I could see more than an inch deep into the gaping wound in my arm.

I stared at the wound, grotesquely fascinated and amazed that the slice didn't bleed much. It was clear, however, that it wasn't going to heal on its own. The gash on my small arm was over a couple of inches wide and deep enough that I could see the layers of tissue and sinews beneath my skin.

Finally! I thought, even as I screamed in pain. *He's gone too far and he's going to be in trouble for what he's done to me. We can't hide this!*

But I was wrong. By the time our folks came home from the bar, Craig had concocted a believable story. To my despair, it was too believable.

Mom and Dad took me to the hospital, where I received stitches to close the wound. Of course, Craig made it all my fault. Clumsy me had tripped and fallen on a bunch of tools we were using to fix our bikes.

Toward the end of winter in the cavern, Craig and I made another discovery. We had been digging more roads and caves for his hordes of tiny Roman soldiers when Craig accidentally punched through to the other side. The only question was, the other side of what? As he shined our one flashlight into the hole, he discovered there was another roomy cavern just to the side of us! It might even be deeper than the one we were in now. As we peered into the dark, immense space, Craig's face lit up with wonder and a lust for more adventure. At the look on my face, he cackled a high-pitched laugh. I couldn't hide my horror this time, and now Craig knew just how terrified of the dark I really was.

Excited, my brother set about digging as fast he could, handing me bucketful after bucketful of dirt to dump into the corner where we were making mountains for our Roman terrain. He checked our progress by stopping and shining his flashlight inside the blackness, and then, grinning, started up again.

"It's pretty deep!" he called from the tunnel. "I'm not sure how far down it goes. I can't see." That didn't make me feel any better.

Craig ran and got a rope from Dad's shed while ordering me to finish dumping the buckets, completely alone and in the dark. I hated him for that. After he came back through the first tunnel, he crooked his finger under the haze of the flashlight for me to come to him at the opening of the second.

Craig held out a length of fairly thick rope. Having me hold the flashlight, he proceeded to tie it around my chest.

"I'm going to lower you down, Gary, so you can touch and see how deep it is." Ignoring my shaking, he explained, "It makes more sense for you to go. You're not strong enough to lift me up with the rope like I can do with you."

"Okay," I said, completely unsure. Slowly, I climbed up into the porthole tunnel Craig had dug out into the unknown. I had to go in feetfirst in order to drop down properly. Craig kept the flashlight, pointing it down and feeding me more and more rope as I went through the lip of the cavern and then down, down, down, trying to peer into the blackest black to figure out the depth of our new discovery.

Suddenly the dirt from the lip of the cavern underneath my support rope gave way. It startled Craig, who dropped the whole rope! As I fell, I screamed the scream of the dying, which no one but Craig would ever hear.

Something beyond terror overcame me as I tumbled farther and farther down. Violently I whacked my shoulder on something hard before finally hitting the cavern floor with a horrific thud. The impact made me lose my breath as a cloud of fine dust billowed up around me. The particles streamed into my eyes and mouth, which had opened in agony. As I struggled desperately to suck in the breath that escaped from my hard fall, the clouds of gritty debris clogged my throat and my nose. I couldn't breathe now at all. I panicked, thrashing desperately.

"Gary! Gary!" Craig yelled, but I could not answer. I couldn't believe it, but it was worse than when he sucker-punched me in the gut. I could not get a single ounce of breath into my lungs as the dust continued to enshroud me. Suddenly, I saw a light. Craig was trying to shine his flashlight, but I couldn't even see him through the murky cloud, and I was sure he couldn't see me or just how far the cavern dropped. It had to be at least ten to fifteen feet above my head.

"Gary!" Craig called again. Still, I could not answer him. I was suffocating.

The light switched off abruptly, and Craig was gone. Alone, with no breath, I knew I was going to die. Craig was leaving me here to die, just as he had left me to get caught at the neighbor's house. All that existed was the intense burning in my lungs, eyes, nose, and throat, and the instinctual knowledge that I could not survive without oxygen. I panicked even more. This was worse than drowning!

And then . . . there was nothing at all.

Sometime later, the sound of scratching from far away made its way into my consciousness.

I sat up and immediately began vomiting. The faraway scratching stopped.

"Oh, my God, Gary! You're okay!" Craig cried. "Can you hear me?" I felt a grain of hope that he hadn't deserted me. Maybe he brought Dad to save me. Fortunately, the moisture in my mouth from vomiting had dampened the dust in my throat enough to allow a bit of breath in.

I started to cough. Then I started to cry.

"Get me out of here, Craig," I begged, surprised at the high-pitched squeak that came out of my mouth between vomit and snot. The walls felt like they were closing in on me.

What is down here? Snakes? Dragons? Huge spiders? Bears?

My imagination was full of dangers, with no light to allay my fears. Completely drenched in the blackness, I was petrified of being left there forever. "Please," I whined desperately. "PLEASE get me out of here!"

"Watch out!" called Craig, cutting through my tears. "I'm going to drop you the flashlight." The fine, dark dust still permeated the air, though not as thick, and I watched the tumbling flashlight as it twisted and turned a few times on its way down. Despite my wounded shoulder, I grabbed it as soon as it hit the ground in a cloud. I hung on to it with all my might, coughing wretchedly again. The flashlight was my only hope in the darkness.

"I've got to run and get another light!" he yelled.

"No, don't leave me!" I cried out, panicked. I shined the light around the rectangular-shaped cavern with its steep, smooth walls. There was absolutely no way I could climb out by myself. Mom and Dad were at work and had no idea of this world under our house. If Craig left me there, I was utterly doomed.

How many times has he told me he would kill me and leave my body where no one could find it?

"I've got to get another flashlight and some belts and stuff to pull you up!" Craig shouted back. "You're really far down there, and we're out of rope."

Then there was only silence.

I covered my mouth in an attempt to still my pathetic whimpering and violent coughing. I vomited again, whether from fear or the dust I didn't know, though, miraculously, I felt I could breathe better again. The tears, though stinging, were cleaning out my eyes and nose as I blubbered. Despite the fine sweat covering my forehead, temples, armpits, and back, it was numbingly cold in the pit.

I wiped my mouth on my sleeve, which was a mistake. I quickly spit out the bitter dusting of particles. And then I just sat, feeling helpless, shooting my flashlight in every direction I thought I heard a sound. With every passing minute, my paranoia built. It felt like a setup. In the horror movies Craig liked to watch, it was always when someone went for help, leaving the other person alone, that horrific creatures or serial killers came out to annihilate the fear-filled character. My body trembled with fear and cold, and my shoulder ached like crazy.

This time I cried out in relief when I finally heard Craig somewhere above me. Having grabbed another light, he said he could now make out my shape as the dust settled.

Suddenly his flashlight caught the reflection of a large, metal pipe, one end buried deep in the earth, the other sticking out of the side of the big hole, not far above where I sat.

"Oh, my God, Gary—this must have been a sewer cesspool a long time ago! What if you had hit your head on that on your way down?" he cried. "You'd be dead now."

The truth of Craig's words showered over me like a bucket of icy water. I was sitting in an old, dried-up cesspool, and had I tumbled just a few inches in the other direction, I could have been killed by the fall.

"Jus-s-st get m-m-me out of here," I wailed with cold and fright. "I d-d-d-don't want to be down here anymore."

"I brought some sheets and stuff," my brother called. "Give me a few minutes to secure them, and we'll get you out."

Sheets? What the hell? But I kept quiet. Craig was smart. Almost every scrape he got me into, he somehow knew how to get me out. Well, sort of. But in that moment, I had no choice but to trust him.

While Craig rustled around above me, I continued to shine my light up the walls of the cavern. The walls seemed made of a rusty metal or something. It was like they were half there, half not, partially obstructed by who knew how many years of untouched grime. I got up and lightly touched a side. A huge chunk disintegrated under my fingers, producing another dark cloud of filth. Panicked, I backed away so it wouldn't enter my lungs. I didn't bother to touch another wall.

Craig finished building and securing his rope. "Do you think you can climb out if I throw this down to you?" he asked.

"My shoulder is hurting . . . and . . . and the walls are crumbling!" I cried. "It's n-n-not going to ww-work!"

"Calm down, Gary," he said gently. "We'll figure something out."

I swallowed as Craig's light went back into the tunnel and the other room. My heart still pounded wildly as I heard more shuffling from above and then silence.

"Craig?" I shouted again.

"Just a second!" came a muffled reply. The light came back out again. Then there was a WUMP! as something hit the floor. My light flashed on a couple of belts tied to some sheets, blankets, and pillowcases. "See the end with the belts?" he asked. "Take the belt, tie it around your waist, and fasten it." He continued his instructions. "Now, see, you can put the other strap under your ass and your foot, and it will help as I lift you out."

I fumbled around for a bit, but then I found a way to do what he asked. Craig started pulling. The light from his flashlight was gone, but I still had the comfort of mine. I began to rise a few inches at a time from the floor. I made the mistake of looking up just as more dirt gave way and landed on me. I cried out, but Craig just kept going. Finally, I could feel the hole we had made in the wall. It was scary, but I was able to scramble out into the relative safety of our old, familiar dirt room.

Once untied, I spoke not a word to Craig, who was excitedly babbling about the other room. I clambered out of our play cave as fast as I could. Racing up the stairs, I sprinted down the hall and into the bathroom, where I shut the door tight, locked it, and turned on the water. I didn't care if Craig would be pissed at me for locking the door.

I climbed up on the edge of the tub so I could look at myself in the mirror, not recognizing one whit of me! From head to toe, I was covered in fine soot—a dark, rusty red mixed with black. My face was smeared with blubber, snot, and vomit, making a muddy, grotesque mask. I looked like a photo I had seen in a history book of a coal miner, so covered with dust that only the whites of his eyes showed true.

I hopped down and peeled off my clothes before tucking into the tub. Under the water, I was mesmerized as the dirt and grime fell off me in waves. I washed my hair four or five times, and my body and hair still weren't fully clean when the hot water ran out. I had to finish scrubbing myself in the freezing cold, the washcloth gross and filthy.

Mom never asked us about our filthy towels or clothes. She was almost delighted to find a ring in the tub two or three times a week because at least it meant we were bathing! It seemed to fit her "boys will be boys" mentality. If she only knew.

In the wee hours of the morning, shivering from cold and loss of adrenaline, I put on clean pajamas and went straight to bed, covering my head with my quilts. I would never go down that black hole again, ever. Craig would have to kill me because I was not going down again.

One day, after weeks of Nice Craig, I just stopped fighting my brother about going in the tunnel and the other things I did not like. I went down and played Roman soldiers and did experiments with our Bunsen burners and some materials I'd snagged at a local warehouse that tested for iron ore in soil samples. Even though I was getting bigger, so was Craig. He was taller and more muscular than ever. Multiple times, he had proven he could kill me on a whim. He had already joked about how he could have left me in that dark hole. Too many times.

I knew he hadn't been laughing when I couldn't breathe. Something within Craig cared about me. I had to hold that in my heart. He didn't want me to die. Not really, even when he said it to my face.

I had to repeat that to myself as Craig's torture took a more insidious turn.

One late night about a month later, after playing for hours in the cave, Craig and I went upstairs to clean up. After my turn in the bathroom, I noticed Craig had plunked himself on top of the bedcover with a magazine he'd been obsessed with for a few nights. This time he showed me a few of the photos in it. They were shocking to me.

Women look like that? I squeezed my eyes shut and turned away. It kind of scared me to think about. The closest thing I'd ever seen was at the lake where I saw girls and women in shorts and swimsuits. This was far different. This was crazy and weird. I was appalled when Craig began touching his privates as he looked at the pictures. I turned the other way in the bed, toward the wall. Finally, Craig went into the bathroom for a while. I breathed a sigh of relief. If I could fall asleep or pretend to, sometimes he let me sleep instead of beating me.

The next night, I noticed Craig looking at the magazine again. *Looks like he's stopped his nightly ritual of reading the Bible.* I got grossed out when he started touching himself again, so I ignored him and left the room to shower.

Returning to the room, I headed to bed, avoiding his eyes. Before I could jump under the covers, I stopped short. Something unusual was strewn across the covers on my side of the bed. I held it up quizzically.

"What is this?" I asked.

"It's a bra," Craig said flatly. "Put it on."

"What?" I cried without even thinking, then snapped my mouth shut. SLAM!

All the air burst from my stomach with the force of Craig's fist barreling into it. I doubled over, and when I could finally breathe again, tears filled my eyes. I just wanted to know what in the world was going on.

I can't put on girls' clothing! Especially a bra! Not now that I knew what it was for. I'd seen some in Mom's laundry basket, but this was a brand-new white one, not soiled and yellow like hers. And it was . . . smaller. I wanted to protest again until I saw the hard look in my stepbrother's eyes.

"I snagged it at King's," he said. "Now put it on."

I noticed it still had a price tag on it. Upon his order, I pulled my pajama shirt back off. It took me several minutes to try, and Craig had to help me figure it out. Why the hell was it so complicated? I was shaking and fumbling, worried I'd get punched again. Then I saw an expectant gleam in Craig's eye.

A sudden and palpable tension filled the room. I didn't understand at all what it was. I just knew it was there.

Craig let it hang there between us like a threat. Then he smiled. "Now take off your pajama pants and underwear."

What? This time I was smart enough not to utter it aloud. Slowly, I removed my pajama pants and then my undershorts. They lay on a pile on the floor with my shirt. I stood there with only the bra on.

"Get on the bed," Craig ordered.

I noticed he had removed his pajama bottoms too. I cringed in terror.

I hated what Craig did to me that night, rubbing his hands over the bra and squeezing me like I was a girl. I was disgusted, but when I tried to squirm away, Craig grabbed my shoulder and pinched my neck until I cried out, my body going almost numb. Then he pushed himself on top of me, where he pleasured himself between my legs. I knew he was pretending I was one of those women in the magazines, but it didn't help.

Before he sent me off to the bathroom to clean up, he whispered the most frightening words in my ear that he had ever said, making my blood run ice-cold in my trembling veins.

Never say no, I reminded myself. *Never say no. Never say no.*
Especially now.

The Beginning of the End

*"The guards sought to deprive them of something that had sustained them
even as all else had been lost: dignity. This self-respect and sense
of self-worth, the innermost armament of the soul, lies at the heart of
humanness; to be deprived of it is to be dehumanized,
to be cleaved from, and cast below, mankind."*
—Lauren Hillenbrand

In the front room of our home, three objects were the primary focal points. Two were Dad and Mom's "Grand-Puba" easy chairs, which were permanently affixed to the floor. They stayed in their position facing the third immovable object—the television. It was here that our family had our Sunday service: a homage to Swanson TV dinners and *The Wonderful World of Disney*.

Ah, I loved Sunday nights! As we settled down for a movie each week, my biggest threat was accidentally spilling my milk on my TV tray, for I was left-handed. Sunday nights meant no beatings. One night a week, I was safe from Craig's violence and his now nightly sexual abuse.

The summer before third grade was filled with many of the things boys usually love. In addition to racing cars and expeditions miles from home, Craig had me help him begin building a pigeon coop. Outsiders looking in on our many adventures remarked that my brother and I lived in a carefree, childlike heaven.

That summer for me, however, began to descend into a greater darkness than I could ever have known existed. I had never heard of Dante, but I could have easily described for him the nine circles of hell. Fishing trips at the lake should have been another escape from abuse. Instead, he pushed me off into the trees or around the bend of the shore to force me to pleasure him. My brother had developed a level of depravity that left me frightened every minute. And now I didn't have to be down in the cavern under our house or in our bedroom to be so terrorized and at his mercy.

Almost immediately after school ended, I started to develop terrible stomach aches. My guts felt permanently tied into one giant knot from which I found it impossible to disentangle. I wasn't sure what was going on, just that I had difficulty eating and sleeping, writhing in pain as the aches worsened over the next several weeks.

I didn't want to bother my dad and mom with it. I thought I might have to go to the hospital, and I felt like a burden already.

In July, our folks took us to visit Craig's sister, Emma. I didn't know much about her but knew she was the girl I'd overheard Craig's father had once nearly beaten senseless. She looked happy enough now, and I did not focus on such things. I was free here, on Emma's sweet summer grass in the golden sunshine, chasing yellow-and-black swallowtail butterflies.

Craig would not openly hurt me here—never with all three of his family members around. I relished the feel of the sun on my face and stopped to catch my breath as the butterflies danced in dizzying flashes of color all around me.

A few days later, I experienced one glorious week. My Grandpa Delbert Price, my dad's father, invited me up to his countryside home to spend time with him. When the train pulled away from the station in Montpelier, I was alone. For once, I was without Craig because he wasn't invited to go with me.

The farther the train chugged up the tracks toward Grandpa Price's home in Wendell, Idaho, the more relaxed and joyful I felt. For an entire week, I was enfolded in the energy, safe arms, and company of a gentle man. He spent time with me, taught me how to fish, and we talked all about life as he instructed me in the intricate art of tying flies. We spent hours in his yard, tooling over iridescent feathers, thread, and fishhooks.

As we quietly wove threads and bobbles, I watched my grandfather carefully. He was an artist, and, once again, I could see where my dad got his gentle, focused, and peaceful nature. I felt safe. I felt like myself in Grandpa's presence.

At the end of my visit, when we pulled into the train station, Grandpa invited me to come back the following year. Tears pricked my eyes. He even promised to teach me to fly-fish! I crushed him with my hug, quickly brushing away tears as he said goodbye.

As I hopped aboard the train, I came to a sudden stop. I hadn't experienced a single stomachache for nearly a week! I realized that my stomachaches had everything to do with my abject fear of Craig. Sitting straight up in my seat, I gathered my courage, making up my mind right then that I would somehow find the strength to withstand him.

My resolve seemed strong after I first arrived home. Everyone, including Craig, seemed happy to see me.

I can do this. At least I thought I could.

The last day I ever dared defy Craig's commands was a balmy summer day. We had been up late working on a racing model car that was sure to beat our neighbors. Craig *had* to beat them. He said he had to show them who was boss even though we had won time and again with our modified model airplane engines and racers. Some of the boys had naturally become more innovative too. Our neighborhood street competitions were becoming more intense.

One early July morning before it got too hot, a large crowd gathered across the street while our parents slept peacefully. It felt like everyone in the neighborhood was out to watch. Working together, we set the parameters of the raceway, using lines of string that would keep our fancy racers on the track, ensuring they wouldn't self-destruct at their great speeds.

The atmosphere was light and fun, but the intensity grew more concentrated when Craig and another boy crossed the finish line within a fraction of a second of each other—and the other kid was declared the winner. I gulped when Craig's face twisted into a snarl, but he covered it quickly and just laughed.

"Lucky break," he said to his opponent. "But let's really see who's boss."

Whenever it came down to close matches, it was always to be determined by the best two out of three. I watched Craig's jaw tighten and his joviality turn somber as he set up for the second race. He briefly did some tweaking to the wheels and the motor of his car before carefully positioning it on the raceway.

A dad at the finish line called it. "Craig!" he shouted.

Relief flooded through me, and I drew the back of my hand across my brow. But I couldn't exhale yet because it wasn't over. One more race would determine the real winner. I hoped it was Craig—and not because he was my brother.

"Five . . . four . . . three . . . two . . . one—BLASTOFF!" the crowd cried, and the racers were off. The cars sped down the street wildly fast, guided only by the strings. The race was again extraordinarily close, but this time the other kid was declared winner. Craig had been beaten two out of three. Immediately, my brother challenged the winner to another race but catcalling and more ensued from our neighbor friends and even some parents.

"Sore loser," someone smirked.

"You can't win all the time!" someone else shouted from across the street as they walked away.

Craig stalked toward the house with a deep scowl on his face. Then he turned and gave me a look before he entered. I pretended I didn't see that he expected me to follow him. Instead, I stayed outside and played around with my buddies for as long as I could.

One by one, each friend wandered home for lunch. Both hunger and the sweltering heat stole our gumption. All traces of earlier adrenaline long gone, my body was exhausted from too little sleep. The house would be stiflingly hot . . . and Craig was in there, somewhere. I had no desire to go inside. Instead, the intoxicating smell of the green summer grass called me to find a cool spot in the shade underneath the side yard's tree or in the back, where perhaps I could take a nap.

I did not even notice that the sparrows in the trees and the pigeons in the small coop were eerily quiet, waiting. It was silent and still as I made my way around the corner of the house between us and our next-door neighbors. Suddenly, Craig appeared from out of nowhere. He grabbed me painfully by the arm and whipped me out of sight.

"C-Craig," I began to stammer. "W-what's wrong? Ouch, that hurts—"

I was slammed onto my back by the force of Craig's shoulder, the breath knocked out of me. My eyes widened when I noticed he had a pillow in his hands. My world suddenly darkened as he placed the pillow over my eyes and face and began pushing—*hard.*

My brother was smothering me, making sure my mouth and nose were blocked. Immediately, I was triggered. The panic I had felt in the cavern somewhere deep below us came back to me, along with the instinctual need for oxygen and freedom from death. I started squirming, gasping, and moving my head quickly back and forth to break free. I needed air! That's when a corner of the pillow moved enough for me to see directly into the twisted face of Craig. His dark eyes were nearly unrecognizable. It was almost as if something demonic had taken over.

Oh, my God! I thought in terror. *He means it this time. He really is going to kill me!*

I screamed into the pillow—which was a mistake because now my last vestige of breath was gone and no one could hear me. My body began to writhe as a mass of the pillow was shoved deep into my mouth and hit the back of my throat, which was now even more constricted. I began to gag, my body contorting in a futile effort to survive. The last thing I remember, I was trying to dig my short, stubby fingernails into his legs.

Then everything went dark.

The message was clear. I was not to defy him.

And from that day on, I no longer would.

***

The stifling summer heat was almost at an end. My neighborhood buddies and Craig grumbled about the start of school. For me, school was salvation. Despite my harsh struggle in nearly every subject and still never allowed lunch, each day that I stepped onto that property meant I was safe from Craig for a full six hours.

My new teacher, Mrs. Gwen Sharpe, quickly became disappointed with my regular schoolwork. Compared to my other teachers, who had been much older, bordering on elderly, Mrs. Sharpe was beautiful and much younger, somewhere in her late thirties, like my mother had been when I last saw her. My teacher was tall and lean with a smaller tucked chin. Her lips were thin but well-defined, and lovely eyes sparkled from behind the still-fashionable-in-Idaho horn-rimmed glasses.

What I loved most about Mrs. Sharpe was that she was extremely outgoing and animated. She made it a pleasure to be in her class despite my test scores. Finding one thing for which she could praise me, she encouraged my art as much as Mrs. Anderson had. Many times, as she walked by my desk during art time, she gasped, particularly at my chalk drawings. Beaming under her praise, I tried to do even better each day.

As the leaves changed and started to tumble from the trees in great heaps, the school prepared for its fall carnival. Mrs. Sharpe asked me to do several drawings of goldfish in chalk for the fishpond. Everyone oohed and ahhed at the results and loved them during the night's popular event. Mrs. Sharpe even carefully stowed the fishes away after, letting the class know they were beautiful enough to use year after year going forward! Every piece of encouragement this woman gave me I tucked away in my heart. I even clung to the remembrance of her warm smile during the ensuing hours of beatings and torture after each school day ended.

Once home, I was under Craig's total domination except for the few hours our parents interacted with us. As the weather quickly grew colder, Craig was strategizing more time in the cavern under our house again. He sent me out to shoplift or steal daily, and I was not to come home without a special find. Even though Craig and I had been delivering *The Grit*, a local newspaper, to purchase the higher-quality toys he wanted, his voracious appetite was never quenched.

Already that year I had been forced to steal another entire train set, this time from King's Variety Store, and a large set from Western Auto, among hundreds of dollars of other toys. All the stealing was starting to catch up with me. Not only had I been banned from King's and Western Auto, but now the drug store too. No one ever told my parents. I was simply outlawed and forbidden to enter ever again.

That didn't matter to Craig. Just the week before, Craig had ordered me to kype something at the grocery store. I was caught and banned from that store as well, coming home empty-handed and trembling. Upon arrival, Craig only nodded.

Oh, good. He understands, and it's going to be okay, I thought. As soon as we heard our folks' car crunch down the driveway to go to work, Craig lunged at me, knocking my chair straight over to sharply hit the floor. Nothing else could penetrate my consciousness. There was only the searing, relentless pain of his kicks. Finally, he stopped and left me lying there. I couldn't move for over an hour, unable to even get off the floor.

Less than a week later, a huge storm blew in. I looked up from my watercolor painting in the kitchen to see Craig bringing in his bike to work on it. He set it upside down on the linoleum floor. My brother had been stealing bikes in town and would hide them for a while, then bring them in and strip stuff from them to use on his master bike.

As I listened to the thunder and whoosh of the wind outside, I heard a sudden snarl. I glanced up to see that a stolen bracket Craig thought would work didn't fit correctly. I watched in horror as Craig's face turned a hideous purple. Seconds later, he smacked me in the head with his metal wrench so hard it knocked me over. Immediately, I began to bleed from the head wound. My hands bloodied as I clasped it, sobbing.

It was only then that Craig seemed to realize he'd gone too far . . . again. "Hey, I'm sorry, Gary," he apologized, grabbing an old towel to stop the bleeding. He didn't beat me anymore that night. The next morning, he even made sure the blood was out of my hair before school and smoothed thick wisps of it over the still-large red welt to make sure it wasn't visible to our parents or the folks at school. He made me go, even though I had a debilitating headache. If I stayed home, Craig knew Mom might suspect something and have me checked out.

Craig wasn't the only one getting highly skilled at covering things up. Not long after the wrench incident, I began falling into a deep depression. Instead of anger or bitterness, I walked around in a state of sheer hopelessness. I started carrying a small pocketknife with me. I never pulled the secret knife on my brother, but I dreamed of brandishing it at him and screaming at him to stop beating me for good.

One day after school, I was daydreaming about it, and a horrific feeling overcame me.

You pull out that pocketknife and Craig will kill you, a knowing voice inside me said.

And with every fiber of my being, I knew that what the voice said was true. Craig would. I would not get away from him. I pondered it as all the kids left the playground. I pondered it even harder as I failed to steal something from the feed and tackle store for Craig. Greeted inside by an angry cashier and one of the managers, even their harsh words and glaring, accusatory gazes were nothing compared to what awaited me at home.

Another place in Montpelier off-limits to me. Another failed mission. The knowledge made me desperate.

As dusk fell, I found myself wandering aimlessly down Clay Street, about three blocks from home near my elementary school. No one was about. It was silent as I walked onto the playground in the growing dark.

I stood under Mrs. Sharpe's unlit classroom windows for a long time, just staring up. As night rolled in, I wondered just how long I had been more afraid of Craig than I was of the dark.

Tears began to cascade down my cheeks and soak into my shirt. I did not want to go home. I did not *ever* want to go home.

Hands trembling, I got out that small, rusty hunting knife and inspected it. It had the words "Calico Ghost Town" engraved upon the handle. It was purchased during the one family vacation we had ever taken together. I clutched the handle, then drew the sharp blade up to the soft skin of my belly, surprised to find that under my shirt, the skin was already slick, drenched with my tears.

All I had to do was fall on the blade. Then it would be over. It would *all* be over.

I glanced up into the shuttered windows of Mrs. Sharpe's classroom. Was it possible my teacher might miss me?

Will it make her cry if suddenly I'm not there?

Picturing my teacher with her angelic smile, I realized the truth. She *would* cry for me. Mrs. Sharpe cared about me. I sobbed even harder with anger and regret. I needed to end this, and yet I could not bring pain to the only bit of sunshine I knew.

I stumbled away from the school and Mrs. Sharpe's windows. My vision was still fuzzy, but I put the knife back in my pocket as the darkness fell more swiftly and the temperature began to plummet. I had my coat but not much else. I had no food, no money, and nowhere to go.

I was going to die at Craig's hands—either tonight or sometime soon. Usually, I didn't know when a massive beating was coming. This time I did.

As I crossed the street, I slipped behind a building and just in time. A car drove slowly down the alley across from me. I recognized it as soon as I squinted in the dark.

Cops! Had the feed and tackle store called them on me? I thought about the many, many items I had stolen for Craig. *If they only knew,* I had often thought to myself—but now I realized they really did know. Whether from the store or from home, the police were looking for me. It was past dinnertime. Dad and Mom would be wondering where I was. Now I was in double trouble—and if I had somehow gotten Craig into trouble, I really couldn't go back.

The police car turned as if to go around the block again. Had they seen me? I took off at high speed and slipped underneath the floorboards of an old barn, breathless, in the midst of cobwebs and thick dust as the car drove slowly by. This barn was located in the field behind our house, so I knew I could fit in the hole beneath the floorboards. Montpelier and the fields surrounding it were full of old barns, and I knew each one of them intimately.

As the darkness underneath the barn deepened in the failing light, my body began trembling violently. I started having flashbacks of the hole under our house. *I have to get out!*

Before I could scramble out from under the floorboards and run in the other direction, another police cruiser appeared out of the corner of my eye. I turned and watched as this one drove down the street, kitty-corner from me in the opposite direction. A couple of policemen got out and began searching, their bright flashlights illuminating the darkening corners. Ducking deeper into the shadows, I was confident they wouldn't find me, but I lost sight of them. A sudden sound made me freeze. It was the groan of the barn door. The old, dusty floorboards above me began creaking as the police made their way inside. I held my breath as I saw flashes of light dart between the floorboards within inches of my body.

I clamped my hand over my mouth so they couldn't hear my frightened gasp. Their lights only looked around the main floor and up into the rafters. Neither of the officers thought to look *under* the barn. Finally, they left in their car. I stayed crouched in the corner under the floorboards for another hour, not daring to emerge even as the temperature dropped. My tears, which had felt like warm splashes on my skin and shirt on the playground, now felt like ice.

I can't stay here. I'll freeze.

Finally scuttling out from under the barn when it felt safe, I knew I had nowhere else to go. Avoiding the streetlamps, I didn't know what I was looking for, except . . . shelter. Safety. Refuge.

Craig kept me isolated. I had no close, strong friends. Beyond school, he didn't allow me buddies unless there was something in it for him. There was no one I could go to. Poking around, farther up the street beyond our house, I noticed the unmistakable shadow of our neighbor's car, a Corvair. Everyone in town knew that car. It was a Portmanteau or mix of Corvette and Bel Air with a hardtop, fastback-styled roof. I loved the way it purred every time it vibrated down our street.

The hardtop was on, but to my relief, the doors had been left unlocked. I quietly worked the heavy metal passenger door to avoid the inevitable squeak of opening and the clap of shutting. Shivering, I hunched down in the seat and tried to get the heater working.

Damn! It won't work without the keys. I searched under the mats to no avail. Resigned, I stuffed my hands back into my pockets and lay myself down on the seat as the shadows pressed in. Hungry and miserably cold, I thought, *it's better than being with Craig. I'm sick to death of what he does to me every night.* At that, I drifted off to sleep.

The next morning, I awoke early, stiff on the seat of the car. It was still relatively dark out, but around me were the unmistakable sounds of people rising and preparing to go to work. Each time an automobile drove by my clandestine hideout, I ducked down while their headlights cast an eerie glow onto the Corvair's hardtop.

Finally, I sat up stiffly, my stomach growling in protest. I had not eaten since the previous morning. I was ravenous, but there was nothing to be had inside this car. The interior was as spotless as the exterior.

Out of the corner of my eye, I caught movement. It was a cat, sneaking into Mrs. Wuthrich's garden across the street. Her garden . . . *Food!*

Brushing aside the fact that it might be too late in the year, my stomach propelled me out the car door in search of snap peas or lingering end-of-season goodies. I knew what was possible to score here because I'd often had to sneak into her garden like Peter Rabbit to find something to ease my gnawing hunger. In all my visits, I'd never been caught.

My stomach growled again, louder. I knew better than to use Mrs. Wuthrich's gate. It squeaked loudly. I hopped the fence instead, crouching low amongst a few shrubs. Most of the garden was bare. Relieved, I did find some remaining carrot tops and tried digging a few of them out with my numb fingers, anticipating the crisp sweetness despite the dirt.

I was about to pull out my hunting knife to use as a tool when suddenly Mrs. Wuthrich's back door opened, only twenty or thirty feet away from me in the growing dawn.

"Gary? Is that you?" she called in her high voice, and my heart thudded in my chest. "What are you doing out here at this early hour?"

Frozen, I didn't know what to do. There was nowhere to run.

"Um, yeah," I replied guiltily and stood up. "Yeah, it's me."

"Well come on in and have a visit," the old woman said kindly. Mrs. Wuthrich was about the same age as Mrs. Anderson but was wizened and bent over instead of ramrod straight. When she saw me hesitate in the light of the dawning morning, she added, "I have some chocolate cake I made yesterday and some fresh milk. I haven't had time to make breakfast yet, but I *know* you like my cake."

My stomach growled louder than Mrs. Wuthrich's squeaking gate. I practically ran into her house, then sat down at the table as she poured me some milk and placed a large plate of chocolate cake in front of me. She excused herself into the kitchen to begin preparing breakfast.

I devoured the cake, gorging and then sweeping up every crumb she offered.

A few minutes later, Mrs. Wuthrich emerged from the kitchen. Her eyes widened at my empty plate. She was just promising more cake and a banana when there was a knock at the door. When she opened it, I nearly dropped the plate I was licking clean.

It was the police.

"Well, thanks for coming to see me, Gary," said Mrs. Wuthrich, still kind, even though she had just delivered me into the hands of the authorities. As they escorted me out of the house without more cake or a banana, I began to quiver at the realization of what the police station and jail might mean for me.

Instead, the outcome was worse than I could have imagined.

After being questioned, the officers simply chuckled at each other. To my utter dismay, they drove down the road a few houses and across the street, pulling into the driveway where they delivered me . . . back to hell.

A Golden Dream

"It's amazing how far you're willing to go when someone believes in you."
—Katie Kacvinsky

For a while, Dad and Mom were really upset with me for being gone all night, but their anger wore off once they believed I was safe—as much as I knew I wasn't.

My folks worked harder than most folks I knew in our small town. Wistfully, I often wondered what it would be like to live the way some of the other kids did—with a mom at home all day, watching over them . . . protecting them. I also had to admit it wouldn't be awful to have a dad making enough money that a kid like me could have his or her very own, brand-new bike—one that wasn't stolen like Craig's, or hand-me-downs made from parts that were stolen, like mine.

As the snow melted, the fragrant smells and sights of spring started to warm me up on the outside. All I could think about was that sort of freedom. When I went downtown or roamed the neighborhoods, I witnessed other kids living the life I only dreamed of. Supported by seemingly healthy, loving families, they were most often perched atop a bike—and not just on any old bike. Oh no, in my dream world, if you were the coolest of the cool, it was all about Schwinn Stingray! There seemed to be a lot of them in town. I wanted one so bad, I would catch myself drooling every time a kid whizzed by with an aerodynamic banana seat.

Between all the errands Craig continued to send me on, one day I stopped short in front of a window, frozen. Inside our local Western Auto hardware store, they had for sale the cream of the crop of bicycles—a brand-new Stingray with three full speeds! In addition, the bike was a luxurious gold—I mean, who had a gold bike, anyway? Oil sheiks? I salivated over the high-tech hand brakes and black tuck-and-roll seat.

Oh, baby, whoever buys that *will be the coolest kid in town! What if it was me?*

Then I looked at the price tag: fifty dollars! That was as out of reach to me as fifty million.

Dejected, I walked away from the window, my head lower than the day they'd banned me from that store. I would have to set my sights for less so I could at least earn some kind of wheels before the end of summer.

As early as anyone would hire me that spring, I began mowing and trimming half the lawns in town. I'd earn a dollar here, and sometimes two dollars there if it was a big job and I was thorough and fast, especially if it didn't eat up too much gas. As long as it wasn't raining, every single day that I was able, I was out mowing a lawn. I loved every excuse to be out of Craig's clutches.

Beginning as early in the day as the neighbors would let me, I'd mow two or three properties in a row before coming home, beet red in the face and sunburned. I never stopped for a lemonade or soda. I was focused on my goal of a bike and put every spare penny away.

The problem was, I couldn't keep all my money. Craig would force money out of my hands for another one of "our" projects. I started to learn how to be sneaky about telling him where I was going and just how many lawns I mowed and trimmed. I would hand over one, maybe two dollars if I could get away with it and privately squirrel away a few in my sock when he wasn't watching.

As summer started to draw to a close, I felt disheartened. I had worked my guts out all season long, and I had compiled a treasure—forty whole dollars hidden in that sock. I knew, however, that there was no way I could earn my beloved Stingray, and surely not before summer turned to winter. I resigned myself to the fact that I would have to settle for a lesser model from King's, but at least I'd have some wheels—and some additional freedom from Craig on a bike I'd earned myself, for which I could be proud instead of feeling shameful.

One early morning after work and before she went to bed, Mom stopped to talk with me. Craig was still inside sleeping, and I was preparing to head out for another hard day with our mower, hand grass-clippers, and the heavy, rusted gas can I used for the jobs ahead.

Mom folded her arms and looked at me sternly. Her hair was a little askew after a long shift, and I could smell the fryer grease on her clothing from ten feet away.

"Gary, come over here," Mom said, her face a mask.

Crap! What did Craig say I did now?

Resigned, I hung my head and walked over.

She perched on the lawn mower to be at eye level with me. I noticed often that she liked to do that, and I always appreciated her for it.

"Do you know what I used to do all summer when I was your age?" she asked.

I knew she had grown up on a farm in Wardboro, Idaho. That's about all I knew.

"No. Not really," I mumbled, embarrassed.

"I rounded up cows and milked the darn things every day, twice a day, all year long," she explained patiently, and if she noticed my pink cheeks, she kindly didn't mention it. "I also had to do a *lot* of herding in the summer. It was ridiculously hard work."

I nodded. Suddenly I remembered what her sister had said, *rather unkindly,* I thought, about her working so hard she looked like a man. At times, under all her hardness was a sense of humor and a tender softness. I thought I understood why Dad liked to be with her.

Mom paused and took a long look at me, up and down.

"You've been working hard," she said finally. "How much did you earn for that bicycle I see you pining over in the window of Western?"

I was taken aback. She was so busy, and yet she'd noticed? A warmth spread over my chest. "A little over forty dollars!" I said proudly. "If I work hard into September and October, maybe it won't be sold by then and I can still get it."

Mom paused and took a long drag of her cigarette before stubbing it out and blowing an equally long stream of smoke from her mouth. Then she turned and looked me in the eye.

"Wanna go get that bicycle this morning?"

I looked on incredulously as Mom, with a big grin on her face, pulled out a ten-dollar bill. I didn't care who was watching, I ran the few steps right into her strong body and hugged her fiercely. "Thank you, Mom!" I cried. And I meant it.

Striding into Western Auto with Mom—a place I had been banned from—stood out indelibly in my mind. I knew I would always remember the glowing, golden, warm feeling I had inside as I produced all the money from my pocket for the bike. I grinned from ear to ear as the clerk shook his head in amazement. I first laid down the ten-dollar bill, then one at a time counted out forty-plus single dollar bills, including tax.

I pushed my new Stingray back out of Western Auto, beaming as I held it straight up and down, careful not to catch the sleek banana seat on the doors. I could smell the promise of a new day. There was freedom in the aroma of the fresh paint on the body and never-used fancy seat.

Mom was equally as proud of this acquisition as I was, and when she beamed at me as brightly, I genuinely beamed right back at her, knowing that no matter what, Craig could not claim this miraculous treasure.

When Mom dropped me off at my job, I proudly parked my bike up against the house where I could watch it from the corner of my eye. I mowed that lawn the fastest of any lawn in my entire life! I did a good job, but as soon as I was finished and paid, I jumped on my bike and sped off, still long before Craig ever rose for the day. Smelling the wind of freedom and loving the taste of it on my air-cooled skin, I was the happiest, most hard-working kid in all of Montpelier, riding a golden dream over every inch of road in that town before I finally made my way home.

Untimely Demise

"God loved the birds and invented trees.
Man loved the birds and invented cages."
—*Jacques Deval*

Fortunately for me, Craig wasn't furious about the purchase of my Stingray. He actually seemed pleased for me. Then, using all my allowance and earnings he pinched from me plus his, he came home with a Honda 90, threatening me within an inch of my life if I touched it.

I had no desire to touch it. After the pillow-smothering incident, I continued to do just about whatever my brother asked. I only hoped the motorbike would be a new obsession to kick Craig's need for me to shoplift to the curb.

It didn't.

That fall, Craig went on a new tangent to expand his pigeon coop. At first, I worried my brother would somehow hurt the birds. In fact, I had seen him torture hamsters, cats, and other small creatures. But there was something about the birds that brought out Craig's gentler side. He would touch them and talk to them as if to his own precious babies, making sure they were well-fed and watered. Secretly, I hoped some of that gentleness rubbed off.

It didn't.

The coop was now a modest four feet long and three feet tall along our fence in the backyard. Craig wasn't satisfied and shared his vision to double or triple the existing project. So, every night after the folks left for either work or the bar, no matter the weather, he sent me out with my little red Radio Flyer wagon, scavenging for supplies.

As another winter turned to spring, however, the expansion of the coop began in earnest; we quickly burned through supplies and needed more. As the town delinquent banned from stores, I had taken to sneaking into abandoned warehouses, commercial properties, and new-home construction sites. There, I scavenged beautiful new two-by-fours, plywood, and more. The carefully oiled wheels of my little red wagon squeaked gently throughout all the dark hours of the night, stopping only due to the risk of being spotted against the brightening dawn sky.

The pigeon cage soon grew into a sprawling, monolithic structure eight feet wide, twenty-four feet long, and sectioned into three eight-foot units. It also now loomed eight feet tall, nearly double my height!

The bottom of the coop included a nesting area for sleep and egg laying. The only thing of great importance left to finish was the roof. I could see the need for the covering, for as I witnessed these unique and beautiful creatures, they deserved to have some freedom. As I gazed upon the beautiful, winged creatures imprisoned in their cage, painful twinges of compassion raced through me. I had to fight back wild urges to set them all free.

Craig, on the other hand, desired to amass many more birds in his cage. The pigeon collection began in abandoned factories at night, shining flashlights into the nesters' eyes to hypnotize them so we could easily grab them and thrust them into burlap gunnysacks. The trick was to keep them quiet while we snuck through the shadows of Montpelier's backstreets before finally acquainting them with their new home.

One night, we found a mother lode of birds in the old Protestant church in Montpelier. The bottom of the ramshackle stone building was still used for services. However, from what we could tell, the tall, abandoned steeple held multiple nesting areas of prized, pure-white pigeons. Craig was elated, and a plan was set for the following night. For this covert sting operation, it was necessary to bring his buddy Mark with us.

As we set about before midnight, it was raining harder than I'd ever seen in Montpelier. Everything was soaked, including the three of us as we went to make our way into the church.

At least it will be dry inside, I thought. *And on the bright side, the frightened birds' cries will be muffled by the sound of pelting rain on the way home.*

The upstairs section of the church had been blocked off, and as soon as we broke into the building, we understood why. The pungent stench of pigeon droppings mixed with rotting wood was overwhelming. Pinching our noses in disgust, we investigated. To our dismay, we found that most of the pigeons were far beyond easy reach, clear up in the steeple.

In the driving rain, Craig had me scour the neighborhood. Fortunately, I found a neighboring home where a twelve-rung ladder hung conveniently off the side of the owner's shed out back. It took me awhile, but finally my small body was able to quietly maneuver the unwieldy contraption off the wall.

Heading back to the church, I stumbled, unable at first to balance the ladder's weight from back to front. It was three times my size. Still, once I got my equilibrium, I made the trek, the water falling from the sky making an almost musical plinking sound as it struck the aluminum.

Without a word, Craig grabbed the closest rung of the ladder to help my muscles hoist it up to the top of the old roof. Rain continued to pour down the slick, slated rooftop as I then scrambled up to the roof, then held the ladder for Craig and Mark. I watched them, amazed by their courage in finding footing up the last couple of feet beyond the ladder, gunnysacks in hand. Watching them slip a bit as they scaled the steep side made me glad that I wasn't tall enough for that part of the journey.

After only five or so minutes of work with the flashlight, they were on their way back down, gunnysacks bulging with the coveted white birds. Mark went first, carefully arranging his feet to miraculously hit the top rung of the ladder, having to let go a little in order to do so. As I held the ladder, the reverberations of his feet slipping and hitting the rungs penetrated to my bones. Still, I held tight, and Mark made his way to safety. Instead of stopping to help me secure the ladder for Craig, however, he was impatient to get off the roof and immediately turned away.

Something went badly wrong when it was Craig's turn to let go and target that top rung. He must have slipped because his feet hit unevenly. I was not big enough to balance the ladder against his error, and it began to topple to the side, where I lost control. I heard a small cry and a sickening THUMP as his body hit the line of the roof at the bottom of the steeple beside me. To my horror, Craig was suddenly gone, having tumbled over the side of the main church!

Panic-stricken, I abandoned the prone ladder and ran downstairs, then outside. Craig's body was slumped near the wall, either unconscious or dead.

"Craig!" I whispered furiously, shaking him. "Craig! Are you okay?" There was no answer. This was all too familiar, leaning over someone I loved, where it seemed all hope was lost and life could so easily be extinguished.

What if he doesn't wake up? What am I going to do?

Suddenly, a loud crash permeated the night sky. I knew it couldn't be thunder, muted as it was from the deluge. Rushing into the building, I half expected to find the police ready to arrest us for breaking and entering. Instead, I discovered that Craig's buddy Mark had fallen through the rotted, pigeon-poop-besieged second floor, all the way down to the main congregation area of the church. I looked around in shock. The previously pristine chapel had been desecrated by the remnants of "rats with wings."

Mark took one wide-eyed look at me, then rose with surprising agility and sprinted away, not even looking back. *Wait*! I wanted to cry out. *I need your help*! But I knew better. The neighbors would hear, and then everything we had been doing would be found out. Craig would kill me for chancing it.

I turned my back on the devastation and raced outside to Craig. Calming myself, I felt for a pulse. He lay unconscious, and as I looked closer, I could see a massive welt on the side of his head. I shook him once more for good measure. When he refused to wake up, I realized I was going to have to get help.

Through the years, Craig had taught me a lot about covering our motives. If we left the ladder out—a ladder that was *not* ours—the evidence of our crimes would ensure deep trouble, birds or no birds. Blinded more by tears than by rain, I stumbled back over to the neighbor's house to hoist that ladder back up on the wall. As much as I was afraid of my brother, the truth was I also loved him.

I don't want him to die! I rounded the corner where the huge ladder was supposed to hang. The hooks had been low enough for me to unhook and lower the ladder fairly easily using gravity, but they were high enough that hoisting it back up seemed impossible. Trembling violently, I raised the aluminum structure against the wooden wall.

Clang! *Too loud.* Clang! Clang! Clang! I kept missing the hooks, fighting my rising panic. *Can it get any worse than this?* Finally, it caught. As I let go of the rails, I cringed in anticipation of the crash that did not come.

Not waiting another moment, I raced back to my injured brother, searching for him in the dark. No Craig. Not anywhere.

Oh, my God! Where is he? All that remained was a tied-off gunnysack full of the pure whites, moving as if it were one, great creature. I didn't have time to question if they had all survived the fall. I ran around the side of the large church, where I found Craig slumped against the wall. It took a moment for it to sink in that he had awakened under the downpour of the eves and dragged himself to a drier area. I had never been so happy to see him.

From the time I heard him drop, I had only been afraid for him. Now, as the impact and relief washed over me, though, I suddenly became afraid for myself. I hadn't been able to hold the ladder. I hadn't been strong enough. I'd let him down.

Dawn was coming, and fast. I wondered what the church congregation would do when they arrived in a few hours that Sunday morning. They would walk into complete chaos—witnessing more than an act of God or pigeons, as evidenced by Mark's telltale footprints.

I grabbed the writhing gunny sack, and we made our way home. Craig, still dazed, let me guide him home in the softening of the rain before the sky lightened. Finally at home, Craig and I secured the white pigeons, not even taking a moment to admire them, for we immediately dragged ourselves to our room and fell into bed, exhausted. Fortunately, it was not a school night. Instead of having to get up in an hour, I would be able to sleep in until my brother wanted something from me.

It didn't take long to hear about the aftermath of our escapade. The church break-in was the talk of the town. It was speculated whether the desecration of the roof was premeditated or just an unfortunate accident. Churchgoers prayed for the hooligan who fell through the roof. I didn't. I was still angry with Craig's traitorous friend for abandoning us when

Craig had fallen as well. As much as I did not know how to pray, I had whispered as pure a prayer of thanks to God as any child that my brother had not died.

Little did I know just how many times I would want to take that prayer back.

Red-Handed

"Men of thoughtless actions are always surprised by consequences."
—*Sarah Addison Allen*

Craig's near-death experience didn't even faze him. Bankrolled by paper routes, chores, and my continued stolen allowance and lunch money, Craig began ordering specialty pigeons before we even finished completing the flight pen. Termed "fancies," he ordered Fantails, Puffers, German Nuns, Snowshoed Homers, and other exotic breeds.

The pigeons we had already captured quickly began breeding, creating little squabs, or squeakers. Right after breaking out of their eggs, they were piteously ugly, but I had to admit they became pretty darn cute in just a few days' time. Craig finally amassed around eighty birds—an astounding menagerie.

A wonder to see in their varied colors, behaviors, and distinct personalities, the birds became my job. I fed them twice daily. They ate a lot, which was expensive. That meant we had to buy a little of food . . . and steal a lot to make up for it.

By day, Craig and I stopped by Walton Feed, where we would buy ten or twenty pounds of grain and corn. Now knowing precisely where the grain was kept, at night, we snuck in, placed heavy sacks on our wagon, and dragged several hundred more pounds back across town to feed the growing flock. Every few days, they needed more.

I was already getting too little sleep, so I was thoroughly relieved when school ended and, by some miracle, I graduated to the next class. Throughout that summer, we continued to steal the birds' food as needed.

Fifth grade for me started that fall. Like every year, I struggled massively in the classroom. I found it nearly impossible to concentrate. I was sleepy, ravenous, and felt under constant stress. Only one blessing remained—that every hour I was in school, I was away from Craig. Daily, he grew more brutal. It was as if he spent as much time strategizing my torture as he did his elaborate battles and schemes. I remained silent, unable to confront his abuse.

As the weather turned colder in late fall, Craig demanded that I steal the supplies for a better roof for our pigeon coop. The year 1965 was an unusual year in Montpelier. As wet as the spring that created our double downfall at the Presbyterian church was, the normally dry region continued to receive record precipitation. The deluge continued for weeks, wreaking havoc on the pigeon coop. Despite my forages for all the heavy-duty materials I could find in the city and surrounding rural areas, it wasn't enough. Mud mixed with pigeon poop made a sludge that oozed into all the feeding and nesting areas. The stench was impossible and as disgusting as the rotten areas of the church had been.

"Gary, I need you to come to the lumberyard with me to buy a sheet of their corrugated roofing tin," ordered Craig. "We need to take note of where it's kept in the yard because you're going to go back tonight and get what we need to finish our project."

I didn't reply, but at my look of exhaustion, he snapped.

"It's a filthy mess in here. You're going tonight!"

I dragged myself across town with Craig and my little red Radio Flyer wagon into the yard of Montpelier Coal & Lumber. There, Craig purchased one sheet of twenty-two-gauge tin, measuring two feet by six feet. Awkwardly, I placed the tin over the wagon and secured it with some twine, carefully noting the location in the yard. Craig paid for it, then left me to drag it back to the yard by myself. I slogged my way home, already soaked and chilled to the bone, knowing that in just a few hours, with dark as my cloak and shield, I would be headed back.

Straight after Mom and Dad left for work, it was time for me to go, despite the deluge. Craig would never think to give me a night off. Strategically, to him it made sense—I would be the only fool out in the miserable weather.

Creeping down the back alleyways, I avoided the town's intermittent police cruisers and a few errant cars as I made my way along the railroad tracks. Finally, I sloshed up to the gates of the lumberyard. Peering into the unknown, lurking shadows, I thought about my father working the night shift. Barely three blocks south of the yard I was about to break into, Dad was sitting in a warm, dry, redbrick RR train depot, where I knew I could not go for help.

Quietly, my heart pounding, I opened the creaking gates of the lumberyard and made my way through the maze of materials to the heavy corrugated tin. Thus began my first of three full trips. Each time, I was careful to stack the unwieldy tin on the side of the coop. Back and forth, chilled to the very depths, I had to keep going until I amassed all thirty sheets according to Craig's orders. I would be severely punished if I didn't finish the task, which I undertook while Craig was home, dry, warm, and asleep.

On the final trip, I kept stumbling, numb with cold and the fever of needed sleep. Hopefully Craig wouldn't drag me out of bed to help him put up the tin when he decided to wake up. I wasn't sure I could.

He might have to kill me. By this time, I was so tired that I did not care one bit.

The eastern sky above the "M" on the hill started to turn a lighter shade as I finished my last assignment. I didn't bother to take off the last load or bring the red wagon in out of the rain as I stripped out of my soaked clothes and lurched into the queen-sized bed that Craig and I now shared. He was still peacefully sleeping after my biggest heist for him, ever. I curled up in the blankets and was out cold.

I had only been asleep for a couple of hours when suddenly I was awakened.

"Craig! Gary!" our parents' rough voices exclaimed. "Wake up!"

Craig jumped out of bed, but I was groggy with sleep and didn't move.

"You need to come out here, *now*," they continued. "The police are here. They want to talk to you."

For the first time, my blurry eyes noted colored lights flashing through the gap in the curtain, pouring adrenaline into my bloodstream.

Oh my God! Police!

Two local law enforcement cars were parked in front of our home. Still, for the life of me, I couldn't understand how they had tracked me.

As exhausted as I had been, I had taken great care that no one had followed me.

By the time I dressed and walked outside, I didn't even need to squint at what the officers were pointing to. There, plain as the new day, were deep and unmistakable tracks in the wet, soggy grass! The police had easily followed my wagon tracks for over eight blocks, right to our backyard. The culprit wagon stood in the grass near the coop, looking less than innocent as the now-light rain made musical notes on the final piece of tin, like a chorus of my guilt.

"Did you do this?" the officers asked.

Craig turned an accusatory glare on me, as if he had nothing to do with it.

I'm dead for sure, I thought. *No getting out of this one.*

However, within a fraction of a second, it seemed the police weren't buying into Craig's playing innocent. I saw the blood drain from his face. While I had been caught red-handed, my only saving grace was that somehow the adults seemed to realize that this project was likely much bigger than a beginning fifth grader could pull off by himself.

"Craig, what is this about?" everyone asked.

Craig stared at the ground. Then he started stammering.

"Look, it's Gary! He's . . ."

"Craig!" Dad said sharply, his face livid and unbelieving. "There's no way this can just be Gary!"

"But, Dad, I've been in bed all night. He's . . . he was . . . he's . . ."

"He was obviously doing something you told him to do," snapped Dad gravely, and Mom nodded. In shock, I peered up at her from the corner of my eyes. Her face seemed more haggard and tired than normal, and I noticed for practically the first time since I had known her that she wasn't jumping to Craig's defense. Her jaw was tight, and her eyes flashed with anger.

"Why did Gary do this, Craig? *Why?*" I noticed that, for once, she was asking him and not me. That was new.

Craig kept stammering, his usual plausibility out of reach in a crowd of unbelievers. Everyone realized he had to have been the mastermind behind it all, but my body suddenly went cold with a dawning realization. *I got Craig into trouble. I'm dead.* It was not odd to me that in the face of all the adults there, I was more afraid of Craig and his repercussions than anything else, except one thing.

I'm probably going to prison, I thought miserably. *I'm probably never getting out!*

Craig kept avoiding my gaze. I didn't know what he was thinking as the police walked all around the yard, scrutinizing the construction, the birds, and asked us what felt like hundreds of questions. Sometimes they wrote answers in notebooks. Craig had carefully taught me to never give more information than was needed, but the police let us know we were getting busted with the worst possible crime. The cost of one lawfully bought piece of tin had not been cheap—but thirty whole pieces?

Trembling, I watched as the cops tried to fit the puzzle pieces of what was going on together. Here I had avoided the police for so long—three full years of pickpocketing and heisting for Craig. Now I just kept my mouth shut, knowing full well that my brother had paid for less than 10 percent of his coop.

Craig didn't give up trying to pin the whole thing on me, but the adults, especially our parents, rebuffed him. He had made it clear to the whole family from the very beginning that this was *his* pigeon coop. *No one else's and certainly not mine.*

When the police were done with their first stage of questioning and investigation, they put us in the back of one of their cruisers. I was shaking from lack of sleep, still chilled but also simply terrified. It felt like the world was coming to an end. Whether they believed Craig over me, the overwhelming evidence from my footprints to my soaked clothes in the hamper pointed dramatically to the fact that I was the one who had done the stealing.

The short drive to the police station seemed excruciatingly long. Once in the lobby, Craig and I sat nervous and uncomfortable on hard benches. Then the officers did the most alarming thing they could have done. They separated me from Craig.

He went into one interrogation room. Trembling, I followed an officer who directed me into another. The tall man in the strict, navy-blue uniform shut the door with a solemn, resounding clang. Then he locked it with a *click* and turned back to me with a menacing stare.

Frozen, I had no idea what I was expected to say. The puppeteer from whom I took all my cues and punishments was no longer present. Despite all the horrors I had experienced at Craig's hands, not since my mother had been shot had I felt this petrified. I felt small.

So I spilled my guts. Immediately.

For the very first time, I told an adult everything—well, everything having to do with the pigeons. I took the blame for all the tin, as I knew was expected from my brother. I was so terrified, however, that the truth spilled out that I did everything on Craig's orders. Still, not once as I sat across from the large, glaring officer on the other side of the stark metal table did I mention Craig hurting me or threatening me.

"I had to do it," I admitted lamely. "I had to do it no matter what."

I was booked on probation for six months. I didn't know what Craig got because no one told me, but I knew he was in trouble too. It was oddly comforting and at the same time deeply disturbing. All I knew was that there would be hidden consequences, of which the adults would have no clue.

God, I'm so tired of the consequences! A tear slipped down my face, and I turned to the wall to wipe it away. Weakness made the torture worse.

When the parents came to pick us up after hours of questioning, there was only uncomfortable, icy silence in the car. As soon as we got home, I crept into bed and under the covers. I slept long and hard. Suddenly I awoke, my heart pounding in my chest. When I sat up, the house was eerily silent. I knew full well I was not alone.

I wanted to avoid my parents.

I especially wanted to avoid Craig.

I sucked in my breath and tiptoed gingerly through the bedroom door. As I came down the hall, I saw the silent family. Craig was in front of the TV, the volume set on low. I stepped out of the shadows, and he glanced up then away. Mom and Dad didn't even bother looking at me from the kitchen table, but it was to Craig my gaze was riveted anyway. He seemed unusually subdued. It confused me. There was no arrogant, half-hidden or sour smile. I didn't breathe out for a long moment because I didn't know if this was a good or bad sign.

Not knowing with Craig was always worse. I turned around and went back to bed, crawling deep under the covers and curling myself once more into a protective ball.

What would slowly become evident over the next few weeks was that getting caught turned out to be one of life's greatest blessings. No one understood the intensity of the coercion I was under, but the adults all seemed to understand that *something* had been going on. The threat to Craig for the heist was decidedly greater than mine, in the eyes of the law, at least. He was getting close to the age where he would be charged with felony larceny.

After that night, all heists, shoplifting, and stealing ceased. I never spoke another word of it to a single adult.

If only the beatings would have ceased too.

For Evil to Triumph

*"Throughout history, it has been the inaction of those who could have
acted; the indifference of those who should have known better;
the silence of the voice of justice when it mattered most;
that has made it possible for evil to triumph."*
—Haile Selassie

After a portion of the truth was out in our family, I was able to get more
sleep than I had in years, with Craig unwilling and unable to send me out
on nightly raids. That helped me concentrate better at school, and as the
weeks passed, I began to have more confidence in my abilities. This, in
and of itself, was a miracle. I could do this thing called school!

Two other miraculous ripples affected school, my grades, and my sense
of well-being. For the first time in *four years*, I was able to eat school lunch.
Craig was not allowed to touch my lunch money. I was flabbergasted. And
I was so entirely grateful.

In addition, for the very first time since I was little, I was able to use my
allowance and earnings for what *I* wanted, including school clothes. Over
the next year, my appearance improved dramatically, and I felt much
better about myself. Although I certainly wasn't fancy by any means, I no
longer looked like the ragtag poor boy at school.

I was positive my reputation would be ruined by my arrest, but, oddly,
as I entered the school doors the following weeks, my name was spoken
in reference to my art, not what I had been caught doing for Craig. It
wasn't just that my teachers were remarking on my artwork, it was that
students were consistently asking me what I was working on, wanting to see
my sketches of missiles and spaceships and lifelike animals.

I pondered the upcoming election for student-body officers. I noticed
that being a class president was a pretty cool thing, rather popular with
the other students. I suddenly experienced aspirations of being a leader,

though I hadn't considered myself one around classmates since my early childhood days in Germany.

Sitting in class one day, I racked my brain. I wanted to figure out what I could offer. Having the ability to race cars or model airplanes was cool with some of the guys but certainly didn't interest most of the girls. I needed something everyone liked. In a hare-brained moment of genius (and perhaps madness), I promised Mr. Rigby's fifth-grade class that if I was elected, I would do a drawing for each person.

The day of elections dawned, and in class, it was announced that I had received the most votes. I was named our new class president. And now I had thirty drawings to do!

I took seriously the importance of being true to my word. With colored pencils, I did full-out, shaded drawings that were studies in depth and contrast and full of creativity and ingenuity. I did most drawings to match my classmates' personalities unless they had a specific request. One of my friends, Dan, came from a rodeo family. He asked me if I would compose a rider on a bull.

I took a deep breath. That was a tall order for a ten-year-old budding artist.

Sure, I had seen drawings of cowboys and some of anatomically correct animals that I liked to mimic. Now the challenge—to put it together. I worked for hours and hours and hours on that drawing, and when I presented it to Dan as a finished piece, his mouth dropped in surprise and delight. He carried it around with him for the rest of the day, showing everyone who marveled at it. Seeing their pleasure made me practically burst with pride. For the first time in my life, I felt a deep level of validation through my work, as well as from my classmates.

That year, as my artistry reached a new level, my confidence reached a high as well. For one thing, I was done feeling ashamed and embarrassed. Now that it was up to me, I wouldn't steal a single other object, even if I could. In a quiet moment of sketching during recess, I realized I had never developed a taste for stealing. In fact, I detested it with everything I was.

Were it only that simple for the other parts of my life. Over the ensuing months, Craig may not have had the leverage to send me out on heists to his heart's content, but it didn't stop him from using me as his punching bag. Craig made sure his ongoing dominion was supreme. He just took it deeper undercover. Missing his tool of entitlement, he took out on me what was being denied him by society and his parents.

I immersed myself in my projects, staying out of Craig's way whenever I could. I'd been working a bit at a time on refurbishing my golden Stingray as my brother slept. I completely disassembled it, painted it a bright yellow, and installed a four-foot sissy bar on it with parts and supplies I'd paid for. Loving the bright color, the artist in me reveled in the fact that no one in the world had a bike exactly like it. In addition, no one could miss me flying down the street! On the chain guard, I hand-painted the letters "The Lemon Peeler." I just wished I could feel as free at home as I did when I raced along the streets.

To everyone's surprise, Mom got pregnant again. In time, she had a baby boy, Troy. I was afraid for him. Craig held both disgust and a nasty rancor for this helpless baby. One morning, he snapped at Mom, and she snapped right back.

"Look," she said sternly. "You're mine, Gary is Wayne's, and Troy ties us together. Now get over it!" In front of her, he didn't have any choice.

There was a short but blissful period when Mom was on maternity leave. I could eat what I wanted and sleep when I wanted, except for the cry of the baby. However, she went back to work as soon as her leave was done. That left Craig and me to watch the baby. With great trepidation, I witnessed my older brother's anger heightening.

Under Craig's orders, we most often left Troy crying in his playpen while we worked on our projects and homework. Although Craig was told he was responsible, he forced me to change Troy's dirty diapers. I didn't mind so much and was gentle with Troy, although I'm certain I made a few ugly faces at the smell.

Troy began wasting away as Craig and I were not trained in what or how to feed him. After all, we primarily lived on cold cereal at home with occasional dinners, along with my miraculous school lunches. When Mom returned from the doctor, she was livid. Troy was suffering from malnutrition. She blamed us—particularly Craig. She also blamed him for Troy's learning deficiencies. Eventually, she quit work to take care of Troy and to address the fact that her blood pressure was too high to be standing at work all night long.

Even when she was at home and saw her eldest son's inappropriate behavior, Mom didn't do anything about it. One day, our two parakeets in the front room were squabbling and making a racket as birds sometimes did. Craig got irritated, reached into the cage, and grabbed the one that was bickering the most. Suddenly, he hurled it against the wall. I watched the bird fall to the floor, lifeless. I was in complete shock.

There was silence in the room. Mom simply got up and walked out. I slinked away as fast as I could, too, shaking. I felt all too often like that poor bird near the floorboards. As much as I didn't want to admit it, sometimes I wished it was *that easy* not to be there anymore.

Now, on the nights Dad and Mom left for the bar, Craig often invited his friends Kenny and Eugene over to drink with him. You would think that with other people in the room, Craig would be on his best—or at least better—behavior. This was not the case at all. I was their slave, and it was my job to cook, serve beer, and keep them happy. It didn't matter what homework or activities I had or what sleep I needed.

Unswervingly, as these drinking nights progressed, things would first grow volatile, then ugly and full of violence. Craig was a wicked drunk. Alcohol did not make him happy but filled him with extreme rage.

One night when the boys were over, Craig's torture and beatings got so bad I feared again for my very life. I didn't know what I had done to set him off this time. Had I not gotten his beer quickly enough? It seemed like I had. Did I serve the TV dinner to him cold? No, I had double-checked, scalding my finger in the hot gravy.

It didn't matter. Craig picked me up and threw me into the corner of our living room. I crumpled against the wall, and he resorted to his favorite pastime of kicking me with his heavy, steel-toed, black boots. As I lay in complete agony, there was silence in the room for about five seconds except for scared whimpering in the other corner from Troy. I knew exactly how my little brother felt. I'd spent so much of my life doing exactly that.

Eugene and Kenny still lounged on the couch, finishing their dinners and beer.

"Please," I begged, tears falling from my eyes as I beseeched them. "Please . . . help me."

Both older boys suddenly burst into fits of laughter—the same maniacal laughter as Craig. Their amusement only continued as Craig began to throw heavy, half-full cans of beer at me. I lay in a pool of red. Blood was oozing from my nose, my hands aching from trying to protect the rest of me. I sincerely hoped one of my fingers was not broken. *What if I can never sketch or paint again?* I warred within myself whether to save my face or my hands. The tears flowed harder.

This isn't fair! This isn't right!

But no one stopped Craig. In fact, his friends only egged him on. Buoyed by their laughter, Craig began his favorite game. He made me stand up, then punched me in the stomach until I collapsed. When I couldn't breathe, he reached down, straddling my midsection, and helped me lift my rib cage and stomach to allow air into my diaphragm. My panic lessened but only briefly because I knew what was coming as he lifted me up onto my feet.

WHAM! He hit me in the gut again. I slumped down, unable to breathe once more. Countless times in front of these two mocking young men, he lifted me up and gave me my breath back only to take it from me again. His face shined in his absolute control and dominion.

When he finally grew bored, my brother looked at the puddles across the linoleum floor. "You'd better clean that beer up, you little son of a bitch, or you'll die!" he snarled. "And clean up the blood while you're at it, you fucking wimp!"

I had no choice but to endure these weekly drinking binges with the same friends who never bothered to stop him. A deep and abiding hatred began to grow within me. The depth of this hatred, however, began to frighten me. I was having daydreams again, although this time it didn't involve a knife. Craig was still too big, and most assuredly I would die. Still, I envisioned in the middle of the torture, me picking up Mom's heavy frying pan and bashing Craig's head in.

That was not like me. I was not a violent person. But my own sense of unfairness and a deep, inner fury was growing. I didn't know what to do with it. I had to do *something*, though, because it was eating me alive.

One night as I was being tortured, somewhere in the back of my mind I made a promise. I would not be silent when I saw someone else being abused. I would never lift a hand to abuse another. *Someday I will help free others from emotional or physical bondage.* I didn't know how, but this time I felt myself lifting my own screaming rib cage to catch my breath. All I knew was this thought: *I will keep this promise!*

How often had I arrived at school trying to hide a black eye or a bruised cheek? Craig didn't care anymore if the bruises were visible. No one seemed to notice I had a hard time sitting, with new welts and marks hidden on much of my body. In gym class, people just thought I was a ruffian and said so. The only good news about that was most bullies stayed away from me. I would have cowed to them, too, for I had no idea how to stand up for myself.

No one at my school or outside of it *ever* asked me what was happening at home. No one ever tried to intervene. It seemed like the whole town had a "boys will be boys" mentality. My bruises, black eyes, and bloody scrapes were easily explained away. No one knew the bleeding on the inside.

Despite how quickly my artwork was improving, despite my paintings receiving acclaim inside and outside of the classroom, and despite the new leader I was becoming at my school, as soon as I was home, I was beaten without mercy.

And my most hidden shame? Since I wasn't out making nightly heists, Craig's attention turned toward his darker, sexual fantasies. These were carried out in our bed almost nightly. It seemed there was no hope of escape from the unspeakable things he made me do to his body. I would run into the bathroom, my hands messy, my eyes filled with tears, sometimes vomiting before I could get myself clean. In my young mind, I was doomed for the rest of my life. Leaving this world early seemed a better option all the time.

And then one day, a girl came into Craig's life. I had no idea what that would do for me as he began spending more and more time with her.

Suddenly, Craig would be gone for an evening that he would usually be at home drinking beer with his buddies, mocking my every move. Any night free of abuse was the greatest boon! I had no words to describe my relief but just waited for the other shoe to drop.

As Craig's relationship with this girl lengthened, I had sudden freedoms in small and wondrous snatches of time and space—freedom from beatings, freedom from his ugly taunting and, because he was distracted, freedom from his continuous mental torture.

And then the unthinkable happened. Now that Craig had a girlfriend, he stopped using me as his sexual canvas of a pretend female. Instead, his focus and energy were drawn away from me.

All these years, I had been waiting for a man to save me—my father, an authority figure, a principal—*someone* who had just *had* to see what was going on, how I was being abused and manipulated and they would therefore rescue me from Craig. Yet my saving grace turned out to be the girl who took Craig's attention . . . blessedly far from me.

The taste of something new was in the air. It was too great to hope, but just the flavor of it on the wind lifted me.

Under the Wide-Open Canopy of Night

"I didn't even know there were stars to look at to not see.
If you don't know that they're there,
you don't know that you're missing them."
—Neil deGrasse Tyson

Like the sudden swish of a magic wand, Craig was gone. He got married right out of high school, barely a month after his graduation. This was not unusual for many of the local young men and women, but even better, Craig and his young bride moved away to Utah and didn't seem to have the desire to come back to Montpelier whatsoever.

At first, I was at a loss. Oftentimes I would still tremble when I came through the door at home, heart pounding, waiting to be beaten for being late or a thousand of the other reasons for which I had suffered. Then in the silence I would remember. He was gone.

With a tentative curiosity, I began to explore what I wanted to do with my time. While there were a few things Craig and I had done together or built together that I enjoyed, there had been far too many things I hated. *What do I want to do?* I asked myself. *What shows do I want to watch? How do I want to spend my very own time?*

Most of my newfound pleasure and freedom had to do with art. As soon as I was done with my chores and mowing people's lawns, I would ride around on my bike and enjoy chatting with friends. But I found myself gravitating toward home, where my sketchbooks, pencils, and watercolors lay. Humming joyfully to myself, I sketched, drew, and painted. Now I could do it as long as I wanted. I was safe.

Early that summer, my family went fishing. It was our first family vacation without Craig. I had been quietly enjoying that fact when I noticed some curious markings on my father's legs. He and I were out on the boat that morning. Visible because of his shorts without waders that day, the marks on his legs were rather distinct, although difficult to see under his dark, curly leg hair. Peering closer, I realized they were *scars*, etched into his skin.

"Dad, what are those?"

"Oh, those?" he said, flicking his skin as if to brush something away. "Those. . . are scars from the lice bites in the prison camp in Moosburg."

Lice bites? I shivered despite the warmth of the sun.

Dad never shared much about his experiences in Europe. I only knew he had been held in a Nazi prison camp in Germany during the latter part of World War II. Even when he'd spoken briefly, I don't know that I really listened. It all felt a little bit like *Hogan's Heroes* to me, disconnected. Seeing his scars brought it home, like Craig's scars on the skin under my shirt.

"Will you tell me about it?" I asked earnestly. "The camp? The lice?"

Dad searched my eyes as if looking for an answer. Finally, he glanced back out over the water and cleared his throat. As he began, his voice sounded far away.

"Moosburg was a terrible place. My buddies and I were huddled together at the mercy of the cruel Nazi guards. They were incredibly demeaning. I can't even begin to tell you what that was like . . . I will tell you it had been a long and bitter winter. We were freezing, our fingers and toes turning blue and purple, and the guards just laughed at us."

His eyes glinted sharply for a moment but then misted over as he went on. "Some of my buddies lost limbs to frostbite. The constant stench of gangrene made me sick. Some of us lost hope. All we could think about was food and the end of the war. They deprived us of everything except scraps and deprived us of our very dignity. We had only our dreams to keep us alive."

He cleared his throat again. "And the lice . . . God, they were nasty creatures that infested our blankets and clothes and bodies. They bit into every inch of skin to feed on us as if our existence wasn't already a living nightmare."

At his words, I started feeling creepy-crawlies on my skin. I had to keep from swiping the nonexistent bugs off my arms.

Dad glanced down at me, then back out at the lake. The water was pristine except where the fishing lines created tiny ripples moving outward. "Two days before we were liberated," he continued, "rumors began flying around camp that the Americans were coming. I can't tell you, Gary, the thrill that pierced me, but I was afraid to hope! We thought for sure the guards would shoot us. We became even more frightened when we heard distant artillery barrages coming closer for the next forty-eight hours. The SS became frightened too, and fortunately for us, most of them ran off."

Then Dad looked at me, an animated spark in his eyes. "I'll *never* forget that day. It was April 29, 1945, when George Patton and his army came barreling into our camp. He was *standing* in his jeep, with his pearl handled .45s at his side. It was a wild day. It was the best day. In one burst of celebration, Gary, the hell was over. One hundred thousand of us prisoners were released. Forever we'll call it 'Liberation Day.'"

That was all he could manage. Dad cleared his throat and changed the subject.

I pondered Dad's story all that day and late into the night. I looked up at the stars, getting drowsy enough to drift off.

Suddenly I sat straight up in my sleeping bag.

The day Craig left . . . the day Craig left our house had been my *liberation day!*

Like Dad, I even had the date memorized in my mind: June 13, 1968—the day Craig was married and gone for good. While he hadn't been scared away by any outside force, the freedom I had the day he left was palpable. I was still discovering it, and I wouldn't take it for granted.

I wasn't a hero like my dad, and I would never claim to be. I hadn't suffered from frostbite or gangrene or lice or work camps or escaping being gassed. But I had lost loved ones in the murder-suicide that still affected me. And I'd had my liberation day from my own prison camp, including physical, mental, and sexual torture, and my fear of death . . . every . . . single . . . day.

This I would not minimize, even though I didn't talk about it to anyone.

For a long moment, I honored my dad in my mind and my heart. There was a part of me and him that made us kindred spirits—a tie to tragedy in Germany, a tie to liberation and freedom. I didn't fully understand what it would mean for my life, but something about it all seemed profound.

On our way home, our family drove around Craters of the Moon National Park, and by way of Twin Falls, the city Dad told me I had been born in, we picked up an adorable little German shepherd puppy. We called him Lobo. Whereas art had most often been my only friend, suddenly this black-and-tan energetic furball became my constant companion and assuaged any lingering loneliness.

As far as I was concerned, the chains of torture were lifted when Craig left, and I never, *ever* wanted them back. In fact, I swore I wouldn't have a thing to do with Craig for the rest of my life. I began dancing around the house with Lobo when I realized something vital.

"Oh, my God," I breathed out loud. "Oh, my God, I'm free!"

I hadn't realized just how captive I had been. I hadn't realized how my stomach was daily tied up in knots . . . until the knots were untied for good. Even the nightmares that had plagued me almost every night for seven years started to dissipate.

My little brother Troy changed. His features were brighter, and he seemed less afraid of life. I was grateful for that too.

At first, I did things that summer just because I could. I was no longer being starved, kicked under the table, or having to sneak sustenance. On one of my first days alone, I went to Teuscher's Market and bought several fruit pies. I brought them home and gorged on them one at a time. I only needed to do it once and got a little sick to my stomach, but the freedom of it was intoxicating.

About a month after our fishing trip, Dad cooked a roast one Sunday. He set it on the stove to cool. Every time I walked by, I took a piece and then another. Within an hour, I had eaten the whole roast! Dad was rather surprised and certainly not pleased. I felt bad, but it was almost a compulsion.

I also loved being able to take long, hot showers and sit in the tub and enjoy the water. It took months after Craig left for all the bruising to disappear, but one day I got in the shower and inspected myself. For the first time since the month of my arrival in Montpelier, I did not have a single, horrific bruise. Gone were the constant red welts and black-and-bluish bruises. Even the last sickly green blemishes had healed.

During those sweet summer days, it was a marvel to enjoy the kiss of the sun on my skin. With no one to smother me with pillows or whack me with a heavy branch, I felt like I was experiencing life anew. Toward the end of summer, I no longer trembled at the sound of a twig snapping behind me in the forest or the backyard. It was just me and Lobo and creation. I began to experience a wild joy mixed with childlike wonder. I felt giddy.

Creation, I decided, *is a marvelous, miraculous thing.*

As the warmth in the air fled and fall claimed its earthly wonders, I became excited about the first day at my new high school. I had begun to grow my thick, curly hair out, and it resembled the cool "fro" that was becoming popular around the country. I continued to eat school lunch every single day, even to the astonishment of my buddies who went out.

I found I still struggled in academics, but I was determined to receive my first-ever A+. My science teacher was a stickler, but I knew it was for my own good, and I tried extremely hard to please him. What names I couldn't memorize perfectly in anatomy, I was determined to show in my drawings.

Mrs. Rigby, my new art teacher, inspired me to get even better at my art. She knew I was drawn to birds and what they symbolized, and so she encouraged me to submit a drawing of a Moluccan cockatoo on a huge, poster-sized cardboard canvas for our science class project. It was the most meticulous drawing I had ever done, with pink-outlined crested feathers—what seemed like thousands of them. It was nearly anatomically perfect.

"Why, Gary," Mrs. Rigby cried, "it looks like it could fly right off the page!"

When my rendering of the bird received only an A in Science, I was extremely disappointed. I wanted to cry. I craved that plus mark on my A! For my art class, I completely redid my bird but positioned it higher on its poster board. This time in calligraphy, I fastidiously scripted the word *cockatoo* in Old English, capitalized font at the bottom of the canvas. I had never been more delighted in an assignment than when Mrs. Rigby gave me my A+.

One late Friday night in September, I went outside in the yard and breathed in the deep crystalline air. I lay down on the grass, looking up at what seemed like pitch-black. My other senses became heightened, and I heard the cooing of some pigeons in the old pen.

I thought about the day after Craig left us for good. Mom and I had let the pigeons go, as well as the hundreds of Western pocket gophers he had held captive in the garage as his personal pets. The gophers showed no hesitation in their instinct to run away into the wild. Many of the pigeons, however, stayed behind. I was floored. It was as if these birds could not taste freedom! Denied it for so long, the very whiff of it startled them back into the safety of captivity. The doors of those cages were still wide open, back there in the dark. It didn't matter. Many of those birds stayed in their confinement, much more frightened of their liberty than their incarceration.

I would not be one of them—a creature with wings yet without the instinct to fly.

I will fly.

With that acknowledgment, I began to weep. Slowly at first, with one tear escaping down my cheek, until sobs racked my body. Huge, stuttering sobs. Unaware of how long it took for the torrent of tears to bleed dry, I finally became conscious of Lobo licking my face as I lay in the cold grass.

I petted Lobo, grateful for his sense of compassion. As I stared again up at the night, I became conscious of something else. The sky was not pitch-black. In contrast, the firmament was filled with the soft, gorgeous light of stars twinkling in a carpet of deep purples and blues. As I stared, I almost lost my breath. Somehow, this universe of masses of color and exquisite light was *pulling pain* from my body. I didn't know what was happening, but I instinctively knew it was good, and I let it happen.

Sometime before dawn, the darkness and I came to a resolution. Rarely was there ever a time of only utter darkness. The artist in me had discovered the stars, and I could no longer go back to seeing shadow except for what it was: a place to harbor the most exquisite crystal manifestations of light. I was no longer afraid of the dark. Instead, I became inspired by its contrast.

Roused beyond the arms of sleep because *I* wanted to be, I went inside.

And there, in the dim light of morning, I began to paint. In the brilliant light of dawn awakening, the brushes became my wings.

The Lift of Salvation

*"When once you have tasted flight, you will forever walk
the earth with your eyes turned skyward, for there you have
been, and there you will always long to return."*
—Leonardo da Vinci

As school progressed, I began, a little shyly at first, to extend myself. I could invite friends over to my house now without fear. Since my experiences with David and the Trout family, I had only allowed myself passing acquaintances.

Taking another big risk before the end of October, I started my first real job. I became a proud cook at the Town Café in Montpelier. At first, the clang of pots and pans, the press of people, and the urgent demand for steaks to be cooked "just so" grated on my nerves. It took me awhile to get used to it all, but soon I found I loved it. It allowed me to witness all sorts of extraordinary human interactions from the relative safety of the kitchen window as customers laughed, joked, cajoled, and hugged one another.

When I worked the night shift, I also got to observe the stick-a-nickel-in-the-jukebox crowd coming from the bar at 1:00 a.m. and playing every Creedence Clearwater Revival song. I memorized Three Dog Night's *Joy to the World* because they sang it at the top of their lungs.

I was warmly welcomed and enfolded in the arms of friends who became like family—safer than family as I knew it. Life in Montpelier became rich, full, and even rowdy for a while. My new friends at the café enjoyed partying, and I certainly didn't have anyone to report to.

I began enjoying girls, friends, and a few beers on occasion. Well, maybe more than a few beers. Our older friends would buy a case for us even though we were only fifteen, and I quickly found I didn't need much.

Despite the partying, I remained sensitive to people and energy. My freedom felt tender, like a newborn's skin. I could feel the importance of every choice—*because now I had them.* I watched people and their habits—and what results those habits led to. It was intriguing. Montpelier was full of hardworking, industrious souls, many of whom blew their hard week's earnings on alcohol and other weekend pursuits. Like Dad and Craig, it would be simple for me to find a girl to marry straight out of high school and settle in. It made me think. It made me feel out choices.

I had nothing against the simple life. In fact, just one summer and fall without Craig was enough to prove to me just how much I adored peace and quiet, pierced only by the rowdy camaraderie of my friends. With very few examples of anything nobler than the wild lifestyle, partying my paychecks away seemed my destiny.

So why did I keep searching for something . . . deeper?

Later that freshman year in high school, I became fast friends with a girl in my class. Instead of partying, Janice and I had long, long conversations. These conversations always seemed to involve the talk of dreams and ideas, and eventually we talked about God and her beliefs in Jesus Christ. You couldn't live and work and go to school in Montpelier without feeling the profound influence of a certain church in the area—The Church of Jesus Christ of Latter-day Saints, commonly referred to during that era as the Mormons. My friend Janice was a Mormon.

Her church had a lot of strict beliefs. It was funny that these beliefs enticed certain people—and created certain rebellious behavior in others. On the far end of the spectrum were the Mormons who believed in the Word of Wisdom, which invited moderation in many things as well as the prohibition of alcohol, coffee, tea, drugs, and anything harmful to the body. They considered the body the sacred "temple" of the soul. On the opposite end were various other folks in Montpelier, believers in other faiths or of nonexistent faith who most often than not imbibed in alcoholic-related pastimes and mocked Mormons for their teetotaler ways.

With such opposing opinions, it was common that conflicts sometimes arose between the "goodie-goodies" and the partyers in the community. I liked hanging out somewhere between the two extremes. Since I liked beer and came from a home where both parents drank alcohol and my mother smoked like a freight train in the Montpelier rail yard, I hadn't ever fit in with the Mormons. Sure, I played church basketball with my buddies, but I never set foot inside their chapel. The only church I "attended" was the Protestant church—to steal their stupid pigeons.

That's why it was rather strange that every time Janice and I talked about these higher aspirations, it felt good inside. Of course, it didn't hurt one bit that she was beautiful! Yet, when I talked to other beautiful girls, I didn't feel *this* way. There was something deeper afoot. I experienced intense discussions with Jehovah's Witnesses, too, and that was wonderful just to open my mind. Still, I kept searching.

Pretty soon Janice and I were getting together with a group of other kids about once a week to talk about God. I didn't protest, as I was truly interested in God *and* Janice. As we talked about truth and faith in God and his commandments, I began to gain seeds of understanding of this thing called life—and how I was an integral part of it. Before, I had kind of felt like I was an accident, and, certainly since my mother had been killed in Germany, I had often felt like a burden. Now, I was learning that I was a marvel of creation—that every human was. There were no accidents among us! This was an entirely new concept for me, and I spent quite a bit of time trying to wrap my brain around it.

One day after group, Janice asked me if I wanted to learn more. I nodded. We set up a time to meet some missionaries at her house once a week. When I walked into the Wright's lovely home, my eyes went wide. It was fresh and clean, and the walls weren't yellowed with telltale, lingering smoke. Suddenly I felt shy again, green to this whole "God thing." I took in everything with awe, including the family's welcoming kindness.

Invited to sit on their couch, I walked by an open window, curtains wafting in the breeze. In that moment, I smelled the distinct odor of cigarette smoke. It was so pungent here in this clean home that it took me by surprise. I was even more shocked when I realized it was coming from *me*. I reeked despite the fact I'd never touched cigarettes. I had just been around smokers my entire life.

Once over my embarrassment, all I could think of was how fantastic the absence of it was! Then I settled in for the ride.

Immediately, the Wright family took me under their wings. As we continued with our discussions, I discovered that one of the missionaries here to teach me was my high school geometry teacher, Mr. Kunz. Where I failed miserably to grasp algebra and chemistry, I *loved* geometry. It was visual and dealt in physical shapes I could relate to. Since I was comfortable in his class, I felt comfortable learning from Mr. Kunz in this capacity too. In time and because of the influence of this spiritual man, I was able to trust another person. His name was David Treanor, and he became my seminary teacher. We rode motorcycles together and talked of God.

Despite everything I had suffered, I had always believed in God. Whenever I heard about this all-powerful being, there was a peaceful feeling in my heart. It reminded me of that part of me that still felt my mother from time to time. Something deep within me knew she was in a sacred and holy place.

God, I felt, was a benevolent creator.

While my parents slept on Sundays, I began watching evangelist shows on television. Billy Graham told stories while I held my sweet and rapidly growing puppy, Lobo, on my lap and Troy played nearby. These shows and my conversations with Janice made me think deeply, and I even began doing this crazy thing called prayer.

That's when I began to get the inkling of an idea. As I tried to make sense of my early parents' murder-suicide in Germany, of being literally imprisoned by Craig, as well as tortured and starved, an idea struck. If God truly loved me, if I hadn't been abandoned by God even in my darkest times, perhaps there was some kind of mysterious purpose. *Could there have been a deeper purpose to my suffering?* A spark of hope was being fanned somewhere deep inside of me.

Maybe I'm not completely broken.

I went to bed early one Sunday night so I could lie in my bed and think. Surrounded by the muted noises of my family in the other room, my head filled with the ponderings of the day. I had gone to church with Janice and the rest of the Wrights and then listened to the televangelists at home until Mom and Dad got up.

I hadn't spoken to them about it, but deep inside I felt a profound and growing hunger for God in my life. Certainly no one in my family had a spiritual or religious practice that I had ever witnessed. In my home, those things were either unspoken or ridiculed. Yet, I kept carrying around thoughts to talk to God about, and the missionaries told me those were actually prayers. If that was so, then I felt my prayers were being answered. Something, or *someone,* was speaking back.

The following Sunday, one televangelist spoke on prosperity. I sent away for his pamphlet. Eagerly, I followed his exhortation to give a portion of everything I earned as a gift back to God. The author swore tithing had created his own wealth. God, he said, gave to us in greater measure when we had the desire to give to others.

The concept seemed crazy to me, but I had to try it. My greatest expense after the fifty-dollar Stingray bicycle had been a $300 Stella ten-speed to get me to work and school. I was currently saving for a car, dates with girls, and perhaps further education after high school. So, for every dollar I earned, I socked a dime away. I didn't know what I would do with it, but it was fascinating to watch the funds grow, knowing it was no longer my money. It was God's.

I started making God my partner in finances. When I needed things like paints and canvases, I prayed as instructed. God always seemed to provide just what I needed. I worked hard too. In addition to several shifts a week as a cook, I started to receive small commissions off some of my paintings. It was a proud day a few months later when I'd saved enough to open my very first bank account.

Imagine my surprise to find out that Mormons had a tithing principle. Ten percent of everything they earned went back to God for church programs, welfare, and humanitarian aid. After all the research I had done on my own, it was as if God was leading me along. The thought was comforting.

In this way I began a tender and tentative relationship with God. Sometimes I just felt awkward. Other times a genuinely warm feeling would envelop me as it had under the stars.

As time progressed and I matured, I studied God more deeply. I monitored how I felt inside when I read the particular works of one religion or another. And then, one day, I made a decision. I chose to be baptized into

The Church of Jesus Christ of Latter-day Saints. It was a huge decision for me, and I suddenly felt very vulnerable.

Only a couple of friends in my whole world knew of some of my early life experiences. Not a single soul, however, knew just how much shame I carried and how tainted I felt. How could I even begin to describe what had happened at six? At eight? At ten?

Dressed in clean white, I stepped into the waters of baptism. My clothing grew heavy with the warm water, but there was a greater weight. It was all of the wrongs I had committed under Craig's oppression and my own human choices with no one else to blame. The waters of baptism represented a cleansing with a promise so intense I wasn't sure I could believe it. I could "become clean, every whit"—every past sin wiped away and forgiven by God and Christ. As I went under the water, I began to cry. I decided to believe Him.

Something happened inside of me under that water. As I came out, I physically felt the weight of the world sloughing off me. Visions of hurting my parents, the years of lying and stealing, David's train, and so much more washed away.

I didn't expect God to do it all for me. I had spent weeks writing and getting accountable, taking full responsibility for my actions. Then I had gone on a spree. Like an addict on their ninth step, I doggedly made my way across Montpelier, making amends to the people I had hurt and harmed. I started with Western Auto, then King's Variety Store, Walton Feed, and Montpelier Coal and Lumber. I was doing a master repentance. I didn't want my new life to look anything like my old one.

Coming up from the water now, tears streaming down my face, I was changed. I let go of all that guilt and shame, and a final shame I just was shown I'd been carrying. I had a flash of it and felt an invitation to release from it. It was deep-seated guilt for my mother's death in Germany. When she'd asked my advice the night of her death, the naive six-year-old in me didn't demand we go get help. As I emerged from the water, I even let that shame go.

For the first time in my life, I experienced what it was like to cry tears of joy.

The Artist's Way . . . to Heaven

*"It is better to conquer yourself than to win a thousand
battles. Then the victory is yours. It cannot be taken from
you, not by angels or by demons, heaven or hell."*
—*Buddha*

I looked back on the last year of my life and couldn't believe what a completely different person I had become. That fall, I celebrated becoming a junior and a legal driver by taking trips up to see my little brother Billy so we could stay close. It felt like another testament to change that Billy and I could move beyond what had happened to our mother and his father.

One bleak winter weekend, where it was too stormy to travel, I noticed a homeless man hanging out near the railroad tracks. A brutal cold had followed the most recent storm, and I couldn't imagine for a minute someone having to sleep outside in such conditions. To my relief, I learned a good person in charge of the local motel had offered the homeless man a stay in a small yet cozy extra room.

Still, I was curious. I'd heard what others called people like him. Vagrants. Indigents. Itinerants. Derelicts. My buddies all said to steer clear of dangerous fools and criminals like this.

I went home and went to bed, but I couldn't shake it. I couldn't get the guy out of my mind. Why would someone choose such destitution?

On a wild hair, I decided to visit this man in the little room tucked away at the motel. I nearly regretted my knock at the door when, upon opening it, his overwhelming stench hit me, yet I didn't sense anything inherently dangerous about him.

Careful not to show a reaction, I watched his eyes, which were filled with deep suspicion. His voice was a gruff bark until he saw the sandwich I carried with me from the café. Begrudgingly, he let me inside, and I was grateful for the warmth of the room, if not from him.

Studying him as he wolfed down his food, I noticed the deeply etched lines around his eyes and mouth. From all my questions, he finally could tell I was just a curious kid, and he let his walls down. As he stiltedly began to talk, I discovered this man had a story and a past he rarely visited in memory. Listening to him broke my heart.

I carried his story with me when I went home. I knew I had to come back.

In our ensuing conversations, I found myself lost in the swirls of the color of his past. I was shocked at the hopelessness he expressed and by what he had come to believe about himself—lost employment as a sales-person, lost opportunities, and worst, lost love. "I am worthless," he said. His vacant eyes reflected his belief.

Still, more than once, I witnessed a flash of longing reach those eyes and emotion fill his voice. My own breath caught at the sound. I wanted to help him.

After I left his room on one of my afternoon visits, I mulled things over. Once, he'd had a dream and a life. He had skills as a salesman—he just hadn't used them for years. When others had stopped believing in him, he'd stopped believing in himself.

I paused on my way home, thinking about the old cap he wore over his scraggly hair. Instead of going home, I turned the corner and stopped at Burgoyne's, the clothier on the main drag of Montpelier. It was set among the small-town shops and proud retailers. As I spoke to the owner, I watched the way his eyebrows shot up at my request and how he took in my modest form. Why would I ask something like this . . . for someone else? Then the owner's eyes misted over, and he nodded.

I left the store overcome with joy. Someone could see the desire of my heart to serve another without an agenda. This clothier made the dream much bigger than my tiny initial vision as he and I conspired together.

A few days later, we presented this man with new clothes for Christmas. Each piece was wrapped in thick, elegant paper. He looked at the warm, cashmere coat with disbelieving eyes. I didn't own anything so fine, and a part of me wanted him to jump for joy or exclaim out loud. Instead, in his surprise, he had almost no words. But his watery eyes told the truth.

He didn't know why anyone, much less a small-town kid and a local businessman, would do this for him.

As the winter progressed, we didn't keep in touch. I was told he left soon after the harshest weather warmed. I often wondered how he was, he in his cashmere coat . . . and I wondered if he'd ever started to believe in himself the way a handful of people in my little town did.

Each of these breakthroughs influenced my art. People remarked how my pieces were nuanced with more light and a growing finesse as I developed a true artist's eye. I quickly went from being famous in my class for my sketches and chalk drawings to garnering a reputation for my acrylic paintings in all of Montpelier and the surrounding areas. Mrs. Rigby continued to celebrate my natural talents and encouraged me to stretch beyond the blue ribbons at the county fair. She had watched me, eager and hungry.

One day in the spring, Mrs. Rigby had an even brighter twinkle in her eye and a spring in her step. To my surprise and delight, she let the class know she was bringing a famous artist into our school from a university seventy-five miles away. My heart felt warm in appreciation of this woman who, like other teachers who had believed in me, kept believing even when I struggled to believe in myself.

The day the art professor came to teach us, I arrived early, with prickles of excitement under my skin. Harrison Groutage was famous for his watercolors: luxuriously rich landscapes and expressions of nature's storms.

In sheer delight, I hung on his every word. I watched every minuscule movement and detail as his brushstrokes illustrated the most amazing dark thunderclouds juxtaposed with breathtakingly beautiful light bursting forth from the clouds to illuminate the lime-green grass landscape below. I had to shut my mouth more than a few times. He brought the canvas to life!

After a while, I didn't care that my mouth was wide open. Mesmerized, I felt that contrast, that juxtaposition *inside of me.* The overwhelming darkness was the backdrop for the exquisite light bursting through the storm.

Until this point, my art had been created with instinct, desire, and 90 percent technical application—a style that ranged between what

Craig and my schoolteachers had taught me. As a whole, my skillsets had ranged closer to illustration, engineering, and draftsmanship, rather than an expression of art. Mr. Groutage's watercolor painting, on the other hand, was filled with passion! It was fluid and flowing. It brought me indescribable joy to see such a master at work.

I devoured every detail of Mr. Groutage's teaching that day and memorized his techniques to the best of my ability. I brought them immediately home and practiced.

And practiced.

And practiced.

Whenever I wasn't at school, work, church, or socializing, I was painting. It took months of this practice, but I was improving by leaps and bounds. It was as if my muse had been just behind a door, waiting to be opened. I was given permission to move beyond drafting composition to *creation*. I felt like a god creating colorful and dramatic worlds with a flourish of my brush. I could see the progression in canvas after canvas. Still, I was scared about what others would think.

Then a couple of things happened that truly boosted my confidence. Our school had been enlisted to revitalize what had been the white icon on the hill above Montpelier for decades. Our principal announced a contest for the new *M* design, and I got excited. The moment I realized John Cook would be designing, too, my heart fell a little. He was an older boy and artist who had talent flying out of his fingertips.

I almost didn't enter. John had ten times the talent I had!

I took a breath and began with my design-builder skills, crafting a strong block-letter symbol, university style, simply revising a bit what was already there. When I saw John's beautiful, flowing-script sketch, I hung my head. It was inspiring.

A week later, it was quietly announced that my revised design had been chosen. I about fell off my chair! In the coming weeks, I loved watching the school's engineers set an enlarged model of the design into the hill. With the addition of the light colored cement, you could see it from miles around.

Most people in town never knew my contribution to it. I don't know if

I even told Mom and Dad. I just felt a sudden, quiet pride having participated in something that benefited the whole community.

Then, late that spring before school ended, I was in First Security Bank in Montpelier depositing my paltry paycheck from the café when the manager of the bank approached me.

"Gary!" Mr. Wright exclaimed, giving me a hug. He hadn't seen me around as often since I finished the missionary discussions at his house a year prior. "Great to see you. Listen, I've seen a couple of pieces of the artwork you've done recently."

My eyes went wide with surprise. I had only been commissioned by a few of my friends to paint something specific for a gift. And I'd gifted a few paintings, especially to a couple of pretty girls (Janice was probably one of them) and a good pal. *Oh, boy. What has he seen?*

"Why don't you put some of your best work up here at the bank?" he inquired, looking at me. "They're high-quality and would add to the ambiance of the bank while at the same time allowing you to showcase your best work—and hopefully make some sales."

I was speechless. I almost had to force myself to look into his eyes to make sure he was serious. "Really?" I cried squeakily, still unsure. "Wow, that would be incredible!"

True artists dreamed of having a place to showcase their work. I was being offered the most upscale building in all of Montpelier and the surrounding area to display mine. It was more than a dream come true—it was a miracle.

This one interaction changed my life and put me on a higher trajectory. The commission from a single painting that I could do in an afternoon brought in twice as much as my entire two-week paycheck from the café.

Still, the cost of coming up with frames for my paintings was a serious challenge until I was offered a job at Cliff Sizemore's Frame and Shoe Shop—shoe repair in the front, frame shop in the back. Since I had a talent for woodworking, he let me craft and build all the frames his customers needed—and build mine for a significant discount.

Working there filled my heart with gratitude. I was creating, and it was all through honest effort. It wasn't lost on me that from the back door I could see Walton Feed, and I knew we were just around the corner from King's. There was power in me now; I had been set free, and I felt good about my work. I was contributing to the shop and to my art instead of being the town thug. I felt more like the "real" Gary than I had since before my mother's passing in Germany.

To my delight, my framed paintings kept disappearing from the walls of the bank, sold to eager customers, only to be replaced with new works. As this progressed consistently, something inside me began to take shape.

I had proven after my short tutelage with a professional how the caliber of my work could be truly heightened. I could only imagine what *formal* training in art could bring me.

I dreamed of it. I craved it. And Mrs. Rigby agreed it was the next step.

Baby Steps of Creation

"All the arts we practice are apprenticeship—the big art is our life."
—M. C. Richards

The next few years passed with exponential speed. I worked full-time for the railroad on the section gang. The railroad gang members swore worse than sailors, but I loved every one of them. It was hard work and paid better than most jobs, making higher education seem a far-off dream for a C student like me. Even then, the entire Wright family, who had taken me further under their wings during my high school years, encouraged me to attend college as their son Greg was doing. Greg had been a mentor to me before he headed off to Rick's College in Rexburg, Idaho. He invited me to come with him the following year.

Because my deceased stepdad, Ted, had been in the military, my little brother Billy and I both had several thousand dollars sitting in an account specified for education. I always thought it would only be trade school for me, but at Greg's invitation, I decided to get a higher education. Deep inside, however, I trembled as I put the packet of papers in the mailbox. I was frightened I wouldn't be accepted—that I wouldn't be good enough.

That fall, I followed Greg two and a half hours north to the college. Unlike my blasé high school scores, working my tail off, I received honor-roll accolades for the first time in my life. They had taken a chance on me, and I wasn't going to blow it. And I discovered that I absolutely loved college. Instead of it being some far-off dream, this new reality invited me to see a full spectrum of possibilities. It was glorious and fed my voracious spirit. In my "spare" time, I listened to inspiring speakers like Zig Ziglar and others whose wisdom surpassed my own and in whom I felt the power of words like an art in and of itself.

When Greg was called on a church mission to England, my vision suddenly expanded further as he wrote letters encouraging me to go on a mission myself. As such a recent convert, I had never really considered a mission, and I prayed about it for some time. *Well, Greg hasn't steered me wrong yet.* That week, I put in my papers and awaited the response.

I thought it was cool that Greg was in England. I would, of course, go wherever the church called me to go. That was part of the culture. You didn't "aspire" to go to some cool, foreign mission, because you might be called up to Montana or somewhere you considered far from exotic. You were supposed to be excited no matter what.

A secret part of me held on to a dream of being called to Germany. What if I could do some good in the country where my stepdad had killed my sweet mother and then himself? What if in the same place where my dad, Wayne, had been held as a prisoner of war, there could be something redeeming? I didn't tell anyone, but I prayed more mightily than ever that I would be sent to that place.

On a school break, I had come home to visit my rather serious girl-friend, Robin, Lobo, and my family, when I received a large, official-looking envelope in the mailbox. It was the call to my mission, addressed to me at 828 Monroe Street. I opened it in front of my folks. It read "Deutschland." I froze.

Oh, my gosh! I am being called to the Germany South Mission!

The moment it registered, I began jumping and down and screaming at the top of my lungs, making Lobo bark excitedly. "Dad, it's Germany! It's Germany!" I cried. His face was stricken until he realized I was ready to go full circle. Tears in his eyes, he nodded, then clasped me to him, hard.

Soon enough, I left for my mission. I touched down in a country filled with so much personal and family legacy it was thick in the air when I walked off the plane. Open-mouthed, I stared at the gorgeous architecture and cobblestone streets overflowing with history etched with both sorrow and rebirth. It felt even more intertwined with my own story, and my fingers itched to paint what was unfolding so colorfully before my eyes.

Like Greg, I loved my mission . . . but unlike him, I also hated it. I loved the hard work of missionary life, serving members and teaching nonmembers about Jesus Christ. I had been transformed because of it, and I wanted others to have it, too, so I struggled with the fact that most people did not want anything to do with Mormonism. I struggled worse when my girlfriend's mother wrote me a "Dear John" letter—the letter of letdown to missionaries that essentially says, "Sorry, buddy, your girl no longer wants to be your girl." I was miserable in Germany. I had something to prove, so I became a workaholic.

I was such a strict rule-keeper that even though Mannheim/ Heidelberg, where I had lived as a child, was just barely outside of our mission boundary, that my companion and I didn't visit there. Nor did we visit a single thing of cultural significance, even when it was right in our own backyard. I even made my companions work during our weekly day off. Sure, we did our laundry, but then it was back to work.

One gorgeous spring day several months in, as my area companions and I were on our way to a zone leadership conference, I looked up to see that our train was going through Moosburg.

Moosburg! That's where Dad was a prisoner of war!

I pressed my nose to the window. As we whizzed by, I shared Dad's story of the camp, General Patton, and Liberation Day. My companions were spellbound, but we never actually got off the train to *see* the place. I just watched it go by, a big lump in my throat.

My time in Germany would have been much more pleasant had I learned how to sprinkle a little play into the work. Instead, I used food and prayer as my only comforts. In doing so, I gained thirty pounds, which didn't help my confidence. Deep inside, I felt that if I just had *more faith*, I could do what God wanted.

There was a small but glorious miracle that warmed my heart and taught me a lesson about my own humanity—and the German culture— in a positive way. As we walked the busy cobblestone streets each day, groups of lovely, smiling little old ladies, or *Hausfraus*, were out shopping and visiting with one another. Heads covered in colorful scarves, they strode about with big, black, sturdy leather shoes under their heavy long skirts. Unlike most people on the street, who completely ignored us as missionaries, these ladies loved to stop and talk. While they never wanted to convert, there was something compelling about the kindness and curiosity in their eyes and the depths of their souls.

We were delighted the first time a group invited us over and plied us with peanuts and pickle-cream sandwiches. After we talked for several minutes, one woman, whose face was beautifully lined with wrinkles, tugged on her bright-blue woven headscarf and looked me in the eye. "*Sympathisch!*" she announced, and her friends all nodded. They thought I was sympathetic, or kind.

They can tell I love them! I realized, and my heart swelled.

What had once been beaten out of me as a weakness—to let my love shine through—I came to see through their eyes was actually a strength. I'd never been taught to do it before, and I had never really known how, until now. My companions would sometimes tease me, but now, everywhere we went, I heard that same word, *sympathisch,* many, many times from these lovely *Hausfraus.*

Despite my stubbornness, some of the magic of that land brought back memories of my mother in a strong and lucid way. For the first time in years, I had vivid dreams of her and felt her presence helping me throughout my mission, wrapped around me as I served. That's when I developed a tangible connection to the place and the people I would never forget.

As I stepped back onto American soil in 1976, it seemed appropriate that it was the two hundredth anniversary of our country's independence. I was still celebrating mine. I could be and do whatever I wanted—within reason. I was very frugal with my money and bought a little Dodge Colt and went straight to work earning money and preparing to reenter college. In the meantime, Greg had been writing to me about an incredible six-month study-abroad program in Israel, where he was going to study the life of Christ. I was intrigued because Christ's life and death now meant so much to me.

Yet, to go from Germany to the United States to Israel was a mind-leap for me. As I jumped on the plane to Israel anyway, history rained down upon me in a series of realizations about humanity—about power and control, and so much of it in the name of God. How mankind could perpetrate the worst of human indignities upon one another was unreal. It made me angry. It made me deeply sad. And it especially sparked new thinking about the responsibility of leaders of nations and peoples.

And then there was Jerusalem. It touched my heart beyond explanation, especially Old Jerusalem. One hundred miles from the Sea of Galilee, thirty students and I stayed in the Hotel Jerusalem near the old city wall. The place called to me as a painter, and my eyes devoured the quaint, antiquated streets; charming old-world shops; falafel sandwiches; and excavation of the city wall.

The Dome of the Rock was exactly what an artist would think it was, and unlike in Germany, here, I finally allowed my artist's eye to run the show. The trip was absolute magic. Instead of continuing my behavior from my mission, I listened to the professors' admonitions that we visit every museum we could and taste of the local flavor, culture, and history. I did all that and more. It was then that a change began inside of me. Instead of seeing only the battles and wars and indignities, I saw a softer side of humanity. There was compassion and beauty and reverence for God in its many forms. The world absolutely expanded before me.

Jerusalem was made even more magical to me because of a certain young lady, Carol, who was one of our study-abroad classmates. She accompanied us on a trip to the Sea of Galilee, where I was absolutely blown away by the natural setting.

This is the place I get to be, I thought, the sight taking my breath away.

It was Carol who taught me how to *relax* at the Sea of Galilee. She showed me how to be present as the breezes off the water lifted her hair from her shoulders and the light from the water reflected equally off her beautiful brown eyes. That semester, I held Carol's hand and felt my whole heart come back alive. I kissed and hugged her in the hallways too. In spite of our growing and deep affection for one another, we maintained our LDS standards of chastity, and our hugs and kisses went no further.

That is, until we arrived back home.

Alchemy and Metallurgy

"Tears are often the telescope by which men see far into heaven."
—Henry Ward Beecher

Upon my return, I was determined to settle on U.S. soil for a while. I began building a life with my new girlfriend in mind and sought ways to receive the technical training I so desperately wanted in my painting. I began attending Brigham Young University's Bachelor of Arts program and became immersed in the glorious excitement of learning new skills.

In the meantime, Carol and I became closer than ever and began to plan a life together. We even got engaged. As the weeks passed, it became increasingly difficult to stay away from each other physically. We were falling hard. For us to continue to attend and be married in the temple, we had to keep promises that our bodies would stay clean, which also meant no sex outside of marriage.

This had not been an issue during or after my mission, and I didn't want to let go of the privilege of a temple marriage or not take my promises seriously. Despite that, Carol and I began sleeping together, and I found myself caught between the heady world of lust, love, and romance and that of my church and spiritual beliefs. I was sleeping with her *and* attending the temple. I was living an excruciating lie, and it all led to a downward spiral that lasted for years until Carol told me she didn't desire to marry.

I was at a crossroads. In my heart, I realized our relationship was coming to a heartbreaking end. Operating as I was outside of my integrity, I discovered I couldn't function at school or in front of the canvas. That had never happened to me before.

One day, I sighed and set the paintbrush down. I knew what had to be done. As soon as I confessed to a priesthood leader, I was immediately brought before a church council and excommunicated. I held absolutely no hard feelings toward these men, a few of whom even expressed sympathy toward me. I knew there was a strict protocol.

Leaving the church council, I was nearly unable to see my way home through my tears. I sobbed for days. I thought my body and my heart would break, but the tears that fell were not only of sadness. As they ebbed, I finally felt like I could breathe. To live a lie after what I'd been through as a child was pain that felt worse than death to me. Tortured by my own mind until I could live that lie no further, I would have paid any price for my freedom.

———

It took some time, but once I got past my broken heart, I began to feel renewed. I had taken a vital step toward reclaiming my integrity and honesty. It was this I began to treasure above all else. I could be *transparent* before God and humanity. I didn't have anything to hide.

However, there were ongoing repercussions of my choices. I was kicked out of BYU because I had broken the standards for admission. But, determined to finish school, I enrolled first at Utah Valley University (UVU), then at the University of Utah (U of U). Then I moved south, where I found a beautiful family to stay with. In Provo, however, I couldn't get away from the feeling that I needed an even bigger change. I was burned out and needed to change the bearings of my inner compass.

A couple of my art buddies from the U invited me to go with them on a one-month excursion to Guatemala. It was inexpensive and safe, and I felt it was the type of immersive adventure that would help me get my head on straight. Working on coming back to church, I had been faithfully setting aside my tithing even though I was no longer officially a member. I knew I would be reinstated at some point, and that's what mattered. My alignment with myself and my relationship with God were my highest priorities.

On the drive out of town on our way to Guatemala, I asked the guys to stop by Stan Johnson's gallery and studio in Mapleton, Utah. He was a well-known, successful sculptor and genuinely great guy. I had met him briefly at UVU in his graphics arts class, where we hit it off as artists, which for me was wonderful. Stan's enthusiasm for life was contagious. Even though he was in his mid-forties, he was like a little kid. He wore snakeskin cowboy boots, blue jeans, western shirts, and it seemed like his grin never left his face.

As my buddies headed outside and piled back into our packed vehicle, I was surprised when Stan stopped me, his face serious.

"Gary," he said, "I want you to come work for me when you get back from your trip."

"Me?" I asked, astonished by the offer—and the fact that he would hold out the offer for an entire month. Inwardly, I celebrated. *This could be a dream come true*!

"Sure." He nodded. "I've got a little place here above the studio you could stay in while working for me, and it will save you a little money while you finish school."

I looked around, my eyes wide. To live in a studio and work under the hands of a full-time professional artist? This was a sure way to cut the professional learning curve. In that moment, I was committed 100 percent.

Stan and I shook hands on the deal, and I left for Guatemala absolutely elated. My head felt higher than the clouds as we wound our way south.

A month later, upon my return to Utah, I felt like a new man. I had used the time to clear my head and was more than excited to learn under Stan. While I was fully aware there wasn't a lot of money in this type of work, I was about to find out just how inspired the decision to learn under this artist was.

Each of my art classes at the U felt miraculous to me. Under expert tutelage, I built skill upon skill in the nuances of form, shape, and function. Better, I was working on my passion. And I had the opportunity to study art history regarding some of the greatest masters to ever walk the planet. It was amazing to see the evolution of art, and I sincerely hoped to be a part of it one day. I primarily studied under Alvin Gittins, a master at drawing and painting the human figure. Under his tutelage, I became even more meticulous in musculature and anatomical accuracy.

Moving in and apprenticing with Stan was a different adventure altogether. In Stan's foundry, I learned firsthand about metallurgy. A complete rookie in this form of art, I was fascinated by what it took to take a clay art form and turn it into a beautiful, bronze masterpiece. First, I watched, spellbound, as Stan created in three dimensions what I would have put on canvas. But that was just the beginning.

Creating bronzes was a highly skilled art, with processes handed down for centuries in many cultures and perfected over time. The Chinese were brilliant at it, and the Egyptians used it to create King Tutt's unforgettable mask. Instead of gold, however, Stan's foundry used 98 percent copper in combination with other metals and minerals like zinc, silicone, and tin.

Creating bronzes required seven distinct processes. First, a rubber mold was made over the clay to hold four coats of hot wax. Once the wax fully cooled, a wax artist repaired any imperfections; this became the wax positive. Next, a ceramic shell was created by dipping the wax positive into slurry and letting it dry. This slurry process was repeated several times to create a hardened, ceramic shell. That shell was then heated to at least 1500 degrees, hot enough to melt out the wax, and refired to hold two-thousand-degree molten metal.

I donned my new, protective gear, hating how rivulets of sweat pulsed down my skin to some uncomfortable holding spot. But the gear was necessary because molten bronze could maim or kill on contact. It took several of us foundry workers to carefully pour the bronze from the two-hundred-pound crucible into the ceramic shell, leaving it to set up and cool.

What I think shocked me most about the process was that the beautiful ceramic shells had to be busted off to separate the metal from the shell. I watched, fascinated as workers used hammers and sandblasters to preserve the surface of the revealed art. The final step was to color, or patina, the bronze. The painter in me loved how different patinas created vastly different effective finishes.

The result? Stan's bronzes were stunning. They were sold in many western galleries across the country. Every process had to be followed with scientific accuracy, but it was oddly satisfying to know that the pieces we were working on would outlast us.

I spent long, hardworking days in Stan's foundry. Often arising by 6:00 a.m., I was welding and grinding by eight. We wouldn't stop working for ten or twelve hours, especially when there was a deadline for completion. Because I was working on getting my spiritual life back in order, to be completely immersed in creation and renewal 24/7, month after month, was an oasis in the spiritual desert I had created.

During this new season of my life, the entire Johnson family took me under their wings. Each day, they nurtured what felt like my fragile soul. Stan was the type of guy who was just *present*, moment-to-moment. The consummate artist, he didn't understand time limits until his body or his belly gave out. His wife was always getting after him. "Stan, you're supposed to be there already!" or "Stan, you missed lunch and dinner, but we saved you some." My boss constantly forgot appointments and where he was supposed to be, but people forgave him because he was not only remarkably talented but giving.

I slept in a tiny room above Stan's studio. After ten or twelve hours of welding and grinding on Stan's Native American bronze sculptures, I would walk up the lane to the house and have a bath. By the time I finished, the bottom of the tub was green from the bronze filings, and I had to rinse thoroughly. After washing up, I was often invited to eat at the table with Stan's gracious family.

In fact, the family's generosity often left me speechless. The artist had picked me up at a time I had knocked myself down, and he had accepted, mentored, and nurtured me without judgment. He also began teaching by example what the life of an artist could be—rich and full, with family and friends and the ability to help others. Just like his nuanced metallurgy brought his artwork to life, his alchemical process with me and my soul was revitalizing my withered spirit. I was determined to somehow stand on my own again, but I had some further healing to do.

One bitterly cold night in February of 1980, I was huddled in my tiny quarters above Stan's drafty studio after another backbreaking, twelve-hour shift and a meal. I was alone with my thoughts and reflections in my sleeping bag. Tonight, as the wind howled, I allowed myself to sink back into memories. I saw my young self with my mother in Germany. Instead of pushing everything away, I let myself wonder what had gone so wrong in her life.

How I wish you were here, Mom. I wish there were someone I could talk to about you, to remember you better.

Dad had answered a few of my questions, but it always seemed too painful for him to talk at all—much less about her. I desperately wished there were someone who really understood her.

Suddenly, I sat bolt upright in my sleeping bag. The thick foam pad didn't offer much comfort from the hard floor, but in that moment, I didn't care.

Holy San Francisco! I have Grandma's address in California!

In my possession, I had a postcard my mother had kept. I remembered that on the top left-hand corner, neatly printed, was Grandma's address.

Hardly sleeping that night, I went to Stan the next morning, filled with excitement. I had worked for months now with no real time off, and he agreed to my twelve-hour road trip to California. The howling wind the storm brought in was brutal, so I prayed for good weather to come.

Rising early that next Friday, I jumped into my little Dodge Colt hatchback and drove straight through Utah, Nevada, and into California, relaxing a bit as the weather grew balmier. My destination: 611 East Folsom Avenue, not far from the Oakland Bay Bridge in San Francisco. I was confident I could locate my grandmother. I would finally have the answers no one seemed to be able to give me.

The closer I got, the more carefully I checked my map. *Could this be right?* As I drove slowly through an older, more dilapidated part of the city, my confidence diminished. I arrived at the old building, aghast. It turned out to be a large, transient apartment complex.

Dumbfounded, I skirted beer bottles, cigarette butts, and a few huddled bodies to get to what should have been my grandmother's door. I knocked and knocked. No answer. I knocked again and again, even on neighbor's doors, but to no avail. I had no idea if she still lived there or had moved away. My shoulders slumped.

I shuffled back to my little car, crestfallen. I had no other way to reach her. Climbing inside, I buried my head in my hands and just sobbed. I had thought for sure that I'd find her. I had been so confident that I would get more information, old memories—*something* that could tell me more about my mom. I needed to know her, this woman I had forever tucked away inside my little-boy heart.

Although I was now thoroughly exhausted, I immediately started for home, disheartened and disillusioned. I felt like I'd been punched in the gut. The whole trip had been a waste. I could hardly stand it.

Upon arriving at Stan's studio, I didn't talk much about my trip. I threw myself back into my work, grinding and welding, until quitting time. I wasn't much for conversation that night around the Johnson table, either, although I tried. February suddenly seemed the bleakest and coldest it ever had. I hoped March would come quickly and bring warmth to my soul.

Two nights later as I climbed exhausted into my sleeping bag, I didn't even remember the moment my head touched the pillow. I fell into a dream . . . only it felt incredibly real to me.

I was standing in a strange but beautiful field of wildflowers surrounded by lush, green trees. At first it was just me, grown-up Gary, but I felt a childlike excitement rise inside me.

Suddenly, in the distance I saw a woman walking toward me. Even from far away, I knew it was her—*my mother*! I immediately recognized her walk and the sound of her sweet laughter on the wind. As she came closer, the color of her lipstick stood out on her unforgettable smile, matching the sparkle I remembered in her beautiful eyes. I could hardly believe it, but my heart *knew*. There was a dramatic moment of connection, and my mother wrapped her arms around me as I did her, and we held each other tightly.

A feeling of great peace and sense of well-being washed over my entire being. I had never felt this much peace, even on my liberation day. This was a different kind of peace, one that permeated me to my core and filled a gaping, wounded hole that had existed since she'd been taken from me.

In that forever-now-moment, my mother and I communicated from one soul to another. Words were not expressed, but it didn't matter. I knew *so much* now, and so did she.

All too quickly it was over. I watched her go, longing for her again, although something within me understood the brevity of our visit. She had places to go, and so did I.

I awoke to the pre-light of dawn filtering into my tiny room, surprisingly filled with the same warmth and deep sense of peace I'd felt in my dream. It had been the most real, visceral, powerful dream I had ever experienced. I basked in the feeling of the love of my mother and the abiding peace that clung to me. I didn't know how, but I had received a gift, and the peace of that gift stayed with me. I just wished her presence could stay forever.

A Greater Purpose on the Planet

"The two most important days in your life are the day you were born,
and the day you find out why.
—Mark Twain

One chilly late-winter evening as I helped Stan set up his classroom for teaching local students, I took a chunk of hard, rusty-brown clay and began to play while the students worked to shape their own. Like I did with my paintings, I first formed a figure in my mind. Once I felt clear, I had fun playing with the hard, stiff substance. As I put more effort into it, the clay melted in the heat of my hands and began to form whatever I decided to mold it into. I mused and folded, mused and shaped, started and restarted.

At first, I was quite whimsical in my creations. I liked the feel of the clay in my hands and often just allowed shapes to form into whatever inspired me in the moment. I began kneading and forming clay as a way to wind down at the end of long, long days of hard work.

As I played, however, in that tiny little room atop the stairs in Stan's studio, visions and pictures began forming in my mind. In great wonder, I began to see them form into the clay.

The next week as Stan taught an advanced class to a number of people from the community, he presented a torso study using an antique sculpture from his *Snake Charmer* collection. The students were to copy, or imitate it, with clay. It was a very classical piece, about two-and-a-half feet tall, and copying it required a critical eye. It wasn't easy, but I discovered that the anatomical precision I had learned under Alvin Gittins came in handy as I sought to re-create the piece. I worked on it at night after my shifts and in between classes for fun.

At one point, a couple of classes later, Stan glanced over at my work, and his eyes widened in shock. He couldn't believe how accurate my imitation of the *Snake Charmer* was.

"Gary," he breathed, "this is perfect! You got every piece of the anatomy sculpted so accurately, so succinctly."

I looked at the shape before me.

Dear God, I can sculpt! Hallelujah!

It was like my soul did a little dance all the way around the room. The confidence and surety of it flowed through me. Deep inside, I knew this ability to transfer something to the third dimension was remarkable. Night after night, as I continued to play with the clay, it was almost as if life and creation itself appeared before my eyes and then sprung into my hands. I was astonished by where my mind's eye could take my hands.

In my off-hours, in my meditations and time with God, my hands kept working and molding, and my eyes beheld in astonishment the creations taking shape before me.

Once again, I felt like a creator, manifesting worlds that had only been in my mind. Now, they were three-dimensional—muscles filled with the action of real life, where anyone and everyone could touch them. It was like bringing not just the vision of art but the reality of it into a tangible, lasting existence—especially if a piece was forged into indomitable bronze.

To me, art was imitating God, and this imitation was the highest form of praise I could give Him. As I continued to sculpt, an overwhelming understanding began to fill me that I, just like every other person, was an exquisite part of the ultimate Creator. Because of my intense desire to be closer to Him, I began having quiet, daily meditations with the clay, asking God to form a better person out of the clay of the *man* as well as the artist. As I worked, memories and emotions sometimes seemed to erupt from the clay.

Dear God, I breathed in realization, *you are helping me to heal.*

As my emotions poured out in the clay, my conversation with God became very real. I spoke to Him about the pigeons who found too much solace in their backyard cage even after they were deliberately let go. Realizing I had once been enslaved, I knew I was now free—free to create, free to make mistakes, free to do as I wished.

The question remained: Where did I wish to spend my hours as a free man?

One night after Stan and his students left the studio, I asked God what it meant to be what I wanted, and what I felt *He* wanted from me: to be a person of love, compassion, and integrity. I cried out, alone in the night, begging to fully understand the gifts of life and creation.

In the hours that followed, the clay warmed beneath my hands, softened and pliable. I added nuances and details, the essences and life and mobility and action and emotion. As I did so, I felt God forming *me* into a better human being.

I was hooked. This communication was not only filling me, it was enriching me and fortifying me. I had more energy to work, engage with others, and be creative.

Then, one day, I realized I wanted to create my first bronze. I still loved painting, with all of its glorious nuances, but I wanted something 3D tangible of the caliber of which I'd been learning over the months— something that would be a true contribution to art and creation.

I first sculpted a buffalo rising from a buffalo nickel. It was a simple piece, but it took me months to complete. I felt it was symbolic of the phoenix rising out of the ashes. It was me taking a stand for my deepest desires and beliefs. The meditation and slumber were over. It was truly time for action!

Unlike painting, sculpting an entire figure was a much more comprehensive process. When it was done, however, I looked at it with a sense of pride. I felt like it was time to show Stan. Not only did he like it, he approved of it so much that he let me cast it there at his foundry! I felt a thrill go through me as I chipped the ceramic off *Buffalo Nickel.* Eight inches wide and over six inches tall and quite heavy, after the final patina, my creation was a marvel to behold.

As a sculptor, I discovered the sense of personal satisfaction that came with the craft when a piece was finally done in bronze. There was only one greater validation, and that was to have someone admire it enough to buy it.

And, wonder of wonders, one of Stan's appreciative clients saw the finished item, and a thrill went through me as I sold limited-edition number one of fifty *Buffalo Nickels*! This was a marvelous opportunity for such a novice, and I thanked God and Stan, my heart exploding in gratitude. It felt like divine orchestration. Even more marvelous, however, was the person *Buffalo Nickel* introduced me to.

I had recently been looking for someone to help me with the wax retouching stage of casting my first few buffalos and was introduced to the talented Lanea Richards by her brother-in-law, Richard Erickson, who also worked for Stan.

"I have to tell you, Gary," Richard said, grinning, "Lanea is a sharp, fun girl. I think you'll get along great! And it may involve more than retouching the wax."

I scoffed at his meaning. "Richard! I'm twenty-six, and she's only nineteen."

"Give her a chance, my friend. It'll be worth it."

Well, to start, I needed an artist. I called Lanea and asked her to come by the studio, where I showed her how to retouch these waxes specifically. Richard wasn't kidding; she was sharp as well as extremely talented. Within minutes, she picked up the technique, and, better yet, she and I clicked.

Lanea began working for Stan, too, while helping me. I enjoyed her humor and the stunning gray eyes that always had something deep behind them. While it was apparent that we hit it right off, we just enjoyed each other in the work environment, and I didn't push it. The irony was that neither of us was currently looking for a companion from the opposite sex, both having experienced relationships that didn't serve us. We felt content just to be friends.

It was fun working around such an attractive, intelligent, and witty young woman, and I liked that she had things to say—despite the fact that she was very private. She laughed a lot yet took her life and talents seriously as well.

As time went on, I wanted to know more about her. I found Lanea very intriguing. One pleasant evening after work, I got up the courage and invited her to take a walk with me. That one walk turned into several nice long walks late into the evenings, overlooking rural pastures, her golden hair shining in the waning sun. Whenever we encountered horses, I saw her natural delight spring to the surface. She obviously adored them and privately shared how she longed to raise them.

The atmosphere between Lanea and me initially stayed relaxed. Pretty soon, however, something was happening between us. Although I was very attracted to her, my feelings were vastly different from what I experienced with Carol. This was not lust. I had a deep, abiding sense of respect for Lanea and enjoyed her company, her moral compass, her vision for her future, and the way she loved and took care of her family. She had not had an easy life growing up, and she had a tendency to take on additional responsibilities, giving to her siblings both emotionally and physically what her parents could not.

I found myself sharing a lot with her regarding my recent past and enough about my childhood, though I didn't feel like the darkest details were necessary. It was enough that we had survived tough childhoods and were each working toward a brighter future.

I was enraptured the day I realized that my growing, deepening feelings for Lanea were reciprocal. We were talking about something when her eyes locked with mine. We drew together not just for our usual hug but a warm, lasting kiss.

It didn't take us long to realize we simply had to be together. I for one was not going to mess *this* up. I had learned a valuable lesson, and Lanea was too important to me to lose. What I loved, too, was that Lanea and I believed in founding a marriage forged in friendship and trust. She was honest, and so was I. I could be transparent with the world about her and my feelings toward her. We felt like we had been guided toward one another and were enthralled with the miracle of our bond and where it could take us.

In great love and honor, five months later, Lanea and I were married. We bought a beautiful Alaskan malamute named Kimuk and took our pup on a modest and joyful honeymoon up Fairview Canyon. Soon, we were planning our lives.

Lanea and I decided it was foolish for me not to finish school at the U since I had such little time left to achieve my degree. It warmed my heart that she wanted me to finish. It had been a dream of mine for so long, and given her emotional support, I knew I could do it. The only question was money. I had been selling copies of *Buffalo Nickel* for $400 each, which helped, but I obviously couldn't take Lanea home to that tiny room at the top of the stairs, so we moved into our own little place. Plus, my sweet wife was always doing for others, and so it was important to me to provide for her. I started working as an assistant manager at Adonis Bronze in Orem, where I got to work on additional pieces of my work.

I finished my new Western sculpture entitled *Sacred Meat*. It depicted a Native American armed with bow and arrow hunting a buffalo. There were so many fine, meticulous details that it had taken me forever to complete. However, I had gotten very positive reviews when I unveiled it. With that boost of confidence, I introduced the piece to the Lido Gallery in Provo. I was shocked and overwhelmed when they bought the rights to the edition of thirty-five for $11,000! It was a miracle because it meant Lanea and I didn't have to scrape pennies to do the casting and final patina.

And we were delighted we now had the money for me to go back to the U and finish school. As Lanea continued to work, I noticed that she would give her mother any extra money she had left over, which wasn't much. She never bought anything for herself. After *Sacred Meat* sold, I took $100 from the bank and drove Lanea to the mall.

"I want you to take this and buy clothes only for you. Can't buy for your mom, your sisters, your brother, even," I gently insisted. "This is just for you."

I stepped out of the department store, heading into the mall to grab a burger. I wasn't supposed to meet her for a couple of hours, but the look she had on her face when I left her haunted me. I wolfed down my burger and immediately walked back to the shop.

Lanea stood off to the side of the walkway near the women's section, right where I had left her. I noticed right away that her shoulders were hunched over. She was crying.

Then my wife saw me. She turned to me with a look of anguish and buried her face into my chest.

"I can't do it, Gary," she sobbed. "Something inside me won't let me spend $100 just on clothes—not just for me."

I held her for a few moments and dried her tears. I knew what that was like—that excruciating feeling. So together we went to pick a few things out. I noticed the receipt when we were done; she hadn't spent anywhere near the hundred bucks, and my heart hurt. When we went home, I praised her in her new shirt and dress, both of which enhanced her beautiful eyes. I hoped that taking care of herself might come easier in the following months.

As I immersed myself back into my final studies, I was gratified to see that when Lanea and I worked together on a common goal, nothing could stop us. I began to understand the concept of "flow" with God and the Universe. I was nearing graduation and got rebaptized in the Mormon church. I felt complete and whole. I also handed over the tithing I had collected the entire time I had been excommunicated: over $2,000 in cash. It was shocking to my bishop but not to me. I had known I would give it back to God someday. Keeping that promise to Him was one of the sweetest experiences I ever had.

Lanea and I wanted to raise a family sooner than later, but I knew I had to have a solid income. In my years of training, I'd heard horror stories of artists' spouses not being supportive or pushing them into work that paid the bills but crushed their spirits. Lanea was the opposite.

One night, shortly after we married, Lanea led me to our little couch in the front room of our tiny place in Provo.

"Gary," she said softly, her eyes earnest, "you know I absolutely love and adore you for who you are. I want you to know that I also see your potential as an artist. I think it's important for you to have the opportunity to fulfill your life purpose and your dream of building a solid foundation and doing your art full-time." She paused and added, "I think *I* should go to work full-time while you work on your art. It will only be until you can sustain us by doing your art full-time."

I just blinked at her. Then I tried to suppress the tear that escaped and ran down my nose. I'd had the great fortune of being surrounded by people who believed in my progress as an artist through the years, but no one had been as supportive as Lanea. In our culture and our church, it was important to start a family right away, but she felt it was important to establish my foundation firmly for us, and she declared it wouldn't take long.

"It will pay off, Gary. I can just feel it."

This time, I didn't try to hide the tears.

"You are willing to do this for me?" I asked, my voice breaking.

She smiled. "I am willing to do this for *us*."

I nodded and promised I would not take this sacrifice lightly. I would put my heart and soul into my work, as I had learned well what day-by-day steps could bring in the form of talent, opportunities, and blessings.

GALLERY

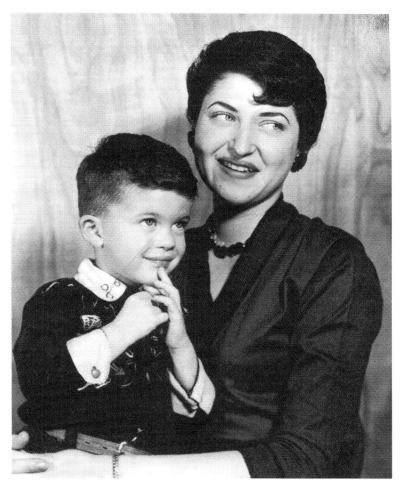

My mom, Betty Jo (here at age twenty-six), and I lived in Mannheim, Germany, a couple of years before her life was snuffed out by her husband. She made many of my clothes, including this groovy western shirt.

My father, Wayne, and Mom holding me as a toddler.
Wayne would later raise me from ages six to eighteen,
even though he knew I wasn't his real kid.

By all appearances, Ted and my mom were happy as hell. Then "hell" prevailed. Later, through military police records, it was revealed that Ted was extremely abusive to Betty Jo. I would learn that my mom attempted at least once to take her life after a horrific beating.

I loved playing with this little dude, my half-brother Billy. Billy was one year old when we were flown back to the States.

*Wayne and Nellie, the father and mother who raised me
from ages six to eighteen, shown here standing in front
of the house on 828 Monroe Street. They never knew
the things that happened in or under the house.*

My first-grade teacher, Mrs. Anderson, in Montpelier, Idaho. Weeks after my mom was killed, she would kindly hold up my artwork in front of the entire class and say, "Look what Gary Price did!" She knew what had happened in Germany just a couple of weeks before.

*Check out that banana seat and those bars, baby! I
bought this golden three-speed beauty at Western Auto
for fifty dollars. My stepmom, Nellie, gave me the last
ten bucks to get it out of layaway. She was as excited
as I was, and my stepbrother, Troy, dug it too.*

I was the first in my family to go to college. After one year, I got burned out, so I took a trip with some college buds to southern Mexico and Guatemala. A month later, I came back refreshed and eventually got my BFA from the University of Utah.

My career took off like a slingshot with my first studio in the basement of our new split-level in Springville, Utah. My next-door neighbor handled my professional photography for years.

*Our family prospered. On our ten acres was this huge
trout and koi pond we'd dug out. Here we are enjoying
the fruits of our labors. Back row, left to right: Raphael,
Isaiah, and Zachariah: Front row, left to right: Tyrone,
Justin, Lanea, and me, the koi and flower lover.*

Through the years, I loved being able to share my creativity with other creatives. This was a particularly fun day in the studio with actor Tim Allen. I sculpted his daughter.

Not only did my boys model for tons of my pieces; every once in a while, I slowed them down enough for a studio shot. Left to right: Zachariah, Tyrone, Isaiah, and Raphael with their papa.

Meeting Dr. Elly Frankl was truly one of the highlights of my life. To have her let me hold Viktor's favorite art piece in all the world blew my mind. Needless to say, I left her a copy of the sculpture I had designed for her husband's vision.

*Elly Frankl told me how her husband was so touched by
this wooden artifact/sculpture that he put it on layaway
after seeing it in a Vienna market after the Holocaust.
He created this niche in his bookshelf especially for it
and entitled the sculpture, The Suffering Man, always
asking, "Where is the hand reaching down?"*

*Little did I realize after I first met Leesa that she had also
suffered severely from the effects of suicide. Here she is as a
single mom a few short years after her husband ended his own
life. Left to right: Jeddadiah, Leesa, Justin, Leslee, and Lynsie.*

*Leesa was not only a bright light to my business but an
even brighter light in bringing me out of depression from
my divorce after twenty-eight years of marriage.*

*My beautiful soulmate proved to be an incredible model for
several of my "Great Contributor" (Women's Series) benches,
including Joan of Arc, Amelia Earhart, and Harriet Tubman.*

*Even though we now have sixteen grandchildren,
this is one of my all-time favorite pictures of some of
our little buds several years ago. So damn cute!*

*One of my greatest successes as a fledgling sculptor
was The Ascent. Every version I created of it sold out.
Thirteen years later, it would become the inspiration
for the Statue of Responsibility monument.*

In 2015, we dedicated the fifteen-foot Statue of Responsibility at Utah Valley University, in Orem, Utah. Here, Leesa and I are being congratulated by President Matthew R. Holland. Alex Vesely - Viktor Frankl's grandson, and Dr. Nancy O'Reilly stand in support while Steve Clark holds the cloth after the unveiling.

As my book goes to press, here is my latest commissioned monument. What an honor to recognize Walter Harper, who in 1913 became the first person to summit Denali–North America's tallest mountain towering at 20,310 feet. An interactive piece which depicts Harper's hand reaching out to assist another as they climb, this historical dedication of the Walter Harper Monument is planned for June 7, 2022 in Fairbanks, Alaska.

Here is an architectural depiction of what the Statue of Responsibility could look like in San Diego, courtesy of Gordon Carrier, Design Principal at Carrier Johnson + CULTURE.

The Messenger was inspired by my guardian angel, my mom. During her creation in clay, I covered my studio walls with my mom's photos for inspiration. I depicted her gifting me with not only life but also the tools to survive it. Our guardian angels do that for all of us.

Indominable Frontier Spirit

*"I hope America can also be the cultural leader of the world,
and use this frontier spirit to lead and show others that we
need courage to go places where we have not gone before.*
—Tadeo Ando

That December, I became the first college graduate in my family. I looked at my fancy diploma from the University of Utah with its "Bachelor of Fine Arts" designation. A quiet sense of pride and a special thrill went through me. This represented so many breakthroughs.

That year as I sculpted and studied, I listened to *Unleash the Power Within* by Tony Robbins. Every time I was afraid to take a step into the unknown world of business because I was such a naïve greenhorn, I remembered him saying, "No matter how many mistakes you make or how slow you progress, you're still way ahead of everyone who isn't trying." These words and others helped me rise above with renewed energy, proving that the voices of my past were neither my truth nor my destiny.

Things felt like they were taking off for Lanea and me. She kept working as she had promised so I could sculpt, which meant the world to me. For starters, she worked a little bit at a foundry that cast some pieces for me. She also went to work at Adonis Bronze and continued to do some wax retouching on my pieces.

Life was busy, and as young entrepreneurs, we were trying to figure out how to handle the business cash flow. It was hard. Each of my pieces took immense amounts of time to sculpt, but it was the foundry process that nearly broke us financially. All of the chemicals, raw materials, and labor had me undone. I traveled door to door in downtown Salt Lake City with my delicate, fragile waxes, asking for the business owners so I could talk to them and show them my work. Many didn't want to buy—but enough did that I was able to keep working.

When I took my new wax piece, *Frontier Spirit,* and others around, I ended up meeting a guy who helped manage a local branch of Merrill Lynch. Gerald looked at my pieces and shocked me by saying, "Yes, I want this one, and that one, and that one." My jaw dropped. Even though I wasn't formally represented by any galleries yet, folks like Gerald made sure I could survive and grow as an artist.

As life progressed, I sculpted a piece called *Range Trouble.* It was another Western, this time of a cowboy who had lassoed a bull with huge horns—and the bull was not at all happy. Wasatch Bronze was casting it and doing great work, but I was about $1,000 short. Still in its ceramic shell, it sat there for six months.

Until I got the phone call. "Gary, we are going to have to auction this piece you have in here. We just can't have it sitting here, and you haven't paid us for casting. What would you like us to do?"

"Uh, I don't know yet," I said, panicking. "I'll call you tomorrow." I sat quietly and pondered for several long minutes. God had never let me down when I needed help with money. I got very quiet and then asked Him what to do.

On a hunch, I went directly to Central Bank in Springville, where I borrowed $1,000. The final work hit the mark in the bronze, and I was very pleased. The professional patina, or final process that enhanced the metal look, set the stage to sell *Range Trouble* editions. The only problem? I didn't really have buyers.

Now, what the heck do I do with these? I have the sculpture in hand . . . and I'm a grand in debt. I have to do something!

I got another hunch. It was the middle of ski season, popular in Utah, so I drove up to Park City to find a gallery. As I drove up Main Street, I noticed one that had a sculpture in the window. The streets were snow-packed and crammed with cars and people. I had to park several blocks away and try not to slip on the ice and snow with a 24" x 36" bronze weighing over a hundred pounds.

When I finally arrived at the gallery, I took a deep breath and walked in, the sculpture heavy in my frozen arms. There I met Darrell and Gerri Meyer, the gallery owners. Right away I could tell they were good people, but they looked at me a little puzzled. They had no idea who I was, nor whose work I was bringing into them. After I introduced myself, there was nothing to do but be vulnerable.

"So, this is *Range Trouble*," I explained, still huffing a bit. "I'm the sculptor, and I just graduated. I wanted to know if you would like to represent me."

"Oh, my God!" cried Gerri. "I love this! It's gorgeous." Darrell took a more careful look, side to side and up and down. Finally, he said, "Yeah, Gary, this is pretty decent quality."

I breathed a silent sigh of relief as they agreed to take it and see if they could sell it for $3,000. I slipped and sloshed all the way back to my truck, deeply grateful and saying a heartfelt prayer that someone would love it and buy it.

By the time I drove down the snowy canyon and home to Springville, the Meyer Gallery had called.

"We sold it!" Gerri cried. "Can you bring us another?" By the end of ski season, the Meyers had sold a half dozen of them. In fact, the gallery started selling them as quickly as we could produce them. The bronze and western markets were kicking, and it was a great blessing for Lanea and me. As I worked on new pieces, I hoped that whatever this luck was, it would continue.

Our financial situation became sweeter as the Lido Gallery in Provo purchased the rights to another of my bronze editions, *Return of Fury*—a thirty-inch-tall Native American warrior chief on a horse, in his war bonnet, fiercely holding a spear. As I sculpted him, I imagined him getting ready to go into battle to protect his family.

When a gentleman in Springville purchased the rights to the rest of my *Frontier Spirit* editions and another buyer bought rights to a mountain-man bronze entitled *The Good Life*, Lanea and I knew we had turned a corner on living in poverty. Now, I just hoped we could get past the struggle with cash flow. Working with bronze meant we often had to rob Peter to pay Paul. As Lanea had promised, however, things began working out, and I was overjoyed that this was money coming from the work of my hands and doing what I loved!

This also meant Lanea and I could finally do something we'd dreamed of—start a family! We'd had a lot of deep conversations on what having a family really meant to us. Due to our rough childhoods, we had to decide who we would allow in our lives as grandmothers and grandfathers, aunts, uncles, etc.

I gulped at the transparency of the conversation. I still had never told anyone about the depth of Craig's abuse, not even Lanea. She knew we didn't "get along," as I would say. I had told her one or two stories so she might understand why I didn't like or trust him, but I held back the details. Of course, she didn't need to know what he had done to me in the dark caverns deep under our home or behind the door in our shared room. I felt like a "wuss" enough as it was, having stuffed down the times I had been cut, sucker-punched, and kicked into a ball on the floor.

It took a few weeks, but as I pondered, it seemed time for me to swallow my old bitterness and anger. Craig and I could just be stepbrothers this time, grown man to grown man.

Tentatively, Lanea and I reached out to Craig and his wife over the phone. At first it was awkward and strange. I almost gave up. But then Craig and his wife asked us questions about our spiritual beliefs. I was blown away when they said they could tell that joining the church had changed my life. I about dropped the phone when they asked if we would teach them.

The moment I was back in Craig's presence, my body went rigid. I prayed no one else could else smell my tangible, deep-seated fear. Sweat ran in rivulets down my back. It had been a decade, but my body didn't care. It instantly remembered the sight of him and the sound of my nemesis' voice. I made myself breathe.

The couple seemed open as I taught the lessons I had learned to give as a missionary. We wanted them to have the same joy Lanea and I both felt in God. Having these common beliefs and hopes in our marriage had helped us so much. As we got ready to leave to return home, it felt great to have tender feelings between Craig and me.

The past was the past. I would let all the old sleeping dogs lie.

One summer afternoon, Dad and his wife called to tell me they had a washer for Lanea and me, which we could really use. We had a baby on the way! Craig was kind enough to let me use his truck and came with me to pick up the washer and take it down to Provo. It was a gorgeous day, made even more remarkable as the entire trip up to Idaho, Craig and I talked about higher, spiritual things and family. Still, something gnawed at the edges of my consciousness.

It was the first time Craig and I spent time alone since we lived at home before he graduated and took off. He was rattling off all the things we did together: the "fun" things we had built including the pigeon coup, our chemistry ensemble, our train sets, and so much more. It would have been great except he made it sound like we had the perfect, idyllic childhood.

As we drove, I didn't know why, but I suddenly wanted an apology for the way he had treated me. By the time we had picked the washer up from Montpelier and were on our way back to Provo, I didn't just want an apology; I craved one.

What is going on with me? I questioned as I tried to concentrate on the road and our conversation. It didn't seem so Christlike to demand an apology, and I fought with myself. Suddenly, I realized Craig had never once said sorry for all the horrific things he had done to me.

I swallowed my feelings as we drove, and I became quiet. Craig also became quiet. Finally, he turned to look at me.

"I shudder to think of the things I did to you."

The silence was palpable. Finally, I nodded. At last, he was acknowledging what he had done. As Craig continued, I could tell the half apology was about as close to a real apology as I would ever get.

God, with your help, it will be enough.

Then he reached his hand out and slapped me heartily on the shoulder.

"And look at what you turned out to be!" he cried. "I taught you how to draw and paint, and now you're a successful artist and sculptor. You didn't turn out half bad."

I gulped again, trying not to cringe. When I came home to our humble little place that night, I wrote optimistically in my journal. In my greatest desire to be a good man and not hold any grudges toward my stepbrother, I inscribed onto the pages that Craig had given me the apology I'd craved for so long. "I feel like he's my brother now," I wrote. I really wanted to believe those words.

In the ensuing weeks, I felt unsettled. It took me over a month for me to realize what had rattled my cage so badly. It was Craig's comment about *his* being responsible for my success in art. Regardless of his past, sickening behavior, he was taking credit for my accomplishments. The thought wedged its way under my skin and would not let go.

But I knew I had to let it go. I wouldn't get anything more from him; it was not his way. With great effort, I threw myself into my art, using the clay as I had so many times before to express unspoken thoughts and emotions. It helped me manage my anger, and soon I felt I was back to normal.

I also had a growing family to think about. Lanea and I contemplated buying our first home. The idea became a reality when our builders, Clark and Dirk Palfreyman, traded statues for a partial down payment. I even sculpted a statue of Clark's hunting dog, Rex. In all my years of art school and training, I had never dreamed someone would want to trade substantial value for my sculptures. Now I was being asked right and left. When Lanea and I needed to purchase something, I began to consider who might enjoy a trade, where value could be exchanged for value and often bring even deeper meaning.

Our new home was built on one full acre in the city of Springville, Utah. It was a split-level we painted yellow. I loved our new place and all the meaning it now had for me and my family. It was particularly special to have a place to call our own, where we could welcome the birth of our very first child. I was beside myself with sheer joy at the prospect of us becoming parents.

What was also special to me was that Lanea, who had always loved horses, got to have a place to start riding and training one, which was pure paradise for her. Unlike the young woman who once could not spend $100 on some clothing for herself, she was allowing herself this beautiful blessing. I loved how her eyes sparkled with so much joy.

As my work was being showcased and sold in three galleries, my career exploded. In the ensuing months, magazines and newspapers cited me as an exciting young artist, "one to watch." I couldn't believe that the wounded boy who was once held captive by fear had not only been freed but now inspired a new frontier of art lovers and art itself.

It proved to me the promise of every lump of clay. It proved to me the promise of every human like me.

The Sacred Clasp

"There are only two ways to live your life.
One is as though nothing is a miracle.
The other is as though everything is a miracle."
—*Albert Einstein*

And then, from one formless lump of clay, I sculpted *The Ascent.*

Every piece of art I had ever created changed and expanded me, but nothing to the degree of this project.

The Ascent was meant to depict a part of my life I rarely spoke of, especially now. As the piece of clay began to morph from formless to form, I felt the need to most powerfully portray all those who once lifted my shattered self-esteem out of the gutter—those who raised my talents to bigger heights and those who reached down to pick me up off the floor after devastation, terror, and ignorance into a more beautiful life. For me, this included the Great Spirit, the One who lifted me most.

In short, the piece would have little or nothing to do with all the tragedies and difficulties of my life. Instead, I hoped this piece could somehow clearly symbolize all those who'd raised me up.

I pondered for days. Reaching for inspiration, I wanted something so visceral and real it would touch people's hearts. So, first, I got vulnerable inside of myself. All throughout the sculpting and experimenting, I saw visions of the people who'd believed in me during my darkest hours: Those, like Mrs. Anderson, who believed in my talents and skills. Those, like the Wrights, who believed in the young man craving divine connection.

Those who raised my capacity for achievement and artistry, like Stan, the man who gave me a job, a home, and a soft-landing place after my soul felt shattered.

Then there was Lanea, who came from an LDS background and yet believed in me enough to marry a man who had been kicked out of the church.

I desperately wanted to portray that *need* we all have for other people to believe in us. *The Ascent* was to be my opus—symbolic of the heroes and sheroes in my life. And I wanted that symbol to change me, because now I wanted to be on the *giving* end of that statue, whatever that giving entailed. Preparing to become a father gave the forming of this piece of clay an even deeper personal meaning. So I gave the statue a tagline: "They rise highest who lift as they go."

The words made my heart beat wildly with the emotion of gratitude. They also made me feel brave, even enough to do a piece that wasn't just a free-standing sculpture. I was dying to push a new frontier—to be innovative. What if this bronze hung from a wall? To my knowledge, nothing of the sort had ever been done. But I had to ponder, to talk to God, to visualize all this meaning in tangible form.

What was the best way to show one hand reaching down to help another? Every muscle, every facial feature, had to be expressive of the struggle and the lift. How could I show in the body's anatomy all those muscles and forearm muscles in the grip and the legs? How could I portray the massive contortions and the juxtaposition of that struggle?

Then it came to me.

Native Americans! And suddenly I saw them. Two Natives in loincloths, exquisite in musculature against the necessity of nature: bold in their freedom, with wild, flowing hair and respect for each other so evident it was etched into their faces.

I went to work on my vision, sculpting the two natives climbing a sheer cliff, one reaching down to grasp the other to lift him up.

While the vision was glorious in my mind, I grappled with positions. Then I finally came up with an idea. Lanea's brother had been a state champion wrestler in high school. So was the son of the guy who'd bought *Frontier Spirit.*

In a fiery burst of artistry and imagination, I had these two young, muscular men hang from the balcony of the little yellow split-level we had just built. I took photo after photo of this crazy pose.

As soon as the photos were developed, I raced downstairs to the little bedroom we had turned into my studio, and, under the ceiling lights, I got to work.

One of my best mentors in sculpture was Edward Fraughton. As I neared completion, I wondered how he would feel about the piece. He wasn't just an artist—he was a master. I had seen a piece he had sculpted entitled *The Anasazi*, depicting a Native American climbing the wall of a ruin with a basket of kindling on his back. So, after I got my hanging piece done in clay, I carefully took the model to his studio in South Jordan, a suburb of Salt Lake City.

"I want to make sure I have the muscular efforts right," I said, holding my breath a little.

"I can see why," Edward said. "Gary, this has a great message, and it's a powerful piece." I let my breath go and smiled. Now it was time to get to work.

Edward was a fellow of the National Sculpture Society who taught classes twice a week. One of the requirements for a fellow was to be actively engaged in teaching the arts. It was a beautiful premise to raise new creators and leaders in the art realm. I was grateful he agreed to give his input on *The Ascent* as he helped me to finesse the finest details of the musculature. I learned a great deal from his critique and put even more hours into the piece.

Things were about to change at home. Lanea was getting ready to deliver our first child at any minute. Fortunately, her whole pregnancy was like magic. She loved being pregnant and was able to stay in great shape, which she loved. After intensive research, she determined it vitally important to deliver naturally, but I got worried when she had a difficult time during labor.

I was so proud of my wife when after twenty hours of very hard labor, our first child, Zachariah, was born. Lanea was exhausted but such a glowing, happy mother. I could not have been more delighted as I tucked our little tyke in my hands, close to my heart.

We had discovered that anyone having a child must invest a fortune, insurance or not. To our delight, both the hospital and the doctor accepted a sculpture in trade, which meant we had no real medical bills after the birth. This not only eased a huge burden for us as a young couple, but it also made Zachariah's birthplace more meaningful to us.

As I held our baby boy, I thought how extraordinary it was that he was a tiny, living, breathing sculpture God had crafted, and I marveled at all the little details, from his face down to his fingers and toes. Zachariah would change my life forever in the dramatic sort of fashion only a parent realizes—when the world becomes enormous and encapsulated at the same time. Sometimes it seemed as if we were the only souls in the world. Other times, the whole world seemed possible and wonderful for us.

So, now, as a new father, I worked on *The Ascent* with even more vigor, and its vision lived in my soul until it was fully sculpted, months after its conception.

As it was going through the bronze process, I discovered some extraordinary things. Little did I know what ancient importance that grip held—two arms clasped beyond the wrist at the forearm. What had come to me in my muse ended up having a significant meaning in several cultures throughout the world. For many Native Americans, this was especially the case.

First, elders from a tribe in Taos, New Mexico, told me that this was *a sacred clasp.* When two men greeted each other in such a way, it meant brotherhood and the power of one lifting another . . . *without letting them fall.* I gasped at the integral meaning they shared with me.

Later I would discover this clasp meant two things to the ancient Romans. Like the Native Americans, it signified not letting another fall, but it also meant something vital to life in their day: that no weapons were being hidden farther up the arm as was often the custom when traveling in enemy lands. Therefore, this clasp meant total transparency, trust, and having no agenda.

Upon each of these discoveries, I marveled at the meanings. No hidden weapons. Transparency. Trust. Lift. Friendship. Bonding. Growth. Possibilities. Collaboration. Partnership. Not only was the final product everything I wanted this piece to exude, but the two natives with their solid, sacred clasp also became symbolic of so much more in humanity.

Like its name, *The Ascent* began to perform remarkably well and quickly rose in popularity. I was astonished by the very real and visceral reactions of the other artists and collectors who got a glimpse of it. The piece had moved me from the beginning. I was hoping but just wasn't expecting that it would move others quite as profoundly as it did, especially those who understood either or both sides of the struggle, which was more common than I ever knew.

The statue became a benchmark to me, another level as an artist, husband, and father. As considerable as they were, Lanea and I had enough income to cover bills and all the foundry expenses for *The Ascent.* I was overwhelmed with emotion and inspired by that knowledge. It got me thinking.

While Zachariah was still a baby, I wanted to take my bride and son to Europe to visit museums like the Louvre in Paris and many other magnificent collections throughout the cultural paradise in so many of the countries there. How glorious to be able to research masterpieces and learn what was possible in the world and in the minds of great artists and visionaries. We made plans with Lanea's uncle, who lived in Europe, to travel in his beat-up VW to save money and afford greater experiences.

And for the first time, I was willing to revisit the past in a physical way—the past that had sculpted *me.* It was strange to walk the very city streets in Germany where my mother held my hand and walked with me, as well as peer into some of the same shop windows she had taken me to. Unlike on my mission, I now allowed myself to see the glories of the region. For the first time, I also shared with another person my long-with-held heartache for a mother who would never return. It turned out to be incredibly healing.

From Paris to Denmark, we spent the next few months studying everything from the Sistine Chapel and the *David* to all the famous pieces in the Louvre and Notre Dame, from Fredericksburg Castle and the Carl Bloch paintings of Christ to Bertel Thorvaldsen's studio and the Protestant Church housing the original *Christus* statue.

I was now twenty-nine years old, but I had long ago made an integral commitment to myself as a university student to never stop learning. My instructors taught that certain artists reached plateaus in their work and never moved beyond them. Other artists constantly stepped outside of their limits, pushed past their comfort zones, and extended their skills, allowing explosions in imagination. Unafraid to make mistakes, they were the masters of some of the most vital works in the history of humanity, and I was often awestruck by what they'd accomplished.

Lanea's uncle, God bless him, was an interesting character. We were so grateful for his willingness to provide his car, we paid for gas and hotels. Having turned sixty-five that year, Darold had never been married, and while a pleasant fellow, he exhibited odd behaviors we didn't understand, like obsessively counting pieces of toilet paper.

I called a friend, and Lanea and I made plans to stay in Egypt for four weeks, then meet back up with Darold in Yugoslavia. Darold beamed, just as happy to be free of us for a while.

Lanea, Zac, and I flew into Cairo, and from there took a cab to my friend's apartment for the first leg of our trip. Paul Swenson had been my roommate in Israel and become a dear, lifelong friend. He had married a most wonderful British woman named Elizabeth. The two were living in Egypt while Paul earned his MBA.

One early evening after dinner, Paul drove us right up to the great pyramids outside the city. I stared up at the legendary structures in wonder.

Paul spoke fluent Arabic by this time and was extremely social. He could talk to anyone—and he did. He was wonderful to watch in the marketplace, and now we watched curiously as he spoke with a guard carrying a machine gun. With excitement flashing in his eyes, Paul asked his wife to watch our baby so Lanea and I could quietly scale the pyramid with him. When she graciously agreed, Lanea and I looked at each other in sheer wonder.

My wife gingerly placed our sweet baby into the delighted arms of Elizabeth. Since it was nighttime and the pyramid had spotlights, the guard instructed us to simply pick a side that was in the shadow so as not to get into trouble. I looked up at the height of the structure, trembling at the wild and exhilarating knowledge that we were actually climbing a pyramid in Egypt! Fascinated by the intensity of the work and beauty before us, we scaled each waist-high block. Unlike a normal hike, we had to jump up and shimmy onto each block to reach the next and the next. Despite just having a baby, Lanea was in phenomenal shape. She scrambled up like Paul and me!

When we reached the surprisingly flat top, a breeze cooled our perspiring bodies, and the full moon illustrated the stunning city of Cairo. It was a glorious thing, and as if I hadn't fallen in love with monuments all over Europe, I was in love with them now. I didn't agree with the slave labor that had built this magnificent structure, but centuries later, the monument served as a historical symbol and made Egyptians proud of their nation.

Going down was more perilous than up. By the time we arrived at the bottom, poor Elizabeth was dealing with an unhappy baby boy. Fortunately, she forgave us as quickly as it took the baby to settle down in his mother's arms.

A few days later, Lanea and I went south to Luxor, where we visited the Valley of the Kings and stayed at the Luxor Hotel. For three weeks on our own, we became integrated into the culture as we navigated the streets and marketplaces, saving money and having beautiful experiences buying our own food. People began to recognize us and call us by name. At first it startled us, but we discovered that to several of them, we had become family.

It deeply touched Lanea and me when we were invited by Egyptian families to dine with them in their homes. We knew they were stretching their meager budgets to feed us, and we didn't take that for granted. We did not speak the same language—and yet we did. It was what would come to be described as "agape love," or deep love for humanity.

So exquisitely touched, Lanea and I felt like different human beings when we arrived back in the States. Our hearts, minds, and ideas had expanded dramatically. I loved that we were closer than we had ever been as a couple.

Within a day of returning home, however, that closeness was about to be tested. We were informed that we owed Central Bank over $7,000! Lanea and I just stared at each other. We had been taking money out of the bank each week, but I hadn't realized we'd gone into the red like that. My heart fell.

Oh, my gosh! What are we going to do? I didn't want this to taint what had felt like such a heaven-sent trip. I had failed to manage resources appropriately.

Then I took a breath and did what I had learned to do from the time I was an intrepid entrepreneur at the age of fifteen. I reached out to God, supplicating Him to hear me and to help me solve this immediate problem. I knew Lanea was praying too.

Later that afternoon, I was surprised to get a call from Jim Sanders, the owner of Sander's Gallery in Tucson. Jim was a great guy and had become one of our favorite clients and friends.

"Hey, Gary, I'm glad you're back!" he cried. "You'll never guess who I just sold your wall-hanging *Ascent* to."

Wide-eyed, I quickly motioned to my wife and put Lanea on the call with me. "Who?" we both asked in curiosity, knees nearly buckling in relief. Our debt had just been reversed—and then some.

"Ever heard of a guy by the name of Burt Reynolds?"

The Beauty of Flight

"I'm still learning."
—Michelangelo

As the leaves on our little acre of Springville paradise turned gorgeous shades of red, orange, and yellow, I went to drop off more statues for Meyer Gallery, enjoying the canyon drive up to Park City. More editions of the wall-hanging had sold, and Lanea and I were overjoyed to be debt-free, with a small savings we were building. I knew the hard work had just begun, but there was a spring in my step as Lanea had announced Zachariah was going to be a big brother. I was overjoyed. I loved being a dad.

I pulled up in front of Meyer Gallery, where Gerri and Darrell had previously ordered one of the eight-foot, free-standing *Ascent* statues to be delivered and displayed high up on the second floor of their stunning gallery. It was over five hundred pounds installed. By far the largest piece I had ever created, it was an extreme investment, for me and for the Meyers.

"Hey, I want to tell you something," Gerri said after I greeted her and Darrell with a hug. "You know we get all kinds of art lovers in here, dabblers and lookie-loos and then our serious collectors. We get people who ooh and ahh all the time, yet seldom do we have folks who get emotional over a piece." Then she pointed to the upper floor of the gallery where the eight-foot *Ascent* stood at the top of the stairs, looking quite impressive. "But I've got to share with you, Gary, we've been watching people. They go up, and they just stand there, staring at your piece. They get emotional, tears in their eyes!"

Darrell nodded solemnly in agreement, his eyes saying everything.

I just gulped, so touched. This was the reaction I had hoped for but hadn't expected. Across the country, gallery owners were giving similar feedback. Each time, I got choked up. As much as I wanted to take full credit for the artistry, which I couldn't, I knew the divinely inspired message of the struggle and the interdependent need for one another was what was compelling to people. My heart sang in gratitude. I turned to Gerri and gave her a huge hug. These two had taken a chance on me that first wintry day I stuck my neck out. The deep, abiding friendship we developed felt like it would last the rest of our lives.

At home, my wife had a series of sonograms showing us a girl was due, yet in December of 1985, our second son, Isaiah was born. We held on to the blessing gown, chuckling that he had tucked himself away, not to be fully seen until he was born, but we were head over heels in love with our little man.

I continued a tradition I had started with our firstborn. Every night, even after a long day's work, I played with Zac and held Isaiah for hours. It gave Lanea a break and was precious time for me.

Our little family visited Montpelier to see Mom and Dad a couple of times a year, although they could never seem to manage coming down to see us. Still busy with their rigorous work schedules, they never took time off except for a day here and there to go fishing. I figured if they were going to see their grandkids, it was up to us, so Lanea and I made the nearly four-hour trek up despite our own busy schedules. I found great delight in watching them hold and play with Zac and Isaiah as we visited in the spring of the following year.

One cool, late fall morning after our return trip, I had just made a bottle for Isaiah when I looked at him in wonder. "I swear, little tyke, you are growing bigger every day!" He grinned at me like that was his job. I enjoyed my morning with him and loved all the noises, half words and half sentences he used. As he crawled across the floor toward me, he stopped and burst into a fit of giggles. I couldn't help it; I giggled back. Isaiah stopped suddenly and stared at me, then burst into another fit of giggles. I began laughing so hard tears streamed down my face.

The bottle finished warming, so I picked up Isaiah and hugged him as I held and fed him. In that moment, he looked into my eyes, and I knew that I was as special to him as he was to me, and my heart melted into a puddle at his feet. It only got better when Zac, awakened by our giggles, sleepily climbed out of bed and into my arms. We both held the baby while we fed him, and blissfully happy, I watched the early-morning light filter into the windows. I couldn't imagine life without these two munchkins. I recognized that because of my childhood experiences, I took some things in life more seriously than others did. Still, it went deeper than that. I was gaining a sense of responsibility for my footprint on the earth, even for how it would affect those who followed.

In the following months, I experienced another monumental success in my work. The Church of Jesus Christ of Latter-day Saints purchased a bronze bust that had been another work of passion for me, *Jesus of Nazareth*. My heart pounded as we went into the church's museum and witnessed the life-sized bust on display. The LDS Church would later purchase another piece called *Pushalong*, a pioneer covered wagon, *The Tree of Life*, and eleven other pieces for their collections through the years. Each time, I felt not only a sense of satisfaction but a spiritual high, knowing so many people around the world would see these pieces at some time or another and perhaps for generations.

But soon I faced an obstacle of a different kind. We were growing so fast I couldn't keep up with everything and still sculpt, even though it was the most important task—our moneymaker, after all. I didn't know a lot about business, but sales had started coming in almost too fast. I was in demand for my Western bronzes, yet I had started branching out into other genres of sculpture, too, in varying degrees of demand and success. I enjoyed learning every step of the way, but I needed help.

I'm going to have to hire a business manager, or we will fail, I thought somberly. More than that, I wanted to keep growing. I saw how art could change people, maybe even save some like it had saved me. One thing I knew—I didn't want to stop sculpting. I needed it as much as I needed air. It was time to take some advice I'd recently heard to "hire what you do not know."

Then, literally, right before my eyes was my answer. Dave Barnett. I didn't know the man well, except that he was a super-nice guy. He went to my local church and worked for one of the wealthiest men in the area. I probably couldn't compete. The more I thought about it, however, the better the decision felt. Dave could always say no . . . but then again, he could always say yes!

I would never know unless I asked.

It turned out to be one of the wisest risks I ever took. The man was beautifully jovial and brought a bright side to all my seriousness. Dave's experience as a CPA created a huge, upward thrust of growth as he knew how to manage the intricacies of cash flow. His new skill set could also be painful at times and create emotional vulnerability for me. Dave discovered that out of my lack of business savvy, I owed the IRS some significant taxes. Fortunately, with his help, we took care of the taxes and penalties in a timely manner. My new business manager constantly showed me how to not let business setbacks become setups for failure. I trusted and appreciated his advice.

While Dave had to absorb a whole new industry, fortunately for us, he was a fast learner and began to take our business to places we couldn't have dreamed of. Thanks to him, my art sales went international.

In 1986, our third son, Tyrone, was born. It was quite a celebration. *Three boys in three years,* I marveled and smiled at my exhausted though exhilarated wife. As I watched Lanea blossom into an even more wonderful mother, I couldn't have loved her more. My daily delight was playing hide-and-seek with our toddlers and reading stories before and after roughhousing around on our living room floor.

When Tyrone came home from Payson hospital, however, he brought a new, tender spirit with him. It was tangible. Everyone who met Ty could feel it. I could feel his intense feelings. He didn't enjoy cuddling or hugging as much as the other boys, but early on, it was obvious that he was a deep thinker and a deep feeler.

Zac and Isaiah were practically glued to one another in almost everything they did those days. Ty, however, seemed to enjoy being on his own as much as he enjoyed tagging along with his brothers. From his first steps in our gardens, he was patient and slow to gingerly pick up a dragonfly. He also loved sneaking up on butterflies.

I spent increased time outside with all three boys as I became obsessed with gardening and landscaping. Lanea and I continued building our savings so we could purchase an additional third acre at a time. We planted hundreds of my beloved aspen trees and made more room for Lanea to house and ride her growing stable of horses. Still, raising a growing family took much of our time, so everything outside of work and the kids was always one small step at a time. But we didn't mind.

Lanea felt it important to homeschool the kids. She researched, took courses, and implemented her findings for the benefit of the kids. She took their education and training quite seriously. Due to our childhoods, it felt vital to both of us that our kids be safe, supported, and learn life skills that would help them for their entire existence. I was delighted that my wife went all-out to ensure this happened.

As time passed, Lanea also began studying Gestalt theory and other aspects of hypnotherapy and psychology. Her fascination with courses of study, her introspection, and her application helped her to be an even more effective teacher at home, and she sought out certification. Our home became even more of a peaceful place as we worked with the boys on positive aspects of behavior while letting them be the creative and brilliant creatures they were.

Although my reputation as an artist had been steadily growing, in 1991, it appeared suddenly as if I had become "known" in the art world. First, I was recognized locally as a Resident Artist, and then I became a member of the National Sculpture Society. At that point, there were a lot of accolades and awards I could have sought, but I was more focused on completing and enjoying my work than being known for it.

This growing renown, however, did have major benefits. The director of the Springville Museum of Art and writer for many features in *Southwest Art Magazine*, Vern Swanson, came to visit my little studio.

"Look, Gary, you've got to get these major pieces in front of an art museum! Plus, you've done a whole bunch of work that's in all of these galleries in the States and abroad now . . . it's time to do this article and get you a gallery show!"

His enthusiasm was contagious. I found my new mentor talking me into doing my first one-man show at his museum in July of that year. Leading up to it, he interviewed me for an extensive article he orchestrated to appear in Southwest Art just a month after the live show.

When I walked into the Springville Museum of Art early in the morning on the opening day of the show, it took my breath away. I hadn't ever seen my years of art displayed in one huge area all at once! With great joy, I welcomed many of the mentors, fellow artists, students, friends, neighbors, and others who had come to mean so much to us over the years.

Later that day, I found it incredibly touching to bring my own children over and let them experience the art Daddy had made. In my studio, for obvious reasons, I couldn't let them touch the pieces of clay I had spent hundreds of hours sculpting. Although I made sure they always had their own clay and we sometimes made things together, it was fun to have them see, touch, and feel hundreds of pieces to their hearts' content.

Watching their eyes light up as they ran from piece to piece was glorious. They loved it, and Lanea and I chuckled at their five-second attention spans. Their delight suddenly gave me an idea. In museums and galleries, the artwork was generally not allowed to be touched. What if we brought the museum outside? We could celebrate art right on Main Street and in local parks with children and others who might not have such access to art. What if we could create sculptures the public could touch and children could climb on, take pictures with, and truly enjoy? My form of art, unlike any other, was made to touch.

My thoughts expanded well beyond my own art. *Wouldn't it be cool to have sculptures all around Springville from various artists?*

Over the next several weeks, inspired by my children and town shows in Florida and Kansas, I took photos of my idea and approached Mayor Delora Bertelsen and Arts Commission Chair Teddy Anderson.

"Listen," I said after I showed them the ideas. "I'll donate a piece at cost to get the program started, and I'll find other sculptors to support us."

I was thrilled when they responded with a resounding "Yes!"

That year we started the "Sculptures to Live By" program in Springville. Our family purchased the first piece from artist L'Deane Trueblood. It was a beautiful bronze of a boy with a wheelbarrow entitled *Will's Barrow.* We donated it to the city and had a dedication with L'Deane, the mayor, and lots of citizens. The program began to take off.

I did a fifty-four-inch, life-sized rendition of Isaiah standing with his nose in a book. It was called *Bookworm,* and it was placed in front of the city library on Main Street. I loved how my kids always called out and pointed to it whenever we drove by.

The project soon grew to over fifty sculptures around town. Eventually, Duke's Jewelers sponsored a large green and very fat frog with a jeweled crown entitled *Royal Expectations*. It was one of my favorites of the sculptures I had designed specifically for children to love.

Springville had been nicknamed "Art City" for decades, and this program added a wonderful dimension and visibility to its reputation. What I loved most was the access to children and adults throughout the town. People even submitted letters to the editor about how much they loved going downtown and educating their children on the meanings and stories behind the art. Art became inclusive and even more collaborative—and evidence that creativity could benefit an entire community with a ripple of greater good.

Lanea and I loved stoking our inner fires with continuing personal development. I was preparing to attend a fire walk Tony Robbins was doing in LA. I remembered how I was able to publicly honor Stan as my mentor and for inspiring *The Ascent* in my gallery show. Tony Robbin's words had inspired me greatly when I was graduating from college, encouraging me to rise, develop confidence, and take risks. It was his words that helped me to get out of bed and to be a contribution, even on my dark days. I told my manager, Dave Barnett, about my wish to thank Tony for his positive influence.

Before I could sneeze, Dave magically arranged for me to thank Tony personally and publicly. On stage, Tony's mouth dropped open in front of his audience of five thousand, when I wheeled out a heavy bronze of *The Ascent* and thanked Tony for his influence in my life for such good. My heart swelled with warmth and joy at the standing ovation Tony got. I hoped it was as singular a moment for him as it was for me.

When we got home from that event, I received an email from Jay Abraham, an affiliate of Tony. It included an invitation to a powerful business-marketing event, but it cost $10,000, something I couldn't afford. Dave gently reminded me that while I had found my niche as an artist, I needed to share my voice and vision more powerfully with the world. "No one understands your unique vision, Gary, unless you tell them. You need to make your passionate 'why' as meaningful for a buyer as it is for you."

I called Jay's office and was able to negotiate a trade—attendance in the class in exchange for a beautiful, tall rendition of *The Ascent*.

"You're on!" he cried happily.

I was delighted. *Another win-win! Especially if I get out of this class what I really need.*

I entered the business conference feeling self-conscious. It was filled with full-suited executives from large, nationally renowned companies. For three days we worked on explaining our individual brands. Finally relaxing into it, I poured my artist's heart onto the page. Under the magic of Jay's tutelage, we were forced to distill several pages of vision down to one page, then one paragraph, and finally, one sentence of fewer than ten words. It was gritty work, and it reminded me of chipping the ceramic shell off the metal cast and grinding away everything that was not a part of the art itself.

I gasped when the distilled sentence came to me. When I spoke it aloud, everyone in the class gasped, too, and clapped. My neighbor in a three-piece suit whispered to me, "Oh, my gosh, Gary! You nailed it!"

It had been a part of my work from the beginning, and it would affect every aspect of my art and my life beyond that moment.

"Lifting the Human Spirit through Sculpture."

The Incredible Journey

You are not here merely to make a living. You are here in order to enable the world to live more amply, with greater vision, with a finer spirit of hope and achievement. You are here to enrich the world, and you impoverish yourself if you forget the errand.
—*Woodrow Wilson*

The next few years, our family experienced the magic of balsa-wood gliders, pogo sticks, and paper airplanes. Each second that I wasn't working, my kids enrolled me in those things about which they were most passionate. As we played, imagined, and dreamed, I saw their fascination—especially Isaiah—with thrust, momentum, and flight. Isaiah became completely obsessed with flight, and something about his passion sparked my muse. How could I capture Isaiah's sparkling enthusiasm, his childhood fascination with flight?

Well, I mused, *I'd want him to be flying* on *the paper airplane, not just launching it!*

When the first life-size piece entitled *Journeys of the Imagination* was finished, I was excited and proud. Nothing thrilled me more than when I saw my boys up close to the finished bronze, their eyes wide at seeing their brother memorialized and on such a cool contraption!

Blessed by my new mantra, with every piece I sculpted, I asked myself, "Does this lift the human spirit? In what way? How can I make this piece even more inspiring?"

As I looked at the boys crowded around the new bronze, I felt myself growing emotional. Zachariah and Isaiah were now close to the age I was when I lost my mother and entered a very dark time in my life. Shocked, I realized that Isaiah's fully enchanted visage flying on the paper airplane represented the freedom I had longed for as a child. More important, this piece represented the freedom *every* child should have from captivity, abuse, and fear. I prayed this particular statue would end up in parks, museums, libraries, schools, and offices around the world, reminding grown-ups to protect freedom and innocence for children. Under my breath, I uttered a prayer of deep gratitude. I would not take one moment of my freedom, or that of my children, for granted.

In 1993, we were expecting again. Pregnancies remained generally easy for Lanea, who absolutely glowed when she was with child. The delivery of each baby, though, was often rough on her, and I found myself getting nervous as the due date approached. She wasn't looking well, and it had been seven years since Ty. When our new son, Raphael, arrived safely, I celebrated wholeheartedly and brought the boys in to celebrate her and the new addition we would soon call Raphy.

That late-fall afternoon remains etched in my mind like a painting; I will forever remember the steeped, golden light coming in through the window as we each took turns holding the baby and the three boys celebrated their mommy, wrapping their arms tightly around her. It was a momentous occasion, and Raphy soon became the boys' favorite little buddy.

Even with a newborn, Lanea was adventurous when it came to the boys' education. She continued to homeschool, which allowed flexibility in schedules. That Christmas, we packed the entire brood in our Suburban and traveled to northern Mexico. Lanea and I had been so moved by our international experiences we felt it vital for our kids to experience the wonders of new cultures too. This was just as critical to their education as art, science, math, and reading. Lanea taught the kids history through engaging stories as we traveled. After we crossed the border, she shared our Christmas surprise—the kids would be giving gifts of their time and Rollerblading talents, and even some of their possessions. Seeing our boys step into the role of teacher was breathtaking.

Like our experience in Egypt, there was an international language of connection, trust, and joy. I watched the boys for hours, proud of their patience and compassion as they taught and offered their gifts of friendship.

Once back home, we prepared for an expanded new year. As a family, we looked for opportunities that enhanced our marriage, family, church, and community. With a new garage and studio going in on our property so I could work from home more often, we felt we were in paradise and would never leave.

The following year, however, through a friend, we happened to find a stunning property, complete with a natural spring. It also had much more room for Lanea's horses. Thus began a new adventure for our family and a turning point in realizing how powerful and inspiring dreams can be to others.

After the success of our outdoor art project in Springville, Lanea and I envisioned building a place downtown we would call "The Incredible Journey Arts Building," which would house an arts school, my studio, a showroom, and more. At the same time, we also created the Incredible Journey Arts Foundation. Our desire was to give to the community as much as it had given to us.

An opportunity came up to purchase the historic 1892 H. T. Reynolds Building—a twenty-thousand-square-foot mercantile building that had been the tallest structure south of Salt Lake City for decades and the first building in the area wired for electricity. However, it seemed to have outlived its usefulness. I discovered that plans were in the works to raze it. Horrified, we wanted to keep what had been a significant part of the community since the 1890s.

Inspired by Scottsdale Artist's School in Arizona and Loveland Art Academy in Colorado, we began renovations on the top floor for artists in residence. The middle floor would house both my studio and the art school. The bottom floor was to be the Starving Artist Restaurant, combined with a store—an outlet for selling the students' art as well as some of mine. We named it Celebration Gallery.

Out back behind the place, we bought the old Kolob Lumber building as well and turned it into our bronze foundry. We started doing foundry tours for churches, schools, and civic groups to show how our art was produced. The Incredible Journey Arts Building turned out to be a delightful educational process for the whole community. It was humbling and a huge step for an artist to own the largest building in town. We felt it would be an art center to benefit the entire state.

Unfortunately, as time passed, it became clear to us that we just couldn't find a way to competently and efficiently do everything we wished according to our grand vision and limited budget. What it boiled down to most was the restoration, which we discovered alone would cost over $1 million, not to mention the equally seismic upkeep and maintenance every year. Lanea and I were heartsick to find that it just wasn't economically feasible. Instead, we sold it to a company committed to do what we could not. I was so grateful. My only stipulation was that they keep all the stained glass and the oak storefront, with which we had lovingly enhanced the Reynolds building.

The company was as good as its word, and people would continue to enjoy that beauty for decades. While the whole project didn't work out as we had hoped, what did take place had a significant impact for good on our community. Through the efforts of an entire community, including civil service leaders, artists, and citizens alike, "Art City" continued to be known for valuing artistic beauty and community creativity.

I learned a lot during this phase that would help me later in life and in business. I never lost the urge to create things in a fashion that would not only support my family but somehow enhance the entire community. The biggest lesson I learned was that contribution didn't have to be lavish to inspire. When people simply *collaborated*, a much grander vision was possible for everyone.

The Good, the Bad, and the Ugly

"Truth is like a surgery. It hurts but cures.
A lie is like a painkiller. It gives instant relief but has side-effects forever."
—*Unknown*

I did not see it coming.

While I was celebrating mostly victories in my career and many precious milestones with my young family, I faced an unforeseen debacle within my stepfamily. It happened over the summer of 1996, when Lanea and I took the boys on a trip to Montpelier, including a stop farther northwest in Idaho to visit my little brother Billy.

Bill and I had stayed in touch since my teenage years when I'd buzz up to see him on my motorcycle—at least before college, mission, and marriage. After that, we connected over the phone, and our family celebrated with him when he married a wonderful, smart, beautiful girl named Cammie. I knew Mom would be happy for him.

The four of us caught up as couples after the boys went down for the night. For the first time in our lives, Bill and I spoke as grown men. The conversation turned toward more personal subjects, and we discussed our lives together in Germany and the fallout of our mother's death. It didn't feel uncomfortable in the slightest for us to have this conversation—until Cammie started to speak.

I was surprised when her voice lowered meaningfully as she mentioned our mother and Ted. I shook my head as if to clear it.

"Wait, what? Can you say that again?" I asked, although this time I turned to Bill for clarification.

"Yeah, you know . . . Dad being a spy and all," Bill replied, looking over his shoulder as he spoke. He kept his voice low too. "I shared with Cammie how Dad was killed by counterintelligence and how Mom sadly got caught in the middle."

What the hell? My mouth hung open in stunned silence.

"Bill," I finally managed. "Can you please start from the beginning?"

Bill did so, and I was floored. Grandma and Grandpa Reeder had told Bill his entire life that because his father's body had come back to the U.S. "riddled with bullets" during peacetime, it was concluded that he was taken out by assassins. The story they developed was that my stepfather was a U.S. operative doing undercover work when he was killed, and the assassins had taken our mother out too.

Grandma Reeder's story didn't even slightly resemble what I'd been told, and even with as young as I had been, I vividly remembered August 1, 1961. Now I was shaken.

Dear God! How I would give anything for Billy's story to be the truth—not the awful story I know all too well.

With a big sigh, and as gently as I could, I explained what I had experienced firsthand. I also shared the clarifying information my father, Wayne, had shared with me within a few months of my return to the States, along with details he later only hesitantly gave me because I asked.

Billy was incredulous. His eyes were as wide with disbelief as mine had been at his words. Our stories didn't mesh at all.

Driving home the next day, still shaken, I wondered why Ted's parents felt they had to make the story more than simply palatable for my half-brother. The thought bounced around in my brain like a pinball. What would I have done in their stead?

Bill had been an innocent baby when our parents died. Although a local newspaper article accurately depicted the truth, how in the world could his grandparents bring themselves to tell little Billy that his own father had murdered his mother and then killed himself?

The answer was obvious. They couldn't.

Instead, they had made Ted a hero.

After arriving home a few hours later in Utah, I sat down and wrote the U.S. Army crime department, requesting the investigative report under the Freedom of Information Act (FOIA). I tried to put it out of my mind from that moment, but I couldn't help second-guessing myself. *What if I had it wrong?* Or what if the U.S. government had a different story?

If, for some reason, my memories of our terrified mother begging me for help were not real, there had to be something very wrong with me.

A large manilla envelope finally arrived in October of 1996. I took it from the mailman and held it in my hand for several long moments. Finally, I sat on my couch in the front room. Inside was a copy of the Army Investigative Service Report on the deaths of Ted and Betty Jo Reeder.

As I read, I discovered that what was recorded about that night coincided very closely, although not exactly, with the specific details in my memory. The report was based on the perspective of the investigator, who interviewed thirteen people.

> Investigation disclosed that about 2000 hours, 6 August 1961, George [Ted] and Betty REEDER were overheard by Edward and Eleanor WETSEL and RUSSELL and his wife, arguing in the hallways of their apartment, 28B Lincoln Street, Benjamin Franklin Village, Mannheim-Kaefertal (Wuerttemberg-Baden), Germany. Shortly thereafter, Betty REEDER requested Edward WETSEL, residing across the hallway from her apartment at 28A Lincoln Street, to assist her in rearranging her bed which had been dismantled during the argument with her husband. At that time, Betty REEDER made the following remark to Edward WETZEL "I'm sorry that this had to happen" and referring to the argument that she had with her husband, she added "He was real wild."
>
> At approximately 2100 hours, 6 August 1961, George REEDER was observed by LONG and BIVENS entering the weapons repair shop of the Marksmanship Detachment, 18th Infantry, building #78 M, Coleman Barracks, Mannheim-Sandhofen, Germany, where he remained for a few minutes and departed. About 2200 hours, 6 August 1961, George REEDER returned to his apartment and he resumed the argument with his wife. At this time, Edward WETSEL who was entertaining RUSSELL and the latter's wife, heard a woman scream in the hallway adjacent to his and the REEDER's apartment entrance. Edward WETZEL looked through the glass view hole in his apartment door and saw Betty REEDER standing

on the threshold of her apartment entrance with her back turned toward him. Betty REEDER was standing, facing toward and struggling with her husband, the latter standing in the open doorway of his own apartment.

At this time, George REEDER fired three bullets from a caliber .45 Remington automatic pistol model 1911 Al, serial #2053033, the property of the United States Government, issued to JOHNS, striking Betty REEDER in the neck, chest, legs, and abdomen. Edward WETZEL still looking through the view hole of his apartment door, saw a flash and heard the report of the weapon fired by George REEDER. When the first bullet was fired, Edward WETZEL felt what he presumed to be a splinter caused by a bullet passing through his apartment door, strike his left arm. Edward WETZEL was uninjured. When the second bullet was fired through Edward WETZEL's apartment door, the latter moved away from the door, and instructed wife Eleanor WETZEL, and RUSSELL and his wife to take cover.

After shooting his wife, George REEDER went into the dining room alcove in his apartment, removed the magazine from the pistol, loaded one bullet in the chamber of the weapon, and after placing the unloaded magazine on the dining room table, and in the presence of PRICE, his stepson (age 6) shot himself in the center of his forehead. After the shooting had ceased, Edward WETZEL again looked through the view hole of the apartment door and noticed that the entrance door to the REEDER apartment was open and he was unable to see anyone in the hallway or in the apartment. Edward WETZEL opened the door of his own apartment and Betty REEDER fell across the threshold of his apartment. Edward WETZEL observed that Betty REEDER, though bleeding profusely from wounds in her neck and body, was still alive. Edward WETZEL left the building to summon medical aid for Betty REEDER from the nearby US Army Hospital, Branch Dispensary #4, Benjamin Franklin Village, Mannheim-Kaefertal, Germany. Enroute he met James DORSEY in front of the apartment building, and requested the latter to notify the dispensary and the Military Police.

Edward WETZEL returned to the scene of the incident, and seeing PRICE standing and crying in the living room of the REEDER apartment, brought the latter into his own apartment and put him to bed. Meanwhile, James DORSEY left the scene and returned to his own apartment where he instructed his wife, Gladys DORSEY to notify the medical authorities and the Military Police. James DORSEY then returned to the scene of the incident and removed a burning cigarette from Betty REEDER'S right hand. At 2215 hours, 6 August 1961, Betty REEDER and George REEDER were pronounced dead at the scene of the incident by LIBEDINSKY. The bodies of Betty REEDER and George REEDER were removed to US Army Hospital, Branch Dispensary #4, and subsequently transferred to the US Army Hospital, Heidelberg, Germany, for examination and final disposition.

Oh, my God! I never knew there was an eyewitness. Our neighbor across the way, Mr. Wetzel, saw them scuffling in our doorway? He actually saw Ted shoot Mom.

Horror and relief overwhelmed me at the same time.

There was no assassin.

It was distressing to read about how my mother had struggled with Ted outside our apartment and how he had shot her three times, producing multiple entry and exit wounds. If anyone had been "riddled with bullets," it had been my mother, not Ted.

There was a strong mention of me in the report further in:

Investigation did not reveal any evidence to indicate that PRICE, Betty READER's oldest son, had witnessed the actual shooting. When interviewed, PRICE verbally stated that he was in his bed when he heard his father and his mother arguing, and that his father did not like the way his mother was, or had been dancing. PRICE further stated that after he heard his mother, Betty REEDER, shout "Help, Gary," he ran into the living room and saw his mother on the floor of the hallway, bleeding, and his father standing by the dining room table. PRICE did not remember seeing a gun or hearing shots fired. The REEDER children, PRICE and William T. REEDER (age 1 year) have been returned to the United States by GAY, who was on rotation status, and placed in the care of Mr. John L. REEDER, [address] Hailey, Idaho, the father of George REEDER.

My stepfather, reeking of alcohol, had come home with a box of twenty-nine rounds of .45 caliber ammunition in one of the pockets of his jacket. I wasn't lost on the fact that in a gun with a capacity to hold eight rounds, Ted had specifically loaded *three* bullets. One was meant for my mother—but she'd fought him unexpectedly.

Who were the other two bullets for? Chilled to the bone, I shook away the thought. While most of the report closely matched my recollection of that awful night, it sure didn't make me feel any better, except to know that I wasn't crazy.

I shook my head in sadness. The way I saw it, God had implemented a system of protecting my tender, young psyche. My brain remembered most of the other details but had specifically removed the sound of gunfire and my mother calling my name.

Between this tragedy in Germany and my experiences with my abusive older stepbrother, I suffered with symptoms of what the world would know later as post-traumatic stress disorder. While I still couldn't recall Ted shooting himself, I remembered the jarring, splintering noise of the silverware drawer crashing just as I passed the kitchen to reach my mother. How would I hear one noise and not another? I decided it was because I had been on a mission to protect and save Mom. Not until I was an adult would I come to understand how the brain remembers snatches of time—snapshots, if you will, in the middle of trauma.

So, now, as I continued to read the report, I realized something important. My selective memory was a gift from God and perhaps saved my little childhood soul from more trauma. It also helped me to remember as much truth as I could handle at the time. The puzzle pieces now clicked into place. It was a terrible puzzle, but it was the truth.

When Lanea came in from outside, I handed her the report with shaking hands. I let her read it while I took over watching our young boys and forced myself to breathe. After questioning my memory for months, it was a relief to read the report. While the kids were occupied for a moment, Lanea quietly pointed to what she thought was most important:

1. That George REEDER did, at Mannheim, Germany, on or about 6 August 196`, murder Betty REEDER by shooting her with a caliber .45 automatic pistol.
2. That George REEDER did, at Mannheim, Germany, on or about 6 August 1961, take his own life by firing a caliber .45 automatic pistol in his forehead.

She looked at me grimly. "It's here in black and white, Gary. What are you going to do about Bill?"

"I don't know."

I sat and thought. Then I sat and prayed. Then I thought some more. To grow up thinking your father was some kind of hero who was assassinated . . .

Bill has never been told the truth.

And, dear God, I didn't know that he had grown up with a lie.

It took several days of the report sitting on my desk before I came to a decision. I had experienced enough of the rotting, fetid energy of lies in my youth and young adulthood. I would not keep the truth from my younger stepbrother. For one thing, Bill was vitally important to me, and so was our growing relationship. I didn't want him thinking I was a liar or that I had made up this sinister story to somehow hurt him. Nothing could be further from the truth. I'd loved him long before we sat on the plane together from Germany to Idaho. And I had too much respect for the man he had become to keep the truth from him.

As I put the report in the mailbox, however, I was more than angry; I was pissed that I was forced to be the one to tell him. *It shouldn't have been me.* I didn't hear from Bill for several months after our visit, and even then, the conversation was stilted. We didn't talk about the report at all.

It crushed me when only a few years later, my little brother died of a heart attack. I had always felt protective of Bill, and a part of me died that day. Worse, however, was the crushing guilt that I might be responsible for Bill's death.

It hurt like hell to be held responsible for a lie that had been told when I was only an innocent boy like Billy. I never even knew about the lie until our conversation. Nothing helped me in my grief. Nothing would bring Bill back to Cammie or me. I didn't look at the reports for a long while after that.

One very early Sunday morning before everyone else was awake, I carefully reread the testimonies in the original report the army sent me. I had deeply yearned for more information about my mother for so long, but I had been desperate for details about her *life*, not her death. Maybe there were some fragmented pieces of her personality I could garner to know her better.

With a more objective eye, I realized that the report was shockingly one-sided, with clear patterns of the male-oriented military culture of the time.

It was obvious that Ted and my mother engaged in mutual jealousy and drama, but as I read deeper into the details, I realized how much Mom hid from me and Bill. In August the year prior to her death, Mom and Ted had been at a club, drinking, went home, and commenced arguing. Ted hit my mother in the face and tried to choke her. She had run to the bathroom and consumed a large quantity of pills the army dispensary had prescribed for a "nervous condition." Afterward, she went out into the room and told Ted he would "never have the opportunity to strike her again." Ted notified the hospital of her overdose, and she was treated and released. At the end of the month, she wrote a statement that the incident was "all cleared up."

Ted also signed a statement, where he even admitted to hitting her:

My wife and I went to the NCO Club located in Benjamin Franklin Village, Mannheim-Kaerfertal, Germany on the night in question. We both consumed a more than usual amount of alcohol and got into an argument over the slot machines. After we got outside of the club, we continued the argument and I slapped her around a little I suppose.

That statement made my blood run cold. *How could Ted be so casual about such a thing?* "Slapped her around a little I suppose." The language left me feeling nauseated.

The investigator described my mother as high maintenance, stating that she had been promiscuous before marriage, made Ted jealous, enjoyed having him fight over her, and that Ted intended to divorce her upon their return to the U.S. because she was "always nagging at him, that her demands were unreasonable, and he could not live with her any longer."

The first time I read the report, even *I* took this at face value.

However, as I gave myself time to absorb the reports individually and in-depth, I clearly saw another pattern. Thirteen people had been interviewed, yet only two gave any indication of my mother's "difficult" behaviors, and even those were rather eye-opening. One man labeled her as "difficult" because she asked her husband to help with dishes from time to time and go to the store. *That made her nagging and unreasonable?* I questioned. The man admitted Ted had told him that when he had occasion to go home early, he would not, especially if it was his wife's day to wash, because he didn't want to help her. I began to reason that Ted was not only violent, he had a selfish streak.

The only other person who negatively described her was a military man from whom she appeared to have had to fend off advances! At a friend's party, this guy had made her extremely uncomfortable when he followed her into her friend's kitchen. She felt the need to call out for help, and it did cause drama.

The very last report was by a woman named Francis Myrtle Pierce. *Francis . . .* I gasped. *Fran!* She was the woman I stayed with after the shooting.

Fran had the longest report of anyone. From what she wrote, I came to believe two things: she knew my father first, and she knew my mother best.

Fran felt Ted was very much in love with my mother. It apparently took my mom several months to open up to her about her past. Mom finally told Fran she'd not experienced a stable upbringing, that her mother had a reputation in town, and that her own first marriage to Wayne had not worked out. It was the first time I realized that Wayne and Ted were friends.

I thought about that for a while. In the small town I was raised in, even in my day, there was a terrible double standard. Boys and men could play around as much as they wanted sexually, even be praised for it, but if a girl or woman did, she was labeled with wicked names and often black-balled from "polite" society.

That double standard was apparent in Ted as well. He didn't like the fact that my mom had dated, even though *he* had dated several other women, Fran confirmed. "Sgt. Reeder could not get over the idea that his wife had been married before, and that some other man had had her. Mrs. Reeder told me that many times, Sgt. Reeder called her a whore and a tramp because her mother was one and also on account of the stories he had heard about her prior to her marriage."

I swallowed. I hated the thought of Ted calling my mother such awful names. My fists clenched as I continued.

According to Fran's report, Mom told her that once she started dating Ted, she never flirted with anybody. "She loved him and wanted desperately to help him overcome his jealousy, and to feel secure in their love," said Fran. It was never enough.

> When our husbands were in the field, we women sometimes gathered at each other's homes to play cards. If we went to Mrs. Reeder's home, we could stay as long as we wanted, but if the card game was somewhere else, she went home no later than nine or nine thirty. Mrs. Reeder was a very sophisticated woman and also quite educated. This did not help his jealousy. Mrs. Reeder was also very attractive and when she was dressed up, she looked somewhat sexy, even if she was not aware of this. . . . Sgt. Reeder had quite an inferiority complex and also had a violent temper. Mrs. Reeder also had a violent temper, which did not help the situation.

Suddenly, I came to a paragraph I had to stop and highlight. It reminded me of something similar to what Mom tried to talk to me about. Months before that night, Ted and Mom had gone out for dinner with friends and had a few drinks.

> ST Johnson and his wife were there and had been dancing. Johnson asked her to dance and she felt it would be rude to say no. At some point, Ted dragged her out of the restaurant and forced her to her knees and bruised her pretty badly. It seems that he hit her several times before they got into the car. Sgt REEDER then drove madly to the woods, where he stopped. She jumped out of the car and tried to run, but he caught her and beat her up some more. She thought he was going to kill her, because he had a wild look on his face. She had never seen him look that way before. Then she begged him to take her home. All of a sudden, he stopped beating her and took her home.

I swallowed again, hard. Fran said Mom begged him to get help for his temper, and he went to the local chaplain. Unfortunately, the chaplain admitted to Ted that he was a jealous husband himself. There was no further counseling, no written reports, no recommendations for help.

I sat in the chair in my living room and thought about that for a long time. Mom experienced Ted's violent, jealous rages, and no one would stop him. She had gone for help and didn't get it. No wonder she had been so frightened the night of her death. No wonder she asked her little boy for advice. She had no one else to turn to.

Finally, she ran to ask the neighbor for help in order to save me and my baby brother. She took all the bullets into her body and could not save herself—*Good God, she was the true hero!*

Story after story swirled through my mind. However, the one that remained in my heart felt the truest. I didn't know how, but after all I had learned about our mother, I wanted to honor her somehow, in some way, for what she had done to save Bill and me.

Divine Orchestration

"Sometimes people don't understand the promises
they're making when they make them.
But you keep the promise anyway. That's what love is.
Love is keeping the promise anyway."
—John Green

One afternoon in 1997, my team and I were busy loading up a large rendition of my *Synergy* statue for a corporate client. Inspired by the handclasp of *The Ascent* and all the meanings behind it, this piece, *Synergy*, depicted six hands, each clasping another's arm in a full circle in a clear symbol of unity and collaboration.

Since *The Ascent*, I had come to recognize how much collaborative effort meant to humanity at large. I was amazed at the number of people who influenced my own children and played a role in sculpting their characters. I realized that there was some idea, talent, or gift in each of us, yet one person could not succeed fully on his or her own. *Synergy* represented the magic that happens when the entire human family becomes unified for everyone's empowerment.

As we finished loading *Synergy* into the truck, I noticed a visitor had arrived and was watching our endeavors. I excused myself from my crew to shake his hand and lead him upstairs to my studio. A bit taller than I was, Kevin Hall was a handsome man with an easy smile. His short-cropped brown hair was graying at the temples, and his sparkling, light eyes seemed to take in everything.

"Gary, thanks for seeing me today on short notice," he said after we were seated and had made a little small talk. "I have to ask, have you ever heard of Viktor Frankl?"

"No," I admitted, shaking my head. "Never heard of him."

Kevin's eyes widened a bit, but he continued. "Okay, well, have you heard of Stephen Covey?"

"Of course!" I said, grinning. "I'm an artist, but I do poke my head up from time to time. I don't know much about him except for the famous Franklin-Covey day planners and his book, *The 7 Habits of Highly Effective People.* That's his, right?"

"Yes," Kevin said proudly, "although he's done far and away much more than that. He carries a doctorate, has been a teacher for several prestigious schools of business, and is also a renowned public speaker. I've enjoyed working with him at Franklin-Covey for a number of years on special projects. That's actually what I came to talk with you about."

I was intrigued but puzzled. Kevin was obviously a storyteller, and he began to weave a beautiful tale. He proceeded to share how Mr. Covey met Dr. Viktor Frankl, a famous psychologist and survivor of the Nazi concentration camps during the Holocaust. Covey and Frankl had met long after the war on the American lecture circuit and held deep, in-depth philosophical and sociological discussions, especially regarding Frankl's passionate belief that there could be no true liberty among humans, unless they also lived the ideal of responsibility.

"Without responsibility, freedom becomes anarchy and chaos," explained Kevin, his twinkling eyes now serious as they stared into mine. "The value of responsibility is necessary for civic and individual freedom and for a prosperous nation. Viktor had long talked about building a monument as a symbol of responsibility in this country. Gary, Viktor had an all-encompassing dream. He wanted to bookend the Statue of Liberty on the East Coast by creating a Statue of Responsibility on the West Coast."

I caught his emphasis, and this time it was my turn to raise my eyebrows. I had not heard of this.

"Unfortunately, Dr. Frankl died this year," said Kevin sadly. "His death spurred a discussion among a group of us, including Dr. Covey, about just how important it is for us to remember Frankl's legacy and the importance of responsibility in this country . . . and that's where you come in,

Gary," Kevin added, looking me straight in the eyes. "I heard about you through a mutual friend, and she let me know just how inspiring your pieces are—like the one I saw today."

Kevin's eyes suddenly sharpened to a greater intensity. "That's why we'd like you to consider being the designer of this very historic monument—a 305-foot Statue of Responsibility, roughly the same size and equally significant to the Statue of Liberty."

At that point, chills cascaded up and down my arms and spine. Equally significant to the Statue of Liberty? This truly was monumental.

I suddenly remembered a night, many years prior, as I gazed out from the top of one of the great pyramids outside Cairo. Monuments were lasting legacies. They stood for something—and the stories and lessons surrounding them could be hallmarks of civilizations for centuries. To have something that could be meaningful for our time spoke to me.

However, I hesitated. At the moment, I was extremely busy, in the middle of several projects. I felt like I had a zillion sculpture requests that needed to be fulfilled. A national monument certainly was a sculptor's dream, but I had many people counting on me already and felt my own measure of "responsibility" to them first.

I also wondered secretly at my ability to do such a thing. This wasn't an *M* on the hillside, and I found myself discounting all the work I had done since then.

"I don't know," I said honestly. "I need to think about it."

Long after Kevin left, I couldn't get our talk out of my mind. Something that represented a vital ideal for our entire nation and the world was intriguing. It was in definite alignment with the values I tried to stand for.

Although other projects crowded my thoughts, this one wouldn't let go. A few days later, I couldn't concentrate when I was in my studio. I found myself pacing and doing everything except work. Quietly, I began to wonder about a few of the things festering inside me. "Without responsibility," Kevin had said, "freedom becomes anarchy and chaos." I had witnessed, been a part of, sometimes helped create, and was clearly at times a victim of the antithesis of responsibility.

I paced and paced.

Just a few months prior to Kevin's visit to my studio, a journalist named Shauna Haehl wanted to write a biography about my life. When I agreed, she had started doing extensive research and interviews when she came across another shocking fact—another lie revealed. In an unguarded moment in an interview with my dad, Wayne revealed that he was not likely my birth father.

When Shauna shared this with me, I was not just shocked, I was infuriated and frustrated. *After all we had been through? Another lie?* I drove straight up to Montpelier that very day and demanded a paternity test.

That's when the father I had known for most of my life talked about the things he had always kept deep inside. He told me he had fallen in love with my mom and married her when she was just sixteen. He was back from the war, from prison camp, and wanted a quiet, peaceful life, especially after working in the rail yard all week long. This was the crux of their marital disputes. His desire to stay home with the woman he loved on the weekends was at odds with what my mother wanted. A vivacious and beautiful young woman, her only reprieve from the isolation and drudgery of the week was to socialize on the weekends. It was a no-win situation.

Finally, Dad told me, she took off to visit her mother in San Francisco. When she came back, she was pregnant, he was sure, with another man's child. Dad stayed married to her anyway.

I just stared at him, dumbfounded.

Bill learned his father was not a spy. I learned that our mother was not a saint.

On the drive home, what stood out to me for the first time was that I still loved and respected her for her love of me and Bill, especially how she sought to protect the two of us. A day or two later, another thought slammed into me as I worked in the studio and pondered my father's actions. Wayne didn't believe he was my father, yet he'd decided to show up for *me*. He had loved my mother, let her go, and then loved her illegitimate child.

I sank to my knees in the middle of my studio. I was alone on the floor amidst my favorite finished pieces of sculpture and several unfinished works, racked with pain and confusion, tears streaming down my face.

"Dear God," I prayed aloud in a hoarse whisper. "*Twice* this man claimed me as his son, even when he knew it wasn't the truth. He took me in as an innocent baby. Then, later, after their divorce, when she had rejected him and he had started a whole brand-new life without her, he took me again as his own son after my mother was tragically slain! Was that irresponsible? Or was that an unprecedented level of responsibility to help a young boy he loved, to save him from more unnecessary pain? To save me?"

I cried aloud, feeling like my torment literally would wrench my soul apart.

"What is the difference between Grandma Reeder's lies about Ted and Wayne's lies about being my father?" I demanded. There were no answers whispered back to me in the space that usually felt so rich and full of symbolic meaning. Instead, my studio felt confusing, isolating, and oppressive.

For hours I remained unable to concentrate. Even a run around the property didn't help. This whole question of responsibility plagued me. Then a thought struck me.

What might Viktor Frankl know about responsibility that I do not?

Soon I found myself in my car, heading straight to the city library. I needed to know. What little I glimpsed of Viktor Frankl came only from what Kevin had told me. I needed more information. The librarians were helpful, and they certainly seemed to know who this famous Viktor Frankl was. When they pulled out a book and showed me several articles and interviews, I began to piece together in my mind the enigmatic life of this man.

Viktor had been a Jew living in Vienna. Early in his education, he had studied Freud, Adler, and Jung, yet Frankl felt strongly that something was missing. He opened his own psychiatric practice and began formulating a book on his ideas while the threat of war loomed over Austria.

I remembered from my German history a popular idea that had circulated before WWII known as *Anschluss*, meaning the idea of binding together the Germans and Austrians into a "Greater Germany"—at least in those early days when it seemed noble.

Fascinated and chagrined, I learned that after the conquest, the Nazis and sympathizers commenced a regime of terror against the Jews in Austria. During *Kristallnacht*, or "Night of Broken Glass," Nazis torched synagogues, looted Jewish properties and homes, and killed ninety-one people. They rounded up tens of thousands of Jewish men who were then imprisoned in Dachau, Buchenwald, and other concentration camps. That was just the beginning. Women and children were next.

It gave me chills to think about it. In my worldly travels, I had made friends with both older Germans and older Jews. In profound conversations, it was difficult to ignore the deep psychological twisting and sheer physical and mental torture of prisoners. My dad, Wayne, had suffered horrifically at the hands of his Nazi captors. I couldn't imagine what it would have been like to be considered a "throwaway, disposable Jew" in Austria during this dark period in human history.

I read on, discovering that Viktor could have come on a visa to the States but stayed behind with his wife to protect his parents. Unfortunately, he was placed into camps alongside his parents, his wife, and his brother. Viktor didn't know his entire family was exterminated, even as he was sent on to another work camp. Unfortunately, guards destroyed the only copy of the book he'd been writing. The only thing that kept him alive in the ensuing three years was the thought of the book he would write again and the woman he loved.

Viktor was one of only a few who survived Auschwitz. After his own liberation day, he went straight to work rewriting his new, full manuscript, which contained ideas that would make him world-renowned. I could see why it was required reading for many high schools—so that we could learn from our past mistakes.

I sat down with a copy of Frankl's book but only quickly glanced through it. What little I did read triggered feelings in my body I didn't like, and dark memories of isolation, fear, and darkness crept in, even in the light of my city's public library. I pushed those feelings back down and concentrated on the article.

I felt the plucking of the strings of God in divine orchestration.

"Yes, I would be interested," I said as I called Kevin Hall from my car. I felt the answer deep in my bones. "Let's see what we can do."

I returned to my studio and picked up my clay. Over the following months, visions of the Holocaust and the suffering haunted me. *Synergy* was international in its energy, but the message wasn't quite right. It was the wrong shape for a tall monument.

The Statue of Responsibility, I knew, was a work of art that needed to be vertical. It deserved to be seen and inspire people from miles and miles away. As Kevin had reported, it had to be equally as tall and significant as the Statue of Liberty.

Over the next several days, I kept having dreams and visions of that sacred clasp from *The Ascent.*

What if . . . ? I mused.

What if the monument people saw on the West Coast was a statue that depicted exactly that? The lift of one human hand to another—in a clasp that represented trust and interdependence. My artist's eye zoned in on my rendering of *The Ascent*, and I realized that if I narrowed the focus down to that one piece, I could design something unmistakable and powerful in its visual form. It gave me chills.

Suddenly, I was filled with the words of a poem written by my friend, Native American poet Howard Rainer of the Taos/Pueblo tribe. He had written it about *The Ascent*, and it had inspired me ever since:

> *Grab hold,*
> *And take this hand that*
> *Reaches out to you.*
> *Look up*
> *Into my eyes;*
> *My spirit*
> *Cries out to you:*
> *Friendship is my thought.*
> *Let us climb*
> *The jagged cliffs of life*
> *And fight the ascent of*
> *Opposition together.*

If I can lift you today,
You will look back
And grab the hands of a thousand more.
That is the way
The Great Spirit would have it!

Chills ran up and down my spine at those words, at that clasp. I couldn't help but ask the most important question: What if an entire nation could be inspired to grab the hands of a thousand others and lift them up?

Why . . . it could truly change the world.

I suddenly remembered being small, hunched on the floor after Craig had knocked every ounce of breath from me. I had made a solemn promise to myself then that I would not be silent when I saw someone being abused. I would not abuse another the way Craig had, and someday, I would help free others from emotional or physical bondage. I remembered promising myself, *I will do this thing*!

I went to work, spending countless hours on the Statue of Responsibility, or SOR. In between my regular clients and my time as a father, I sculpted . . . and sculpted. Then I sculpted some more, pouring visions and memories and thoughts of Viktor Frankl's powerful ideas of humanity into the clay.

Finally, the day arrived when I set down my plethora of sculpting tools. I remembered the saying that at some point, every painter must set down the brush. The same was true of every sculptor. It was done. Well, at least this first rendition was final.

I stepped away from the work and felt the magnitude of something far bigger than me in it. I sent a message to Kevin Hall. Would he and Stephen like to see it?

Excited about the response, I was surprised when there was no follow-up.

Nothing happened.

I called and left a voicemail and was saddened to get no answer. Days passed, then weeks and months. I wasn't sure what had happened or why the Statue of Responsibility had fallen off the radar. Still, I was far too busy to let it get to me.

I had no idea that this hot-cold energy would plague the statue and its proponents for years to come. It represented the absolute height of passion and virtue, and, therefore, opposite qualities would often try to test it. It caused me to reflect on Frédéric Auguste Bartholdi and what I'd been taught he had to go through to bring the Statue of Liberty to light. If Bartholdi hadn't been massively persistent, his dream would never have been made manifest. Because it also required something much bigger and higher than immediate gratification, it was a struggle. Would the Statue of Responsibility be a journey of struggle too? Most importantly, would it end in triumph?

On the Wings of Angels

"I have need of angels. Enough hell has swallowed me for too many years.
But finally understand this—I have burned up
one hundred thousand human lives already,
from the strength of my pain."
—Antonin Artaud

There continued to be no word on the Statue of Responsibility. My obsession with it quickly got swallowed up with the children's activities and family life, especially with the addition of my younger stepbrother's child, Justin. His father, Troy, had become a drug dealer in Montpelier but eventually couldn't handle the pain or stress and completed his own life. *Another brother lost.* That broke my heart.

There was nothing we could do about Troy, but with great compassion and genuine love for him, we brought Justin to live with us when he was just four years old. I was proud of how my wife insisted we take him in, as my mom Nellie and my father Wayne were really getting along in years. Both still worked those long night shifts. It seemed to me that Lanea's therapeutic work also helped us understand him better.

I watched with tender pleasure as our boys enveloped Justin with love and acceptance and as one of our own. Like each of the other boys, Justin had his own unique gifts he brought to our family table. Day by day, we grew to appreciate this beautiful boy for exactly who he was. Not only did he blend right into our embrace, but we were also richly blessed for having him.

On Christmas the following year, Justin stood at the window, fascinated. Over the years, I'd become friends with Matt Packer, the CEO of Central Bank. He requested that we put on a Polar Bear Plunge in the spring-fed pond on our property, which people liked to call "Price Park." I agreed—although I had no desire to do it personally. Little Justin and I watched with our mouths wide open as grown adults plunged into the freezing water to renew and refresh themselves physically and mentally. We had no idea it would become a time-honored tradition, with hundreds of people and lots of press.

Shortly thereafter, we faced unfortunate news. Nellie, my dad's wife and the mother who'd raised me since age six, passed away. My heart was heavy. Nellie had become Mom to me in every way, shape, and form she could. I felt her loss deeply.

Dad did too, and his health slowly declined. Lanea and I went up to Montpelier and brought him down to get settled in Utah. He was in a better situation, but I could tell he'd lost the will to live. In our visits together, we chatted a lot about life, prisons, freedom, and memories.

I loved this man with everything in me. I certainly had been angry with him when I learned he had lied to me about being my father. Since that time, I'd come to know he loved me as his own son. He always had. He was my dad and would forever remain that way in my heart.

While I was enduring these massive changes, I started to feel an extremely strong influence from the other side. It didn't take me long to realize it was my birth mother. I could tell because she touched feelings so tender, like the dream I'd had in my tiny studio at Stan's. Oftentimes, emotions welled inside of me. I began to count on her presence, especially when faced with difficult decisions. When she showed up, it seemed a "coincidence" would happen that profoundly affected my decisions and abilities to solve problems.

Her presence was so comforting; I could feel her guardianship. What bothered me, however, was that I couldn't remember my mother's voice anymore. That fact drove me crazy. It felt like a vital piece of me was fragmenting and fading as time went on. I wanted to grasp every tendril, but it kept slipping out of my hands.

I decided to sculpt a piece that would honor my mother and the heavenly influence I continued to feel strongly from her throughout that year. In my little studio on the east side of our property, I went through my fading pictures of my mom. On a whim, I had the local copy shop print life-size portraits, which I hung in my studio as inspiration for this first piece in honor of her.

As I worked the clay, thoughts took me back to that small apartment at the army base in Germany. I poignantly remembered sitting on Mom's lap as she guided my crayons, pencils, and pens into shapes that felt like they could jump off the page in my imaginative, young mind. Tears filled my eyes now as I worked, realizing that my mother had given me the ability to express myself through art—and that *this* had given me the ability to survive all the upcoming horror I would face after her death, and the joys I would face in becoming a parent myself.

Aptly, I named my new twenty-eight-inch piece *The Messenger,* with my mother depicted as the youthful angel, the focus of the piece itself, her arms extended, palms up with a message to deliver. I couldn't count the innumerable times I was literally handed the exact person, place, or thing that I needed. In the description of the piece, I wrote:

"Some believe we receive gifts from emissaries that we might call guardian angels or spirit guides. However, we may describe or explain it, I am convinced that we are not alone. I strongly feel that my mother has been one of my guardian angels throughout my life. *The Messenger* is about the one who is unseen, but forever real. She is a messenger of light, of truth and comfort. This youthful angel radiates purity. Her appearance is pristine with her elegantly outstretched hands. I offer to you 'The Messenger.' who is delivering to you a very specific, personal gift when you are ready to receive it."

This art piece ended up being incredibly popular. It touched me deeply when cemeteries bought large renditions of it for children's areas and when grieving folks around the world bought it for their children's or spouses' headstones. I was asked to do a male version as well, which I wholeheartedly sculpted.

While the end of 1999 brought a ripple of panic into our society as the world thought it might come to an end—either through technology or doomsday prophecies—I couldn't help but feel watched over, protected, and blessed. On the advent of the year 2000, I felt my mother's presence everywhere I went.

The Messenger continued to inspire. Later that year, the Icelandic Association of Utah requested an eight-foot-tall rendition of the sculpture as a monument to be placed in Iceland, depicting all the Mormon pioneers who came to America via boat from that great country. I couldn't believe it! My mother's visage would be the ultimate symbol of purity and connection.

As honored as I was to have my piece as this monument, I was shocked when one of the top leaders of the LDS Church demanded that I take the wings off *The Messenger* because of teachings that angels did not actually have wings. To me, the wings were symbolic of the energy and immediate power of God's messengers. It was the first time in my life where I saw how religion could get in the way of meaning instead of adding to it. Only momentarily disheartened, I agreed to compromise and was thrilled to attend the dedication in Iceland.

At the end of the year, I even got up enough courage to take the polar bear plunge on our property, and Justin laughed, like the rest of my family, at the look of joyful shock on my face as I rose out of the water. I whooped and hollered. Matt was right; it was a terrific way to cleanse the past year and reinvigorate for the coming one, which everyone felt so uncertain about.

The year 2000 was a boon; we didn't collapse as a society, and I was truly enjoying the association of many other artists in our area and across the entire country.

I'd love to say that I continued to learn the power of compromise and teamwork, but over the next year as my business, reputation, and pocketbook grew, so did my ego. I began to feel that all the growth was due to my own brilliance. Sadly, I soon forgot just how vital a role Dave Barnett played— the same talented man who had helped to systematize and bring greater prosperity to my business. After 9/11, as every American felt devastated and experienced either major or minor bumps in the economy, I falsely believed Dave had grown lazy and was taking advantage of sales and his considerable commissions. My arrogance placed me in a precarious position.

One day, Dave and I sat in his office, arguing about a business conflict. I felt completely taken advantage of. When he bustled out the door in a huff, I became angrier because I knew Dave was right; I was wrong. Still, my ego! The truth was that I was pissed I hadn't won. In my selfishness, I let Dave go. It was one of the worst decisions of my life because it affected a magnificent relationship. Still, I wouldn't admit that for quite some time. I hired a new business manager, and a man named Daniel Bolz to help with foundry sales.

I was asked to do another one-man show at the Springville Museum of Art. It was a great honor, and I was able to keep my promise to honor my mother and how she had saved me and Bill. I dedicated the entire show to her and brought the beautiful, life-sized poster that had inspired me to sculpt *The Messenger*. Both the poster and the large bronze greeted everyone as they walked into the Springville Museum of Art, my sculptures now filling two major rooms.

As part of my exhibit, I did therapy. I sculpted my past tragedies, including the night of my mother's murder. Alongside it, I laid out a copy of the police reports. This was the first time in my life that I quite publicly talked about it all. In the display was a tender favorite, a separate sculpture depicting my last, precious moments with Mom as we sat in the living room and she asked me for advice that fateful night.

While I shared the tragedy, I also shared the angel my mother had been to me since and how I felt her loving, guiding presence in my life to that day. With the help of a talented team, I was able to show a nostalgic video we called *Celebration*, dedicated to Bettie Jo Reeder and our spiritual reconnection. I was amazed that the public seemed to get as much out of the exhibit as I did. I was asked if I would leave the exhibit up for months longer than expected.

On the final night before I turned the lights off in the museum, I glanced over at the tall bronze of *The Messenger*. I had another in my studio that would be going off to a client the following week. I was so grateful the wings were intact on both, but it was her face I paid attention to that night.

Thanks, Mom. I know so many opportunities are coming to me on the wings of angels, and I feel you out in front of them all.

The Burning

"What is to give light must endure burning."
—Anton Wildgans

"Death is a stripping away of all that is not you.
The secret of life is to 'die before you die'
—and find that there is no death."
—Eckart Tolle

Another personality was brought into our loving circle, but this time it was not a child. Reggie was a large, beautiful Doberman Pinscher I had picked up from a famous breeder in Tennessee. This pup was fun for the boys to play with, although he sometimes got a little rough.

With great affection, I sculpted Reggie in clay and named the sculpture *The Guardian*. I loved the distinctive, clever look in his eye set amidst the hair around his streamlined face. I also attempted to add an essence of his sometimes-boisterous behavior.

Within a few months, however, Reggie began engaging in overly protective behavior regarding the boys, the horses, and Lanea and me. He rapidly became suspicious of strangers.

Well, at least we have trained him to be good to the boys, I thought reasonably. Deep inside, I was grateful he was particularly protective of the youngest, Raphy and Justin. They were still small and innocent. They could not yet protect themselves against others. We didn't live in a dangerous place, but I always felt the unconscious need to shield them, and I didn't always understand why. Instead, I blew it off.

Surely, we can train Reggie to act appropriately to strangers. When it was just him and me, the dog behaved nearly perfectly every time.

One beautiful summer afternoon, Reggie began barking at the approaching mailman as we were all outside. To my horror, as the innocent man stepped into the yard to deliver our mail right to us, he was only able to take a few steps before Reggie immediately jumped up and nipped the man's elbow hard enough to draw blood.

What the hell?

I was not only horrified, I became angry. Quickly, I strode out across the yard and snapped at Reggie. "Bad dog!" I cried. Apologizing profusely to the mailman, I grabbed Reggie's collar.

The mailman curtly strode away, clutching his elbow. I didn't blame him but felt sorry that he'd ignored my invitation to come in so we could bandage it for him. "I can either call the cops," he raged, "or you can do something about that dog!"

Sudden emotion welled up inside of me. I felt embarrassed, angry, frustrated, and ashamed all at once. Slamming the mail onto the steps, I held tightly to Reggie's collar and took him behind the house. There, I smacked the dog's snout, yelling, "You don't ever do that again! You hear me? He wasn't doing anything to you! Not anything at all. Why did you go after him? Never again!" And I smacked him some more. Pretty soon the poor pup was cowering, so I backed off.

I left Reggie chained outside to be with the "consequences of his behavior" before I came in the back door, my hand smarting a bit and my temper still flaring hot.

Suddenly I stopped short. My wife had come inside, too, and now was looking at me, shock and bewilderment clouding her pretty features.

"Gary," she said slowly, her eyes still registering disbelief, "where is this coming from? I have never seen you lay a hand like that upon *any* creature. What is wrong?"

I almost snapped at her defensively but then shut my mouth. I looked down at the ground, ashamed. My face felt engulfed in flames. Certainly, I got upset at the boys sometimes for silly things, but I had never physically abused them. Even when they hurt each other and I panicked, I still refused to beat them. Now, to hit a dog? Lanea was right. This was *not* in my nature. Because of my past, I had always refused to lose my temper.

I won't ever sink to that level, I told myself countless times. *I will not!*

And, yet, I just had . . . with poor Reggie.

I crumpled into a chair. "I don't know," I said, my throat tight. And then the tears came, hot and wild. "Lanea, I don't know. I don't know . . . but I feel this *rage* coming on, especially when someone does something that another doesn't deserve. Like now, the mailman wasn't doing anything, not *anything*, and Reggie just attacked him! It was so wrong, and I just became out of control. It's . . . it's scaring me."

"Gary," my wife gently said, "I think we need to do a session on you." She was referring to the Gestalt method she'd worked to become proficient in over the years. Her eyes held a knowing look, though her tone was still soft and kind. "You are holding things inside that need to come out. If you don't, I'm afraid it will get the better of you." She touched my arm and walked toward the door. "I'll get the kids squared away, and you meet me downstairs in the family room."

"O-Okay," I said sheepishly. Shame completely overwhelmed me. *How could I have lost my temper like that?* I was worse than embarrassed. Only moments ago, I felt justified, but now I was humiliated for my wife, kids, and even the mailman, though from the looks of it, he would probably be happy knowing I'd punished the dog.

Slowly, I rose from my chair and made my way downstairs, still hanging my head. I lay on the couch and focused on my breathing, willing my adrenaline to slow and my heartbeat to stop beating so wildly. At the moment, it felt like it would burst straight out of my chest. I paced and paced, hating my reaction. I hated myself for smacking the dog. I hated everything about me in that moment. I had sunk to that level. I was a piece of shit.

I am worth nothing.

Soon Lanea quietly emerged from the stairwell and walked over to me on the couch.

"It's going to be okay," she said firmly as she perched on the couch. "The kids are at the neighbors. Gary, we just need to get to the bottom of this." Her voice now held the firm knowledge she'd been acquiring through the years that helped others to heal.

"I know," I quietly acknowledged. "I do need to get to the bottom of this." I closed my eyes against the pain and terror welling up inside of me.

For the next several minutes, Lanea walked me through a process of grounding and finally getting calm. When my heartbeat slowed, she began to guide me to go back in my mind's eye to a safe place in my childhood. In her comforting voice, she encouraged me to acknowledge any feelings of my inner child. I knew from her trainings this was a common psychological practice in therapeutic settings across the world, but I had never experienced anything like it before.

Suddenly there he was: little Gary, dark-haired and rambunctious, innocent and joy-filled in every way. Surprisingly, at one point, he took my hand and led me to a time in my childhood. I thought he might lead me to my mother's murder, but that was not the case. Firmly, he led me back into my house on Monroe Street in Montpelier, with my dad and stepmom at work, when I was so afraid of Craig that I often crawled up in my covers, hoping not to be found. Little Gary walked with me into the dark cavern under the house when I thought I would die, and time after time when I really thought Craig would kill me.

My brain was suddenly filled with violent flashes of yelling, punching, cutting, kicking, molestation, smothering, and the words that he would kill me repeating over and over and over.

I launched up from the couch, tears streaming down my cheeks, and my face contorted in rage.

"I just want to *hit* something!" I cried, my voice high, shrill, and full of fury.

"Here!" said Lanea without judgment, and she grabbed a large, heavy pillow from the couch, which I started to punch with my bare hands. She raced away for a moment and came back with a thick, old oak shovel handle, handing it to me as I stood shaking and overcome.

"AAAUUUGGGHHH!" I screamed, my voice filled with anguish. "AAAUUUGGGHHH!" I screamed again, my emotions exploding.

And again.

And again.

And again.

All the years of abuse, of never having a voice, of being afraid for my own life . . . It all welled up beyond any control.

I screamed as if my very life depended on it. And I could not stop. I screamed and beat that pillow over and over and over. I continued to beat it with the stick until my palms were blistered . . . and still I kept on beating.

Never one to swear, four-letter words poured out of me as easily as from a long-haul trucker, momentarily stunning me and my wife. But I went on.

"THIS IS WHY PEOPLE TURN INTO MURDERERS, YOU MOTHERFUCKER!" I bellowed, and I realized I meant every word of it. "THIS IS WHY THERE ARE SERIAL KILLERS IN THE WORLD—BECAUSE OF PEOPLE . . . LIKE . . . YOU!"

I kept shouting the pain of that truth over and over. The screaming and beating the large pillow seemed to last forever.

Finally, when I had no more voice, when I had no more blubbery hysterical tears, when I had no more energy to destroy this pillow, only then with trembling hands did I drop the heavy wooden handle. Clenching my fist, I no longer felt the slivers in my palm. I dropped the rest of my body to the floor, where I curled up in a little ball, heaving and dry heaving until my pounding heart finally stilled into silence, wetness still staining my cheeks.

Just as I had no idea how long I beat that pillow, I had no idea how long I lay there on the floor, still sobbing until, mercifully, I fell asleep.

Sometime later, the sounds of happy children at the dinner table above roused me, and I found a blanket tucked around me in the dusky light. I was eternally grateful for Lanea in that moment. Still, haggard and worn, I wasn't ready to face the kids. Quietly, I picked myself up off the floor, my knees raw and bloody under my pants and my entire body aching. I made my way to our bedroom, where I collapsed for the rest of the night.

The next day, I felt like I was the one who'd been beaten instead of that poor pillow. Lanea asked me how long I thought I had beaten it.

"Maybe twenty minutes or so?" I replied hoarsely.

"No, Gary," she murmured, looking me gently in the eyes. "You were at it for nearly a full hour."

I shouldn't have been surprised. My whole body felt black and blue—and, indeed, some areas where I'd hit myself going after that pillow were purple and bruising. I still had some splinters in my palm that needed to come out. I could barely speak; my throat was so raw. But I didn't care. A tsunami of emotions had broken open inside of me. While they continued to flood me, something had changed—for the better. Now they felt . . . *controllable.* Now I could identify them for exactly what they were: betrayal, hurt, confusion, and pain. Oh, so much pain. Instead of pretending they weren't there, however, I wasn't hiding from them or hiding them from Lanea. I was no longer afraid of them. There was a sudden surge of relief in knowing they no longer had power over me.

The first thing I did when I climbed out of bed was to go outside. I spent some gentle moments petting Reggie, loving on him, apologizing for my behavior, and making a promise to him and God that I would never touch him or another creature like that again. He forgave me quickly and easily, but it would take a long while for me to forgive myself.

Later that day, I had to go back into my bedroom to be alone. In my deep and heartfelt pleading to God, I was shown that I had held on to all this emotion and rage for two reasons. The first was that I had no choice. As an adult, I could now see things through different eyes, but as a child, *my truth* was that Craig could and would have killed me if I'd opened my mouth against him. Whether true or not, I didn't know. As the child, I stayed silent because of Craig's continuous threat that our parents and police would never find my body in the black hole of a cave under our house. Craig had told me multiple times that what happened to my mother was nothing compared to what he could do to me.

Second, I realized that through the multitude of tortures, I had promised myself even at very young age that I would never fall to the level Craig had. I refused to vent my rage upon another. Having all boys of my own had felt vulnerable—and empowering—to me, but I had tightly contained that rage, had been hypervigilant so my boys would never become the victims of what had happened to me.

I took in large, deep breaths. Now that I was looking at everything clearly as an adult, having protected my inner child, I wasn't sure what to do with what I had learned about myself. No one in my circles of influence *ever* talked openly about abuse. The only thing that felt remotely as real and brutal to me were the stories of the concentration-camp victims, though I couldn't fully interpret or understand them. I knew full well they had been dramatically different from mine, and I couldn't compare. I also recognized that while the circumstances were different, the emotions were the same.

Just who could I talk to? There were details I didn't want Lanea to know. I felt alone.

Battles raged in my head for the next several weeks. *Am I the only one walking around in everyday society who has endured abuse like this?*

With great sorrow, I gave Reggie to a single man in Salt Lake City who accepted him and adored him. The new owner didn't have kids of his own and felt that perhaps the pup's aggression had to do with him being overprotective of our children. He never had an ounce of trouble with Reggie.

That also helped heal my heart. I didn't realize at the time what a blessing Reggie had been. He'd opened the door to something putrid that had festered deep inside of me for too long. He was the conduit that allowed it to come to the surface as it really needed to, and I was so delighted he was now in a loving, protective, and nurturing home, just as he deserved. Just like every child deserved.

A few months later, as the weather began turning and I would normally be outside, I was sick in bed with the flu, including fever and chills. Like many men, I was being a real baby about it. I hugged everyone and sent them out of the room so I could sleep and not be whiny or cranky.

I dozed on and off, but when sleep wasn't working, I turned on boring daytime television in an effort to get my mind off feeling sorry for myself. I snoozed again to later awaken to a recognizable voice—Oprah Winfrey's.

I stopped shuffling around to get comfortable so I could listen to a woman I'd admired for a long time. Oprah had worked her way up in business, earning every opportunity. And, like Lanea and me, she worked hard to build a community of people and continually give back to that community. As I lay there under the blanket, Oprah's words filtered into my consciousness.

Suddenly, I pulled the blanket off and sat straight up. I shook my head.

Wait, what? Oprah Winfrey was abused in her childhood?

I stilled myself to listen, the internal dialogue in my head bouncing back and forth across my brain. As it turned out, Oprah had been physically beaten by her grandmother, forced to sleep outside on the porch by a caregiver, and, beginning at the age of nine, raped. She had been sexually abused until fourteen, forced to leave her home not knowing she was pregnant. Her child died two weeks after being born.

Stunned, I sat there with this revelation. A woman I so admired had been mentally, emotionally, physically, and sexually abused, like me. And she had been blamed for all of it. It did not escape me that a woman so many greatly admired was *openly* talking about it on *public* television. And as I listened to her voice and saw the firm set of her jaw, I realized she refused to be ashamed of her story.

Dumbfounded, I watched the rest of the program. When it was over, I snapped off the TV so I could think despite my stuffy head. Oprah was an icon, and yet she was vulnerable in her sharing. I felt a surge of strength. She was not afraid.

For weeks, I couldn't get the images and her voice out of my head. Not because it was disturbing, which it was, but because the overcoming of it was absolutely empowering.

Her abuse does not make her any less of a human than she has ever been!

In fact, I knew she had probably worked very hard to prove that she was more than that abuse. It didn't make it right, but she used it to make her stronger.

Something clicked with that realization. I felt a literal, physical shift inside my body, like the puzzle pieces of all the atoms inside me had just snapped back into a place I didn't know existed. I felt young and pure again. I was astounded as years of shame cascaded out of me like a waterfall. I felt freer than I had since I was that innocent, little child playing on the swings in Germany and jumping from the fence as if I could fly.

Unveiling the Kaleidoscope

"Everything can be taken from a man but one thing: the
last of the human freedoms—to choose one's attitude in any
given set of circumstances, to choose one's own way."
—Viktor Frankl

Over the following weeks, I continued allowing the walls and fortresses I had built up inside me to come tumbling down. It felt *so* good! I became a voracious reader of personal development material, alongside Lanea.

With great insight, I realized just how much I had hidden from the shadow of my abuse because of how I thought I would be judged—especially as a male in society. Added to this was an unspeakably dark shadow of my deepest fear that facing it might trigger me to be a violent person. Therefore, I had never been free of the terror of the abuse or the seemingly impenetrable shadow it cast over my life.

Continuing to take steps to heal, I could distinguish clear choices, including distinctions between anger and violence. A person could be angry and not violent.

An artist friend introduced me to a book by Eckart Tolle entitled *The Power of Now.* Tolle's words about intense, emotional pain caused me to ponder deeply. If not fully addressed, this pain could be carried around with a person like a living energy field.

"Just like a parasite," Tolle described, "it could stay alive, feeding on one's energy." I had so recently experienced how this could be true. The author shared the vital importance of shedding this pain in order to obtain the power of the present moment. "You . . . realize that all the things that truly matter—beauty, love, creativity, joy, inner peace—arise from beyond the mind. You begin to awaken."

I would read his words and work on my clay—my greatest form of meditation. One day, I closed the book and began to ponder as I worked in my studio, and I came to a profound realization. When I hurt Reggie, I had not been present. I was stuck in the regret that I had not trained him better. Even deeper and unconscious, however, I had been stuck in that pattern of "not fair." The mailman had been completely innocent, not inciting the attack, just as I had not incited Craig to attack me.

I was beginning to awaken, and it felt glorious. But as I continued to mold the clay, I could tell I was not yet complete.

A memory came up from a few years after Lanea and I had been married. She'd joined me on a trip to Montpelier, where I'd lovingly but honestly confronted my father and stepmother. How could they have allowed Craig to treat me the way he had? While I didn't share all the dark details, I had to know the answer. Hadn't they noticed how I'd obeyed Craig's every whim? Did they not realize I had stolen half the town for him? Did they really have no clue about the train sets and pigeon coop? Hadn't they been tipped off by my constant bruises and battle scars? Hadn't they witnessed the way Craig controlled my food? Why hadn't they stopped it? Why hadn't they stopped *him*?

My dad and stepmom had just looked at each other, bewildered.

"We honestly didn't know," my stepmom had replied, her face contorting in a mix of divergent emotions.

"To be quite frank, Gary," said my dad carefully, "you hid it very well. I think we chalked most of it up to roughhousing and a 'boys will be boys' mentality. I'm sorry for that. But you didn't let on. The only thing I witnessed is that you wouldn't let me in, no matter what I did. You didn't give me a chance to listen. You didn't trust me."

"Can you blame me?" I asked softly. "You rescued me from Germany, but you put me into the hands of a monster. You . . . let him do whatever he wanted to me."

Dad's face fell, and I saw tears mist his eyes.

"We didn't know. I'm sorry, Gary. I'm truly sorry."

Dad was right. I was so afraid of Craig I wouldn't open my mouth. Then, when he left, I became stubbornly and fiercely independent. Even as a teen, I controlled my environment, becoming self-sufficient. Seething in so much resentment under the surface, I hadn't let my father anywhere close to me. I didn't realize how enraged that little boy had been that they hadn't protected him. Somehow, I had expected them to be omniscient, to know everything that I had been unwilling, and unable, to reveal.

Tearfully, I apologized to Dad and Nellie for my behavior. Looking them in the eyes, I thanked them for all the good they had done for me, which was considerable. "I love you," I said, even though this phrase wasn't often spoken in their home. Then I hugged them hard and kissed them as we said our goodbyes.

That had been years ago, and now both of them were gone. I had long ago forgiven them, but it still hurt.

Several months after my incident beating the pillow, I asked Lanea to support me in a final confrontation of my past. We drove from Springville up north to where my stepbrother resided. This time, along the way, I revealed to her some of the deeper abuses I had never, ever, told anyone about. It felt freeing to let light into the shadowy caverns of my life. Lanea listened quietly, although at times she visibly gulped at my revelations. I didn't need to scream now, although I got choked up a few times. She did too.

The closer we got to Craig's house, the more nervous I became. I hadn't seen my brother in quite a while. After I nearly destroyed the pillow in my basement, I hadn't trusted myself to talk to him . . . until now.

At our knock, a surprised Craig answered the door. Dressed in jeans, cowboy boots, and T-shirt, he was still a striking figure. He invited us inside their lovely home. While Lanea and his wife greeted each other and their kids, I asked if he and I could go somewhere to speak in private. Puzzled, Craig led me down a hallway. He was still taller than I was, and we entered a bedroom. Once I saw the bed, all other details faded. I realized this was the first time I'd been alone with him in a bedroom since he'd left our childhood home.

My face flushed with embarrassment, and I had to fight the strong instinct to cower and run away from the coming conflict. Instead, I took a breath and pushed aside all intense emotions. I looked into his eyes and got straight to the point.

"I need to talk with you about what you did to me as a kid," I said flatly. "I need you to acknowledge that it wasn't right and it wasn't fair. It was ugly and horrific and mean. I need you to acknowledge what you did to me. I need you to do it so . . . so I can forgive you."

Craig started to object. "Hey, I told you that I felt bad about those times."

"'Those times?' Craig, it was *all* the time!"

"Naw, I mean there were sometimes when I got a little mean, but we had lots of good—"

"Craig," I cut in, "you hurt and threatened me every single day. When I was little, you took my lunch and allowance money, forced me to steal, and beat me if I didn't. You threatened to kill me so many times I couldn't count them if I tried. You made me do everything you ever wanted and if I didn't, I paid for it." I reminded him of his smothering me, dropping me down a black hole, and cutting me wide open with a knife. "Later you threw full beer cans at me and beat me in front of your friends, for hell's sake!"

By now, everything was pouring out of me, and I was unable to stop. "Do you remember how you would punch me, lift me up, and give me a second to catch my breath before you punched me harder, leaving me on the floor, turning purple and afraid I was going to die? You were downright vicious, Craig. You were mean and malicious. It wasn't just every once in a while, and you know it! It was Every. Single. Day." Then I looked at him with great meaning in my eyes and added, "And that doesn't include the *other* stuff . . . in our bedroom."

Craig's face had already gone white, but with my last words, I could tell he wondered how much his family could hear.

"Look," I continued, "this has been troubling me—how and why you were able to do this stuff to me. I realize your dad was an alcoholic. I know he beat *Emma* and your mom. Was that part of it? Did you take it out on me? Did you resent me coming into the family?"

"Well, I had problems then too," he started in and suddenly brightened. "But look at how you turned out—"

"Oh, no," I said without malice, but my words firm and clear. "You will take absolutely no credit for my success. I was not able to do anything I've done because of you. I love you, my brother, but I did what I did *despite* all the hell you put me through. You will NOT take credit for that."

He nodded, and the room went silent. There was a long, long pause. Craig remained speechless.

In that silence, I felt I could take a breath now.

I'd said what I needed to say.

I no longer needed or even wanted his apology.

Even though I had once craved it, it was fueled by the simple need to speak my truth to his face. With resilience and even a sense of pity, I looked him in the eyes one last time and rose to leave.

Craig started visibly; his eyes went wide. He went to put his hand on my arm, then thought better of it.

"Wait a minute, please. Please, Gary, sit for a moment?"

I hesitated. Then I nodded. I sat back down and waited in an equally long silence as Craig gathered his words.

"When I think of . . . when I really think of what I did to you . . ." He shuddered, his voice soft. "I'm sorry, Gary. Believe me, I know it wasn't fair. I look back and, honestly, I can't believe the things I did to you. I'm sorry." He paused, his voice filled with pain. "I know words don't do it justice, but I am really sorry."

I let his apologies run through me. They were not the healing balm I thought I had needed for so long, but they were an acknowledgment of the truth I had spoken.

I also felt the truth of his apology this time—different from the last. He had not blown me off—nor been able to take credit for the sculpting of my character when he had not held the chisel of creation, only weapons.

I took a long, deep breath. "I forgive you," I said. And this time, I meant it.

When I got home, something happened. The world around me became miraculously filled with wonder. My world began to change because my story had changed. It was breathtaking, the new colors and even the energy I could see all around me. It was as if a veil of gray I didn't know existed had been lifted from my eyes and heart. There was still the acknowledgment of everything I had been through, but there was also this breathtaking beauty in everything and everyone around me. As an artist and lover of life, I thought I had seen it all, but now it was as if I was looking at things through the eyes of that innocent child, little Gary, again. The world seemed to explode in a kaleidoscope of color; the palettes were grander than I had ever known. It showed up in my sculpting and artistry, and it began to strengthen most of my relationships. Just not all of them.

The Biology of Belief

"When you know better, you do better."
—Maya Angelou

For the very first time in my life, I wasn't afraid to speak, even about my past. I could look into the eyes of my beautiful children and stay present with them without needing to hide from their innocence. The more transparent I became, the more empowered I became. For some people that was a wonderful thing, and we had a more open and honest relationship than ever. For others it was disconcerting and frightening. I didn't realize that with vulnerability comes raw power, and sometimes those who are in the throes of their own deep and private hells struggle to be in the presence of it.

As part of her studies, Lanea was becoming more empowered too, which I loved. She became involved with an internationally renowned personal-development group. The organizer did retreats all over the world. The empowering parts of the training were very good. I enjoyed many of the teachings and received tremendous growth and healing in my own life and even more motivation and inspiration in my work. Most of all, I loved that it was something my wife and I could do to grow together.

Over the next few years, so much growth happened in our little family. First, Lanea put the boys in a special charter school. She'd always taken their schooling seriously, and we'd had innumerable discussions on what constituted a good education and what didn't. I was pleased with the school, as I saw what the kids were gaining from it by the discussions we were having. They were thriving. It also freed up my wife's time to take more trainings for herself and trainings from the facilitator we both enjoyed.

As time passed, however, I began to disagree with some of the teachings of this facilitator. Lanea began to step away from our church, feeling that our religion was not what it was supposed to be.

Over the last few years, I had recognized that organized religion was at best complicated. Religions that chose to rule through fear and guilt were problematic. On the other hand, I had personally witnessed and experienced so much *good* from religion, including the values of integrity, positive behavior, family, community, service, and contribution. I myself had been so transformed as a young man through religion I felt it certainly had its merits and place in society. It was then I understood the phrase, "Don't throw the baby out with the bathwater." I would honor the place of religion in my life, my family, and my community. I would enjoy what these other trainings had taught me, too, but I could draw the line for myself.

While Lanea embraced the training's beliefs wholeheartedly, I simply became less rigid, which my wife welcomed. It did surprise our kids and a few friends when I began to indulge in an occasional glass of wine after a long day of work. Perhaps hardest for me was letting go of the fear of being judged. In our culture, if you imbibed alcohol, it was more than a minor indulgence—you were breaking a commandment. To me, it simply didn't feel that way. I passionately believed in a higher power and trusted that. I trusted God.

I would never let go of my faith in the beings who had saved my body, mind, and soul. In my newfound freedom from my darkness, in my deepest soul ponderings, I no longer believed my spirituality had to be the fear-driven journey I and plenty of others experienced—of having to get it "right" or be damned. To me, my personal relationship with God was far more precious, more tender, and more valuable than other people's judgments.

Unfortunately, not everyone agreed with my decisions, including the writer who started my autobiography. Shauna had helped me so much on my healing journey, but I crushed this wonderful woman's dreams for the book when I stepped away from the strict teachings of my church with things like that occasional glass of wine. That autobiography with her as the author would never come to fruition. I realized that people often had deeply varied and beautiful thoughts about God, life, and the afterlife. Like the angel with her beautiful wings, if it didn't look a certain way, for some, the wings had to be clipped.

In the past, a rejection like this would have made me feel less than whole, like I was not good enough because I was not reaching someone else's ideal of divine potential. Now, however, I was developing a new and powerful compassion for myself and others. Along with that came a deep, abiding respect for others and their beliefs, whether those who were on "the straight and narrow" path I'd once considered myself on or those with beliefs incredibly divergent from mine. I released the disappointment and blessed the lessons.

For the first time in my life, I began to appreciate much of me for me. I was still acutely aware of my faults, as I seemed to face them often. In fact, I saw how often I made mistakes. I also began learning more deeply from them when I had the eyes to see and to forgive myself. In that light of compassion came a beautiful unfolding inside me, miraculous in nature. I began to see myself and other people . . . through the eyes of love.

Only now it didn't matter if they accepted me or not.

I could love them anyway.

Quite suddenly, for the first time in years, the voices of the *Hausfraus* in Germany came back to me: *sympathisch*. I finally recognized the exact meaning behind that sweet German word and the calling of my soul to love—in the gorgeous, miraculous, meaningful, and sometimes fractured kaleidoscope of the Great Artist.

My boys were growing and changing fast. Zach and Isaiah were moving from the charter school into higher education and thinking of serving church missions. Lanea and I supported their desires for education, careers, character development, and choices for their spiritual paths.

In the meantime, I still had three boys at home, and it was fascinating to see how different they were from their older brothers. Now that I was free from so many of the chains of the past and could be more present, I noticed in my boys even more personality traits and characteristics I adored.

During my formative teen years with my own father working nights and sleeping days, I didn't have a father walking or working beside me. He taught me to fish and other things I would always treasure, but I never got to learn father-son skills or leadership from him. Fortunately, there were other men who had been tremendous examples to me. Now, as a father, I sought a different relationship with my boys than what I experienced.

What I didn't realize was how I had gotten used to the easy camaraderie with Isaiah and Zachariah. The two boys were charismatic athletes. They excelled at most things and got along with just about everybody. I thought my relationship with them and how they were making their way in the world was what my experiences with my other three boys would be. I was naïve.

In our hearts, Justin had grown to be one of the family. When he first came to us, we had to help him overcome so many fears. In the process of caring for him, I realized he and I had much more in common than we originally thought.

Justin was experiencing panic attacks when boating or swimming. I spent time teaching him how to relax in the water and let the physics of his body teach him to trust himself. Seeing him learn to have a great love for swimming was a particular joy for me. Watching him grow and trust Lanea was also touching, as was how she set everything aside to create a safe home for him.

Our youngest, Raphy, was turning into quite a character. He had tremendous confidence and a desire to succeed. Even as a little guy, if he needed money, he would get eggs from our chickens and walk around the neighborhood—quite a trek—and sell them for a quarter apiece, coming back with wads of money stuffed in his pockets. When he set his mind to something, he was unstoppable.

Tyrone, our third son, was his own man. Often quiet, he was fascinated by things the other boys weren't, like butterflies, dragonflies, and cats. Ty loved cats when no one else in our family did.

Ty also loved movies, so we surprised him by picking him up, along with six or seven friends, to take him to a movie. For our socialites Zac and Isaiah, that would have been a celebratory highlight. Ty, however, quietly cried to Lanea and me that he had wanted to see that movie by himself.

Sometimes this son was a terrific instigator of trouble. Ty would push the older boys to their limits, knowing they weren't allowed to retaliate. He kept at it until Isaiah swore he was going to pummel him if he didn't stop for good. With our hard, fast rules against violence in the home, I was as shocked and surprised one day when Lanea finally said, "Okay, Isaiah, I see you've had enough. If Ty does this again, you have our permission to pummel him."

I trusted my wife, and so I didn't breathe a word into the silence in that room, but I had to manually close my mouth and turn on my heel to hide my surprise. It changed the dynamic in the house. Suddenly knowing there were boundaries changed the rules of the game enough that Ty stopped, and the epic arguments ceased—for which we all were grateful.

I didn't always understand this son of mine. Ty certainly didn't enjoy being out in the yard with me like the other boys. As he got older and the other boys were often gone with sports and other activities, Ty's reticence to help me got under my skin.

One day, after he became a teenager, Ty and I were laying sprinkler pipe under the hot summer sun. At my same height and build, he was stocky and strong, but his attitude sucked. Here I was, trying to be jovial, and he was expressing not only reticence but also being pissy. On top of that, he kept doing what I perceived to be dumb things, like not lining up the sprinkler pipe properly, allowing each one to fit inside the other. I figured it was time to have a come-to-Jesus meeting. He sure needed to learn a thing or two.

"Ty, why can't you put a shirt on?" I blurted irritably.

"I don't want to," he replied, his jaw set in a stubborn line above his stocky shoulders.

"And why can't you make these pipes line up?" I said, ignoring his previous comment.

We stood there, both of us "hot under the collar," even though he wasn't wearing a shirt. Our faces were inches apart, his as red as mine with anger . . . and something else.

Suddenly, I recognized it as hurt. *Oh no. I am hurting my son.* What he said next confirmed it.

"Dad, I have never been good enough for you!" he cried out, his voice cracking. "I always feel like I can't do anything right."

Suddenly, I recognized what I had done. I looked at him—really looked at him, and my heart broke. I began to cry, tears streaming out of my eyes and causing rivulets in the dirt upon my hands.

Oh, my God, I get to own this!

In my young son's face, I read a lifetime of hurt and frustration. It wasn't just my words; it was my expectations of him. He was right. I had never truly seen him or appreciated him for who he was—even though I thought I had. I was so used to Zac and Isaiah that I hadn't been comfortable with Ty just being Ty.

The dam really broke when tears started streaming down my son's face, too, and we cried together. We threw our arms around each other, sobbing. Finally, we hugged hard and genuine. The deep, heartfelt tears cleansed our grimy, sweaty faces.

Suddenly, I ripped my shirt off. Ty just looked at me in surprise, and we laughed harder than we had cried.

Our relationship changed in that one interaction. It was a beautiful gift to me and one far more important than the silly sprinkler pipe. I was also grateful that for my part, learned behavior could be unlearned. Beliefs passed down from one generation did not have to be accepted by the next if they didn't work.

I discovered things about my son I hadn't discovered before. Despite his somewhat aloof personality (and my sometimes overbearing one), Ty was the warmest, nicest kid. I began to enjoy watching him mature into an incredible adult with a unique contribution to make. I also began to appreciate his terrific powers of introspection and observation, along with other things that I could love, trust, and certainly learn from. From that day forward, I never took his differences for granted again. Instead, I learned to celebrate them.

Ty's gift of frankness paid other dividends. I began to notice the glorious differences in all of my children: Raphael, Justin, Ty, Isaiah, and Zac; and I could celebrate the unique and awe-inspiring qualities each one of them brought to the table.

A Monumental Experience

"Freedom is in danger of degenerating into mere arbitrariness
unless it is lived in terms of responsibleness.
That is why I recommend that the Statue of Liberty
on the East Coast be supplemented by
a Statue of Responsibility on the West Coast."
—*Viktor Frankl*

I had some tough decisions to make. Our business model had changed drastically. Daniel Bolz, whom I had hired for foundry sales a few years prior, now faced the end of his tenure. I really liked Daniel, but he just couldn't get the Reynolds building and foundation going, and I struggled because I knew I would have to let him go.

One day we were having a heart-to-heart talk in my studio, and he was contemplating something I said when he began to stare at my sculpture of the Statue of Responsibility.

"Gary, will you tell me the story behind this?"

Almost grudgingly, I told him about Stephen Covey, Viktor Frankl, and my part in the national and international dream for the monument. By then, it had been close to four years since I had heard from anyone regarding my proposed design. As I spoke, Daniel's eyes nearly popped out of his head.

"Oh, my gosh, Gary, we've just got to make this happen! I mean, would you let me run with this? I'd really like to help make this a reality!"

Daniel's enthusiasm was contagious. In his passion, he reached back out to Kevin Hall and Stephen Covey, then introduced me to Bill Fillmore, a renowned local attorney known for supporting public interests in the community. Bill had worked for BYU as associate general counsel under President Jeffrey R. Holland before going back into private practice in the early '90s. By the time I met him, Bill's firm, Fillmore-Spencer, LLC, employed nearly twenty attorneys and was involved in several high-profile projects.

Daniel introduced us, and Bill was immediately enamored with the story of the Statue of Responsibility. It didn't hurt that Bill had served a church mission in Austria, and loved Viktor Frankl's extraordinary story of surviving the Holocaust, along with his book and the teachings that had come to change the world.

In meeting Bill, I felt like I'd found a long-lost friend. As many attorneys do, he had a way with words and storytelling, but his agenda somehow always involved making the world a better place instead of tearing it apart. I quickly came to appreciate his self-deprecating sense of humor. I valued ability to make big ripples in such a humble manner.

That afternoon, Bill said something that would forever change the face of the project. "Gary, Daniel, if we are going to be doing such a monumental work, then we need to get an endorsement from the Frankl family. I firmly believe the three of us should plan an immediate trip to Vienna."

As chills washed over me, I knew Bill was right. To build a solid and ethical foundation for the Statue of Responsibility, we needed to go to Vienna and seek the blessing of the Frankl family. It had been Frankl's dream, after all.

It also made perfect sense. The sculptor of the Statue of Liberty, Frédéric Bartholdi, had also gathered endorsements and letters of recommendation. The first endorsement he sought was that of Ulysses S. Grant. Why? Because the Statue of Liberty was a gift from the citizens of France in honor of the abolishment of human slavery. In addition to Grant, Bartholdi sought other prominent, ethically minded individuals in the U.S. to back his proposal before successfully bringing his creation to fruition in 1886.

This trip to Vienna for another historic monument was beginning to feel like it could be equally significant in its own way. Even though Viktor Frankl had passed away seven years prior, his dear wife, Elly (Eleonore Katharina Schwindt Frankl) was still alive, along with their daughter, Dr. Gabriele Frankl-Vesely and her two children, Katharina and Alexander

Vesely. Every family member was still highly involved in Viktor's ongoing work, and of all people, they would understand the deep significance of our endeavor.

When Kevin Hall heard, he got reinvigorated by the project and invited us all over to his home, where we planned the trip. It grew from Bill, Daniel, and me to include Kevin Hall, Kenneth Linge from *Utah Valley Magazine*, and John Farr from CMG Productions. Unfortunately, Stephen Covey was on tour and couldn't make it, but John included his daughter, and I included my wife.

We were all delighted to discover that Bill knew a prominent business, civic, and church leader in Vienna. He had formed a friendship with Johann Wondra during his Austrian mission. "If anyone can get us in to see the Frankl family, it will be this man," he said. "Johann Wondra is the former director of the world-famous Burgtheater and is well respected in Vienna." Indeed, Wondra worked his magic, and we were grateful that a meeting was soon arranged for our group and the Frankls at the Viktor Frankl Institute on the 20th of November 2004.

On the flight over, I discovered that this time, I could read Frankl's book without being triggered, and I knew it was all the inner work I had done. Tears poured down my cheeks while Lanea slept, and I would not tell a soul the depth of compassion I felt for the prisoners in the WWII camps and the deprivation and humiliation they endured at the hands of their Nazi guards. I had only a taste of what they had suffered, and my abuse had affected my entire life, just as my dad's taste of the Nazi's cruelty had forever affected his. Millions of Jews like Frankl and others lost not only their way of life but everyone and everything precious to them. In addition, their entire culture and people were nearly decimated in Europe. No wonder Frankl felt so impassioned to help all people find meaning amidst their suffering.

As the plane crossed over the Atlantic, I realized in awe that there was no greater work for me to be involved in. In fact, the efforts I had put forth felt even more sacred.

As we touched down in Vienna, the crisp, chilly air had a distinctive smell, especially the open-air markets with their strong cheeses, exotic spices, and freshly caught fish. We sped along cobblestone streets and alleyways to our lodgings near the center of town, where I drank in the sights and sounds and smells so reminiscent of Germany. Still, I could tell Austria was unique in its own way.

Vienna had its own flair, and it was easy to fall in love with it. I concentrated on the fact that each street we passed held sweeping architectural masterpieces—palaces, opera houses, grand parks and gardens, and monolithic statues—that took my breath away.

Yet, while the scenery was breathtaking, I couldn't shake an underlying anxiety. I fought to hold my body still. My heart pounded. Inside, I was trying to hold down something bubbling to the surface—a deep fear.

What if Dr. Elly Frankl, Dr. Gabriele Frankl-Vesely, and their family don't like the statue? What if the deep meaning it now holds for me means nothing for them?

I suppressed a gasp and gulped. Now I said a silent prayer that they would see the symbolism for what it was and why it had inspired me. I tried not to be nervous, but my palms were clammy, and I kept forcing myself to stretch, breathe, and try to relax in the cramped cab.

All of a sudden, my eyes lit upon a tiny group of older women huddled together as they slogged down the street in the crisp November air toward the market in their black, bulky leather shoes. I smiled. A warm, beautiful feeling of peace washed over me. They reminded me of the *Hausfraus* in Germany who had taught me that I could be *sympathisch*. I was brought out of my fear and into what this trip was all about—love and service. This trip was about Elly, her family, and their dear Viktor's dream. This was *not* about me. All I had to do was listen and be authentic and show *sympathisch*. Everything else would be okay.

Upon arrival, we found that Johann Wondra had arranged the conference with the Frankl family to be at an office near the center of town in the historic section where the Viktor Frankl Institute was housed. Frankl had died in 1997, but his family and a committed group of volunteers from the Viktor Frankl Foundation were committed to seeing that his profound legacy live on.

Our entourage walked into the beautiful old building and gathered around a huge conference table near the front. Elly Frankl was an older woman who was a bit reserved in the beginning. Dressed in a black skirt and top with a powder blue suit jacket and matching black piping, her hair was thinning and gray. I noticed, however, that she had a most captivating, youthful appearance when she smiled. Her daughter was warm and lovely. It took only a moment to see her mother's and father's brilliant minds in her as well. As polite as they all were, their eyes held a degree of reservation about us and curiosity regarding our agenda.

Bill took the lead, speaking for the most part in German, although we soon found it wasn't entirely necessary. Elly and her family spoke remarkably good English. Herr Wondra also spoke briefly. The Frankl family was cordial but still somewhat reserved. I was quietly concerned watching Elly's rather somber face.

That's when John Farr, our documentarian, played a video for them on a small television set. It was of Stephen Covey extending a warm welcome to Elly and her family and explaining the dream for the Statue of Responsibility—Viktor Frankl's dream, which had begun to form in his mind decades before when he first imagined and wrote in his famous book about a Statue of Responsibility needed in America. This was many years before he and Covey met on the American lecture circuit and became fast friends.

The always charismatic Covey then quoted Elly's husband: "'Freedom is not the last word. Freedom is only part of the story, and half of the truth. The positive aspect of freedom is responsibleness. That is why I recommend that the Statue of the Liberty on the East Coast be supplemented by a Statue of Responsibility on the West Coast.'"

Watching the video was the first time I learned that Covey was impressed with my recent design for the Statue of Responsibility. He said he felt the world needed to lift each other and respond to each other's needs.

As the video concluded, I was delighted to sense a marked change in the energy of the room and a rising feeling of anticipation that was not just mine. Now it was time to unveil our reason for coming to Vienna. I was shaking and had to clear my throat, but after I spoke a few words about my inspiration for the Statue of Responsibility, I nervously turned to the figure I had created and then hand-carried 5,522 miles. It was hidden under a black silk cloth.

Without too much flourish, I whisked off the cloth to reveal a seventeen-inch model complete with two hands clasped and cast out of glimmering stainless steel. I explained to the Frankls that I wanted the monument to exude bold and brilliant light.

There was an immediate and audible gasp of appreciation. As all eyes beheld the statue, I teared up. *They love it! Thank you, God!*

I couldn't help it. The moment overcame me, and I wept openly as I witnessed the Frankl family embrace my concept for the statue.

Suddenly, Elly came forward, her eyes now brimming. "Gentlemen," she announced, "I am astounded by this concept! You simply must come with me to our apartment. I have something to show you."

In an effort not to overwhelm Elly with our big entourage, a small group of us strode after her in the growing cold of the late afternoon to the apartment she had shared with Viktor. It was not far. *We discovered it was the same flat that she and Viktor had moved into upon their marriage, after his release from the Türkheim concentration camp, a subcamp of Dachau. They were certainly as poor as church mice when they first moved in.*

"Viktor came back to Vienna penniless," explained Elly, her eyes solemn as we entered and she removed her coat. "Absolutely penniless and not in the best of health—but highly motivated. His parents were gone, and his wife was gone. He immediately began writing his book *Man's Search for Meaning,* which he finished in just nine days. He had it in his head, you see," she explained, grinning as she pointed to her own.

Nine days, I breathed to myself. His book was like a magnificent sculpture he had carried in his mind all those years in Auschwitz, Theresienstadt, and Dachau before his own Liberation Day. Frankl understood liberty and the ugliness of its total absence.

"When Viktor came back from the camps," Elly continued, "he had a completely different view of life. He believed that at the core, people yearned to find real meaning to their existence. During the war, he observed that those prisoners who found meaning tended to survive if they were not killed by the guards. Those who could find no purpose or meaning, however, lost hope. It was they who shriveled up and died or ran into the electrified fence. You have probably heard this, but Viktor said, 'Everything can be taken from a man but one thing: the last of the human freedoms—to choose one's attitude in any given set of circumstances, to choose one's own way.'"

Reverently, Elly led us straight from the living room into Viktor's open office at the far end of the apartment. There was a large desk and chair. Off to the left, an open doorway revealed his study, the bookshelves on all four walls filled with books from floor to ceiling. Then Elly took my arm and brought us over to the most prominent wall, where there was an alcove carved into the bookshelves.

Sitting inside that alcove in a place of honor was a wooden statue. It was just a few inches taller than the seventeen-inch statue I held in my hands. The image took my breath away.

Viktor's statue was a painted, wooden carving of an anguished man, sculpted from the waist up. He was covered in dirt and sweat, bloodied, his hair disheveled. Flames licked at him from below, and in his anguish, he looked beseechingly toward heaven, hands raised as if in supplication to God.

"It's called *The Suffering Man*," said Elly, her voice soft. "When Viktor came back to Vienna, he wandered into *der Wiener Marktplatz*, you know, an open-air market, where he saw this." She explained that as he had no money, he asked if he could put the statue on layaway. "He paid just so much every month. After many, many months, Viktor brought it home. It became his favorite statue. Gary," she continued, still holding on to me and now looking straight into my eyes. "Viktor would always ask the question, 'Where is the hand reaching down? Who will reach down to lift the other?' And you, my American friend, you have answered Viktor's lifelong question!"

The whole room gasped.

As Bill Fillmore later put it, it was almost as if you could hear the Halleluiah Chorus of angels behind us. I was totally blown away. I had been inspired to come up with this concept, one Frankl had envisioned in 1945—the very act of reaching down to lift another!

"Oh my," I breathed, staring at the statue, chills running up and down my neck, back, and arms. "That's beautiful, Elly. May I touch it?"

"Yes, of course," she replied. "Not only that, will you pull it off the shelf and place it on Viktor's desk?"

I carefully plucked *The Suffering Man* off the shelf. It seemed like an ancient relic filled with so much symbolism and significance. Quite suddenly, this moment meant everything to me.

I was moved by the feel of the light, wooden carving in my hands. I placed it next to the prototype of the Statue of Responsibility on Viktor's desk. There, the image of *The Suffering Man* was forever imprinted on my heart. I knew all too well the devouring flames and torment of a personal hell. I also knew how it was to have that hand reach down again and again to lift me up. It was a spontaneous gift of love. My eyes again welled with tears matching Elly's.

That would have been the exclamation point of the whole trip, except for the transformation that overcame Elly as she became filled with light. Her eyes flashed with laughter and joy and tenderness. I noticed she also had a wicked little twinkle as she told us how the world thought she and Viktor would never make it—she the dyed-in-the-wool Catholic and he the Orthodox Jew.

"But we did in spite of their thoughts!" She chuckled, her twinkle even brighter. She showed us around the rest of the apartment, sharing photos, treasured moments, and memories.

That night in Vienna, exhausted and blissfully happy, I went to lie down next to my wife but found I could not sleep. Not wishing to disturb Lanea, I grabbed the book on my nightstand. I turned, many pages in, to Frankl sharing about those souls who found meaning enough to stay alive even amid the "slow dying," as well as about those who perished quickly because they could not.

I knew that slow dying. I rose from my bed and grabbed my journal, where I penned flashes of things that had happened to me throughout my young life. Then I focused on what Elly had shared—that Viktor and I were alike in the optimism that drove us both beyond the suffering. And suddenly visions of the Statue of Responsibility came fast and strong, beautiful and poignant:

I envision the statue very simple in design and very powerful in its meaning and symbolism. I see the statue several hundred feet tall in order to lift upward not only mankind's heads and eyes but their thoughts and ideals as well. I see the statue in a gleaming material and radiating light in order to be a visual beacon of upward motion and inspiration. I see the silhouette of the statue unmistakable in its meaning and message.

I see at the base of the statue a gathering place for peoples of the world, a peace garden with other sculptures from many different cultures depicting their unique expression of the higher ideals of humanity. I want those of all ages to be empowered by the statue in one way or another. And finally, I see smaller satellite Statues of Responsibility placed throughout the world in strategic areas to further life, give hope, and inspire humanity. Another great man, Victor Hugo said, "Nothing is more powerful than an idea whose time has come!"

I believe the suffering Viktor and I endured was for a reason, and that as we all couple our trials and ideals with optimism, we will be able to leave behind in our global hour of need, a monument of great significance.

Gary Lee Price
November 20, 2004
Vienna, Austria
5:43 a.m.

The Frankl family ended up endorsing the project wholeheartedly. To me, it wasn't just the endorsement but the very precious friendship we had established with Elly, her daughter, and grandchildren that felt like the greatest success.

Before we left, we enjoyed a remarkable dinner and celebration at Beethoven's ancient residence. There were about fifteen people between our two groups, and we now toasted one another as we had become one in purpose.

Upon our flight home, I couldn't help but sense a growing excitement within me. This truly had been a historic trip. The symbol that now held even greater significance for me seemed something our country really needed. I was delighted that Covey and his people were all behind it.

Now, the only question was, would the rest of America get to see it?

Upgraded Peeler and Humble Pie

"The mountains you are carrying, you were only supposed to climb."
—Najwa Zebian

It's been said that God does some things to make you humble, other things to keep you humble, and yet others to make sure you stay humble.

Upon our arrival back in the States, the entire team was on fire. With Bill's help, a Delaware nonprofit was set up and a solid board of directors put in place. Now it was just a matter of finding significant financial support, which I figured would be a no-brainer. America's economy was strong. Who could resist a project of national and international scope that involved both Viktor Frankl and Stephen Covey?

As the year 2005 dawned, I was feeling rather accomplished. I had an incredible marriage, remarkable kids, and a great home with ten acres and a natural spring. I was living my passion as a sculptor and had a profitable career. I remained industrious, creating anywhere from ten to fifteen finished marketable pieces of art per year, my library of bronzes continued to sell, and our foundry had to keep up with our rigorous schedule and demand for fine quality.

After the high of Vienna, I felt so good that I didn't care I was turning the "big 5-0." In fact, I had the sudden desire to mark half a decade in a very big way.

First, Lanea helped me plan a huge celebration our community could enjoy. Next, I had a little secret. There was one thing I wanted, something I had never allowed myself. Some might call it a midlife crisis, but it didn't feel that way. I'd had a passion for muscle cars since I was a kid. I'd even restored a couple of vintage cars in my day. But now I felt the urge to push the accelerator into an even more glorious future.

If I was ever going to own my absolute dream car, now was the time.

What embodied that for me was a bright-yellow 2004 Porsche 911 Twin Turbo. I loved the German design and engineering.

As my birthday neared, I hesitated a bit, then finally bought a round-trip ticket to Scottsdale, Arizona, to look at the possibilities. It didn't mean I had to buy. The showroom of the Porsche dealership was familiar from our visits during Arizona art shows.

I fully intended on just looking when I found *her*. She wasn't yellow but a rich, merlot burgundy with a gorgeous, camel-colored all-leather interior, including the dashboard and headliner. The leather was luxurious, soft to the touch, and smelled beautiful. As I walked around her, her color, like a smooth glass of rich wine, had me hooked. This Porsche had a few thousand miles on her, but for all intents and purposes, she was brand-new. I walked around her for hours, inspecting every square inch. I opened the door and just sat in the cockpit, imagining . . .

After a few hours of visualization, I called Lanea and told her, "I think I've found it, the car of my dreams!"

Still, it took me about five more hours at the dealership. Did I dare? Part of the issue was justifying the purchase.

Am I worthy enough? Am I nuts? I'd always been a guilt-driven person, a characteristic I hadn't been able to shake. Even now, forty-four years later, I had to remind myself that losing my mom was not my fault.

Come on, Gary, you can do this! You do deserve this. You have earned it!

Just in case, I gave Lanea a final call to make sure. It meant I'd forfeit the other half of my round-trip airfare. She gave me her blessing.

"Go for it!" she cried.

I had support from all sides. Still, I vacillated. The old guilt and shame washed over me. Every time I went to sign the papers, I felt like the kid in front of Western Auto. But now, in this dealership, I had every dollar bill I needed that I earned myself, and I was the only one standing in my way. Finally, my very patient salesperson came up to me as the dealership was only an hour from closing.

"Are you ready for that test drive?"

A huge grin took over. "Hell, *yes*, I am!"

Soon I was flying down the freeway going triple digits toward home.

Just before the on-ramp, I pulled up to my final stoplight. I was surprised, when, windows down and enjoying the breeze, another gorgeous Porsche pulled up beside me. A handsome, silver-haired gentleman winked at me while giving the thumbs up.

"Nice color," he crooned, and I grinned. Yeah, I'd made the right choice. I felt like that little kid flying down the streets of Montpelier on my golden Stingray, then upgraded Lemon Peeler.

Lanea came out to greet me in her bejeweled jeans. I was sad all the kids were still in school. I couldn't wait to take them each on a ride. My wife and I hugged and kissed in a celebratory reunion.

When Lanea went to rest her bejeweled backside on the car, all I could see was the ruin of that perfect paint job. I stopped her just in time—but would never forget the look she gave me.

That night was my glorious fiftieth birthday celebration. We'd hired a band and rented a giant white tent that covered our entire front pasture. Adjacent to one of Lanea's horse barns, it came complete with a guest book for the hundreds of family members, neighbors, and friends to sign. We'd hired two different restaurants to cater the food so everyone would be well-fed no matter their tastes. I felt on top of the world during the celebration.

The next morning still on a glorious high, I popped out to visit my new baby. As I looked into the passenger side of the car, I noticed something on the floor that I couldn't quite make out. Puzzled, I opened the door. To my utter dismay, I found six dried horse poops, all stacked neatly on the floor mat.

No one ever owned up to it, but I got the message: not to be too big for my britches. Eventually my family and I would laugh about my extra "present." I was just grateful that my humble pie wasn't the fresh, bright green, and terrifically stinky kind.

After turning fifty, I began spending more time in gratitude, meditation, and prayer. In the mornings, I often arose early for a walk, run, or bike ride. Tapping into nature helped sustain my gratitude. It also helped me see stress as a natural cycle of life. Instead of fighting it as vehemently as I once had, I changed my strategy. I gave to the Master Sculptor anything that was not in my control. I also asked for guidance with the things that were and found myself listening more intently than ever.

One fine early spring morning in 2007, I came home from a run hearing a message so loud and so strong it was as if it were branded on my heart and tattooed on my forehead. *"Save more. Spend less. Continue giving."*

Allowing my breathing to settle as I stretched, I pondered those words. While my muscle car was extravagant, I had carefully strategized and saved for it. The economy was up, and our line of credit was down to zero. People were buying my art more frequently, and so it surprised me to be getting this message.

I looked out over the full ten acres of land we were stewards over, the buds bursting on the beautiful trees we had planted over the last several years. The smell was intoxicating, and I was so grateful for this slice of heaven. I also realized we had more than enough space for our family and Lanea's beautiful horses. Five of the acres we weren't even using. I certainly didn't need to continue in my over-the-top landscaping of Price Park. As I looked out, for once I didn't see all the work that "needed" to be done. Instead, I felt a sense of great peace wash over me. There was no need to prove anything to anyone.

Beginning that morning, I committed to simply enjoying and maintaining what we had. The older boys, from Zac to Ty, had grown into their early twenties and were beginning adventures of their own. With only Justin and Raphy at home, I didn't have the daily help on the land. The promptings even caused me to consider trading in that sweet Porsche in the garage for a lesser model or something else entirely. I truly enjoyed it, but I didn't need it.

Lanea and I continued being big givers and contributors, and it felt important to honor that spiritual side of our family. Still, we had some looming personal debt, so anywhere I could personally trim back, I started to do so. For years, I had been so focused on growth it was strange to feel this pressing, urgent need to trim and reinvent rather than expand.

As we progressed into summer, I used my worries as a catalyst to become even more productive in my business. *I can just keep working harder and harder to eliminate our personal debt.* That was easy. I'd done that all my life.

After one particularly long day of sculpting from early morning to dinner, I had taken a break and was musing in the deepening glow of sunset with a glass of wine. I looked over at my beautiful wife, who was enjoying the same view.

"Honey," I said, "I keep having the feeling to cut back on expenditures for now. We have more than enough, and we could even cut the property in half. We'd still have five full acres to maintain and enjoy with the horses while making better use of our resources."

Lanea shot me a look of absolute horror, then fury. Without a word, she rose and quickly stalked into the house.

Wow, I had just hit a nerve. Worse, I didn't know why.

She wouldn't talk to me about it, so I left it alone. A couple of days later at the foundry, she unloaded. "No, Gary, we will not sell a single acre!" she snapped.

I blinked. "Okay," I said in confusion. I didn't understand where this sudden intensity was coming from. "Look, I just want to be wise with what we have. What if we sold just half these acres—the five we are not using—and paid everything off?"

"Again, we are not selling one single acre, Gary," she said coldly. "You get that out of your head right now!"

"Honey, wait. I'm not suggesting anything rash. I'm just burned out on ten acres. And we don't have the money to finish the other five like I would love. We could take a big trip around the world like we once did together, with all of our bills paid and money to spare."

Lanea just stared at me, her face stricken. "You just bought that freaking expensive machine out there." She then gave me a most malevolent look, one I was not used to seeing on her features. "You're getting lazy," she said. "We will not sell anything. Just go out there and make more sales."

My mouth popped open. Lanea had never talked to me like this, and it stung. I was overwhelmed by it.

Over the next several days, she became increasingly cold. We had never had such a terrible disagreement. It was so unnerving after so many happy decades that when two more weeks went by of her not speaking, I went to a friend who knew us both well.

"Lanea did not have much growing up, Gary," he said. "You know that. What you and she have built is phenomenal. But you need to understand, it's also her security. Many women need to have a place that feels safe to them and that they know is *non-negotiable*. When you threaten to sell half of it, you threaten to undermine half of her security. Do you see?"

"Yeah," I said, the light beginning to dawn. "I do see. I hadn't thought about it in that way." I thanked him and went home, remembering my teen obsessions with safety, security, and money. Lanea had walked with me as I'd discovered my self-worth. I would walk with her now.

Deliberately, I backed off from any thoughts of selling the acreage. The last thing I wanted was for her to feel unsafe. Instead, I trimmed my budgets again. The only problem was that I just couldn't shake the prompting I kept having. I bit my tongue as Lanea kept building and spending money on her growing stable of horses, feed, corrals, and more. It was important to her, and she was important to me, so I would support her in any way that I could. I was grateful when Lanea became warmer again.

In the meantime, as the boys got older, she traveled frequently. She was following her personal growth journey with her favorite facilitator, a teacher who had a special charisma and a vast following. Lanea had twenty or more journals of notes on this trainer's teachings. I was glad she was finding fulfillment in personal development and healing, and I supported her wholeheartedly.

Unfortunately, Lanea became deeply offended when I began refusing to attend the trainings with her. I had learned to listen to my gut, and I just didn't like how I felt when I was there. I thought it was just easier to decline, but Lanea's upset became as big as the old acreage issue. I loved my wife dearly, and I desperately wanted to support her. At my wits' end, I joined her on a medium-sized cruise ship with her beloved facilitator and the woman's most loyal followers, about four hundred of them, all headed for Tahiti.

It's going to be okay, I kept telling myself. *You don't have to buy in. Just support your wife and leave the teachings at the door.*

After a very good meal, the members of our group all gathered in one of the ship's finely appointed meeting rooms. A deep reverence for the charismatic facilitator swept over the open-minded students. I didn't mind that at all. However, I was shocked by what happened next. One by one, the students filed up in front of the trainer and got down on their knees, reverentially bowing before her.

I couldn't do it. I wouldn't do it. I did carry love and respect for this woman and the fact that my wife adored her, but it seemed I was the only one on the entire ship who wouldn't bow down to her.

I had no intention of being disrespectful, but Lanea was embarrassed and flummoxed by my non-worshipful behavior. She glared, silently fuming, as I refused to do what everyone else did. Back in our cabin, her demeanor grew extremely cold again. In my mind, I tried to think of how I could explain to her what was going on.

It wasn't just the many times Craig had made me feel that groveling was my role. It was a bigger, wider scope of humanity I saw before me. *My father suffered as a prisoner of war in Germany that we might not have to bow before anyone! I certainly bow my head to my deity every time I say my prayers, but I will not put one person above another anymore!* In my heart, I knew that no one human was either above or below another. I could not raise another to godlike status in my mind or through my actions. Only One belonged there for me.

Only, I couldn't share these feelings with Lanea because she refused to speak to me for the rest of the trip. It was hell. While I would not bow, I tried to placate my wife and please her in multiple other ways. As we walked off the ship, the icy void that gaped between us made me shiver. I could hardly stand it. What was happening? More confusing, I could tell she was having severely negative thoughts about me. Whispered conversations with her sister over the ensuing days, weeks, and months confirmed it, and I grew weary.

I was unable to be my bright, optimistic self, and I didn't know how to function when Lanea and I were not on the same page emotionally. I wanted her to be happy and have a rich, full, beautiful life. She deserved it. My wife had every right to believe what she wanted to believe. I just couldn't be part of something that felt false to me. It saddened me that she took it as a personal affront.

I tried to pour myself into my work but found it hard to concentrate. Even the statue project floundered. When we had first arrived home from Vienna, everyone on the board had come up with a fair amount for my commission of designing and overseeing the project. Regrettably, we ran into immediate issues. The enormity of the situation quickly became evident. Steven Covey's health went downhill. Kevin was struggling with some personal things and Daniel was put in charge. While Daniel did everything he could, the scene in America began to change drastically.

I was somewhat surprised and further saddened that my promptings about saving more and spending less had been spot on. By the end of 2007, the nation had fallen into an irreversible financial crisis. There could not have been a worse time to raise money since the Great Depression and the Dust Bowl. As stocks fell and houses, jobs, and businesses were lost, the last thing people were thinking about was giving to the Statue of Responsibility when their families needed basics like food on their tables.

My business was hit hard, and so were many beloved friends and customers. Once-wealthy buyers lost nearly everything. Nationwide, suicides were up, bankruptcies were at an all-time high, and everyday people were losing faith in establishments they had trusted for generations.

Everyone on SOR knew this was *precisely* what the monument was meant to instill—greater accountability and responsibility for citizens, government, and organizations, but as a country, we had to pick ourselves up first. We needed to pick our ethics up off the floor, dust them off, and put them back into play again.

Another blow to the project came when Stephen Covey's advisors talked him out of donating a significant sum. Schisms appeared within the original group. Other monies weren't coming through as promised, and there was a question of what had come in being used wisely. We had to part ways, which was painful.

The tearing apart of the board was excruciating for me, and now I had nowhere to go and no one to talk to. Lanea remained cold. Every day, no matter what I did, she looked at me through eyes of suspicion. I tried to make up for her upset by doing other things to please her, doing all I could to empower her. Unlike backing off on her spending, I could not stomach those trainings, and she would not get close to me again.

Finally, Lanea came to me one day and said, "Gary, you need to find something that's for you."

Relieved, I found a core-accountability training program all about personal responsibility and empowerment. Very quickly, I discovered I loved it. It rang so true to me. Instead of blaming parents, religion, predators, governments, and other outside forces, all accountability sat squarely on my shoulders, as it did for every individual.

After a time, our son Raphael went through the training, as well as Zac and his wife, and they loved it. I begged Lanea to take it, but she refused. Since none of us could talk her into it, I backed off.

Instead, Lanea and I took a trip back to Germany to try to rekindle the flame in our marriage. We tried some things we'd never done before and went to see parts of the country neither of us had seen. Unfortunately, it didn't melt the ice between us for more than a few hours at a time, and the deep sadness I felt deepened.

Back at home, the debt compounded and my income still suffered from the economic collapse in the country. I supported Lanea in her dream to take a trip to India with two of the kids despite the tens-of-thousands-of-dollars cost our now-struggling family could ill afford. I wanted her to see I was willing to sacrifice for her and the boys. To my chagrin, I was accused of being a horrible person.

Worse, I began to believe her. My self-esteem plummeted, and I began tripping over myself in everyday activities that were once so easy. Overanxious that anything I might be doing was selfish, I began to lose myself. Friends worried for me, but I could not seem to find my way back home.

The Shattering

"Some things have to be broken so new things can be built.
Destruction is just construction in disguise."
—*The SW*

As our marital problems worsened, I became increasingly depressed and despondent. I couldn't create in my studio. I tried to do sales calls only to break down in tears and rush myself off the phone. I knew there were two sides to every story. I wanted to hear her, but it was difficult to have even a simple conversation when she kept walking away.

How could something that was once so good have gone this badly?

In my eyes, my wife was near-perfect. If something was wrong, it had to be with me. I wrote Lanea a series of letters, apologizing for not supporting her the way she wanted and for so obviously taking advantage of her kindness as she told me I had multiple times. I hoped and prayed that we could come to an understanding.

I thought it had to be my fault when my wife instead filed for divorce. I was crushed.

I wasn't the only one. Seeing the faces of our sons crumple in grief at the announcement felt like it would kill me. It felt like I had failed them. All I had ever wanted for them was safety and a stable foundation of deep, abiding love.

For their sake and my enduring feelings for my wife, I desperately tried to see what we could do to work things out. I begged Lanea to go to marriage counseling. Finally, after many pleadings, we went. Within just a few sessions, I could see she had already made her decision. Regretfully, everything I tried to patch our failing marriage was futile. Even the letters I had written during my deepest depression, meant for me to take personal accountability and to buoy her up, were now used as accusations—in the relationship and the courtroom.

Several loved ones tried to show me that her arguments were colossally one-sided. But I couldn't see it and instead felt massive guilt and took all responsibility for the failure. The voices that had taken up residence in my head since childhood knew exactly how imperfect I was.

Finally, after loving intervention from family members and friends, I started going to see psychiatrist and coach Brad Chapel, who helped me see that because of my childhood traumas in losing my mom, in stealing for Craig, in having to leave both of my little stepbrothers, and finally in caring so deeply for Lanea and the boys, I was unbalanced as far as responsibility. On the pendulum, I tended to live in *over*-responsibility, taking *over*-accountability for other people and for anything that went wrong.

Understanding this took time, but finally I began to recognize the pattern, and I realized it was time to come not only from balanced responsibility but also to recognize our humanness. Both Lanea and I had made mistakes, and we both had hurt feelings. Though I was now beginning to see things in a healthier light, the question remained: How did we move forward? This was a question I would never hear the answer to because for Lanea, it was already over. She now wanted what she felt was her due.

Our fortunes were not what they had been. Expenses had been cut in the areas I requested in my business, but it wasn't enough. I wasn't receiving the promised commission from the statue, either. Twice now, the SOR mission had floundered, and Lanea was suddenly furious about our financial situation, even though she knew the truth that the mission held significant meaning for me. The hard truth for all of us was that the project was stalled indefinitely.

Finally, I moved out of our beautiful home to my small studio away from the ten acres, the horses, and my family. My heart was broken. Lanea was the mother of our beautiful children. I recognized how she had homeschooled and then busted her butt to get them into private school and worked with me to provide support for their biggest dreams. In our future, we would forever be raising beautiful grandchildren together. But we were no longer partners in anything else. I was bereft and spiraled into even deeper depression.

In the midst of my despair, I felt life would never be rich and full again. I didn't know how it could be. It felt as though I had lost everything of importance. My career certainly didn't matter if I didn't have a family to share my blessings with. I spent hours, sometimes days, drenched in tears. My dearest friends, who were already anxious and worried, began to fear for me. I lost my will to sculpt. I almost lost the will to live. It was the first time I realized just how hard it had been for my dad to lose Nellie.

I started fasting, hoping to get my head on straight. Unable to sculpt but needing to move, I spent hours walking and talking to God, even in the most inclement weather, anything to release me from my anguish.

The divorce dragged on for two years with no sign of resolution. I was stunned when my former life partner picked the attorney with the most brutal reputation in the valley. I had hoped we could end amicably and that more fighting wouldn't be necessary. I was already battle-weary and shocked by betrayal, but now my attorney warned I had better hold on to my shorts because that's all I would have left.

One day, I met with my accountant. I was so distraught I couldn't physically write out a check to pay a bill. I was so torn apart inside I was almost immobile. It was incredibly embarrassing to ask the accountant to fill out the check correctly. I couldn't believe I was that pathetic.

From the ashes, I had no earthly idea how I would rebuild anew. As often as I sank my fingers into the clay of who I was to mold myself into something better, it seemed only an act of God could put me to rights again.

Like Melted Chocolate

*"I suppose that since most of our hurts come
through relationships so will our healing,
and I know that grace rarely makes sense
for those looking in from the outside."*
—Wm. Paul Young

One blustery winter morning, I was not too surprised when my friend Jeff Kroneburger stopped by my little studio in Mapleton to see me just before the holidays. I was surprised, however, what a beautiful gift he would give me; it was unexpected and perfect.

With 2009 just around the corner, I felt like I had nothing to celebrate. I was back living in a small space above my studio nearly as tiny as the one I lived in when I worked for Stan. The irony wasn't lost on me.

The last few times my friend Jeff stopped by, I had dissolved into tears. He now removed his long, outer woolen coat to reveal his business attire, then ran his fingers through his delightfully thick, slightly graying hair. He was years younger than I was, but I felt more like I was his grandfather—haggard, old, and sad.

"Look, Gary, I am extremely worried about you," he said, a wrinkle between his brows. You're not doing all right. You've got to move on— new dreams, new goals, new people, and maybe even a new relationship with God."

I looked at him and felt the tears threaten again. I appreciated this man so much. He was a professional in real estate, and my rapid decline from Price Park to this tiny studio shocked him nearly as much as the despair in my eyes. I also knew that as my friend, he thought that if I just went back to church, all my problems would be solved.

"I love you, man," I answered him seriously, "but church won't solve my problems. God and I have made peace. It's just the rest of the world I can't figure out."

Jeff paused, but only momentarily. "Okay, then do me a favor," he pressed. "There's a girl I know—the most positive woman on the planet. She's been through rough times too. A widow. Lost her husband when she had small kids at home. But seriously, she'll lift your spirits."

You mean she will bring me back to church, I thought.

"Look, Jeff . . . a woman's not going to do it for me, either. I am not going to date. I know it has been a while, but I will never get into a serious relationship again. You can't convince me of this because I simply don't want to. I don't want to date, and the last thing I want is to lead anyone on."

"Just call her," he pleaded, handing me a business card. "She's amazing, and, dude, you *need* a good friend right now." He paused, looking at me with unusual frankness in his eyes. "Leesa can be that kind of friend," he promised. Then he left.

I glanced at the card he'd given me with her picture on it. The woman was beautiful—you didn't have to be an artist to see that. As I peered closer, I liked the lilt to her smile, and I really liked the unusual way she spelled her first name: *Leesa.* Leesa Clark.

I rolled the card around my fingers for a long while, setting it down about a million times over the next few hours. But then I always picked it up again. Jeff's voice rang in my head. *You need a good friend right now.*

Finally, like a coward, I didn't call but texted, my fat fingers on my tiny flip phone.

> Hi, it's Gary.
> I like how you spell your name.

Little did I know that in all her years, never had a man given Leesa a compliment about her name before anything else. She was delighted. Soon I would discover that when most men flirted with her, they texted things like, "Oh, you're the boss?" and "Wow, you're really hot," and "How much do you make?" I didn't know she was the head honcho at Keller Williams, a large real-estate conglomerate in the area. I also didn't know Jeff had to completely twist her arm to accept an invitation from me since she and I were a lot alike in our grief and total resistance to dating.

My text seemed to intrigue Leesa, and I was heartened by that. I felt a bit of levity. This levity continued, refreshing to me, as Leesa and I bantered back and forth in our texts for a couple of hours. Finally, I got the courage to ask, "Can I call you?"

The moment I heard the sound of Leesa's voice, warmth spread over my heart like melted chocolate. Her beautiful voice matched the beautiful face on her card, and the sense of humor I had glimpsed in her texts came out immediately in our conversation. As much as I enjoyed her quiet laughter, nothing charmed me more than when Leesa laughed out loud. This woman had an unrestrained quality to her that I admired. It had certainly been far too long since I felt that way.

"What are you doing right now?" she asked.

"I'm supposed to be sculpting," I said honestly. "Though I haven't done it in a while. Right now, I'm just thoroughly enjoying talking to you."

We spoke for well over an hour about life and our kids, in whom we each took significant, adoring delight. Talking about our kids warmed the awkwardness.

"When Jeff rolled into my office," Leesa admitted, "I was certain he was looking for a place to put his license. Suddenly he was trying to convince me to talk to his amazing friend, Gary. Well, I got up right then and opened my door. I told Jeff he could leave. 'First, I'm not going out with anyone *you* know,' I told him, 'and second, I have zero interest in dating again.' Well, Jeff rose, but instead of leaving, he shut my door and sat down again! Can you believe the nerve of that guy?" Leesa chuckled.

Then her voice softened as she continued. "He mentioned that you have been alone for a while, and he knows I know what that's like. He promised me, 'Gary is the kindest, most beautiful, sensitive man you will ever meet, and he's heartbroken.' Jeff even got a little emotional as he was telling me. Still, I told him 'Nope, I don't want to know. I'm not going out with him,' but he just wouldn't stop. I thought I was going to have to physically remove him from my office!"

I suddenly burst into a giggle, imagining Jeff cajoling her into this call like he had me. With a small gasp, I caught myself, my eyes widening. Leesa made me laugh in a way I hadn't laughed for years.

"I like that giggle," she said, and I felt my face grow red. Lanea couldn't stand my giggle, and it sometimes embarrassed my kids. Lately, I hardly let it out at all. Now I relaxed. *Leesa likes me. She even likes my giggle.*

As our conversation continued, it was just easy to be me. My tight chest loosened a bit. Out of the blue, my fingers felt an itch that had been absent far too long. I glanced over at some unfinished clay.

"Hey, Leesa. Is it okay if I call you later tonight?"

"Sure!" she said brightly, and I was relieved as I quickly made my way over to my sculpting chair. I could breathe, and the clay felt at home beneath my fingers again.

As I mused and molded, I was reminded of the first professional mentoring I'd ever had. So many years ago, I'd been taught how to paint light in a darkened, storm-filled sky, creating an intense and unusual contrast.

Leesa had been a contrast intense enough to knock me out of my rut. If nothing else came but friendship, I would be forever grateful. As my fingers worked the clay, I realized *she* reminded me of what light could look like and feel like, and I hadn't even met her yet.

To my delight, I sculpted all that afternoon and into the evening. A good five hours passed, and I was still in that chair. It was more than I had been able to do for months. Then I called Leesa back, as promised. We started chatting right away, and when the clock struck midnight, we found we were just getting going! Hours had passed in what felt like an instant. It was the first time in several years that I'd engaged in such a long, in-depth, heartfelt conversation with a woman—and the first time in twenty-seven years I'd thought about any woman other than Lanea.

This time, our dialogue wandered deeper, and Leesa and I began talking about lost loves and dreams. She shared how she had picked herself up from the ground to move on and had been at it far longer than I had—and certainly was much better than I was at it, despite the fact that she could have been justified to stay a victim of circumstance and sadness—yet she didn't. I was intrigued.

Leesa's first husband left her widowed with several young children at home when he completed his life one fateful night. What knocked my socks off, however, was the energy in her voice when she talked about her ongoing determination to create a better, healthier life for her children, now all adults. Her tenacity and intention poured through the phone. Even when some in her congregation at church once ostracized her as a widow, Leesa only emphasized the gracious friends who were incredibly compassionate and saw her through. She spoke of miracles that happened through her faith and of her focus on her children.

I sat on the other line, completely mesmerized. The woman was so positive, and her words delighted me. *She's special,* I thought. *Anyone who meets her must know this within seconds.*

"You know what's interesting," she said, musing, "I feel like I've been growing infinitely deeper as a spiritual person outside of church. My kids don't understand it, but it's like an entire, beautiful world of clarity and joy is unfolding before me." I could hear the passion in her voice, and I was about to agree when, all of a sudden, she stopped and I heard a gasp on the other line.

"Oh, my gosh! Gary, I've got to go shower and get ready for work!" she exclaimed. "I've got closings today!"

I looked at the clock, and my eyes widened in shock. *Holy cow, it's 6:00 a.m.!*

"Call you tonight?" I asked, a little tremulous.

"Absolutely!"

Although I should have been exhausted, I spent a productive day in my little studio. Muscles delightfully sore, I was determined to take a nap but awoke with too much excitement just a short time later. My being was filled with nervous, excited energy. I got more work done, determined to wait again until 6:00 p.m. to call her . . . but I couldn't.

At 5:15 p.m., I dialed Leesa's number. When she answered, I breathed a soft sigh of relief when she was equally excited to talk to me and didn't mind that I had called early. In my tiny flat above the studio, I settled in. The wind howled a lonely sigh outside, making sounds through my thin walls, but I paid no attention. Instead, I felt cozy, safe, and warm in our new friendship.

This time it was my turn to talk about my nearly thirty-year marriage. I blamed myself for the shattering of it all, and then I spoke to Leesa about all the good times, for there were so many. I shared triumphs, tears, and tenderness. It was refreshing just how easy it was to simply share with her and know she appreciated my stories.

"I love that you loved her so deeply, Gary," she said with a small sniffle. Had she shed tears while I spoke fondly of the good times with my family?

Leesa and I talked again through the night a second time and then all through the third night as well. This extraordinary creature and I had already become good friends. I really liked her. At one point, she shared that her picture on her business card was old, but I didn't care. Her soul was gorgeous. I knew I could be friends with her forever.

Finally, after three nights of no sleep, I asked if we could meet in person. Instead of dinner, we agreed to meet informally. Leesa was surprised when I asked her to meet at a copy shop, but then she realized I'd said, "Coffee shop." That was an immediate obstacle because she was a strict Mormon who not only didn't drink coffee, but felt it was akin to sin to enter a coffee shop! Just for me, however, she agreed to settle for a hot chocolate.

Oh, boy, we'll see if my coffee breath blows this meeting. In fact, I knew many things about me that might blow it for her. I was intrigued with her enough already, however, to give it a shot.

I drove to Art City Coffee in the blizzard, arriving a few minutes before 4:00 p.m. I went inside and sat down. They knew me well there from my months of anxious visits and long walks. My cold fingers twiddled anxiously.

When Leesa pushed open the door moments later, I lost my breath at the sight of her. I jumped off the stool to greet her as she strolled into the shop, knocking me out with her classy, knee-length, high-heeled, fur-lined boots. I loved her equally furry but classy coat, reminiscent of Cruella de Vil, keeping her snug in this blustery, snowy December weather just before Christmas.

Leesa smiled warmly, although she raised an eyebrow at my soft pajama pants and slippers. It was all I had been wearing for months. When I planned to come, I didn't want to give the wrong impression or falsely convey something I wasn't.

I looked down. *Yeah, I'm successfully not conveying anything but sloppy . . .* I sighed inwardly. *Oh, well.*

In the next few seconds as we crossed the room and met to genially shake hands, I realized my forehead came up to her chin.

"Oh, gosh, I'm sorry," Leesa announced a little hesitantly. "I know my height is usually a dealbreaker—"

"Oh no, honey!" I cried. "No, no, no. Are you kidding? This is a dream come true!"

I watched as her cheeks flushed with pleasure, and I could only think how adorable she was. A tall drink of water, Leesa was trim but curvy, with medium-length, dark, thick hair styled with unmistakable flair. One look into her beguiling, chocolate-brown eyes gave me an immediate urge to sculpt her angled, attractive face. I had never felt that way about a woman except for my mother. And, well . . . Leesa was definitely not my mother.

In comparing heights, we discovered we were actually close without her heels on. When she admitted she loved her heels, I said, "Don't you dare take them off!" That's when her grin went wide, and she cocked her head and looked at me curiously.

So far, so good.

We plunged into conversation, and it was as if everything and everyone in the coffee shop went away. Leesa had her own delightful giggle, and she seemed to like mine as much in person as she did on the phone. It was just the two of us, hot drinks and magic in the forbidden world of a coffee shop.

When we next looked around us, we were the only customers in the shop. It had grown dark outside. The coffee shop had closed, and we were about to get kicked out. We gave each other a look, knowing we weren't ready to leave each other's company.

"Would you like to see my studio?" I asked tentatively. After my past two magnificent studios, I was slightly embarrassed by my tiny little place, but it was now or never for her to find out about me.

"Sure," she said, smiling warmly, and we thanked the owner and braced ourselves for the biting cold. Outside, only two cars were left in the parking lot: my Porsche 911 Turbo and her 2006 Dodge Charger, which I knew was equipped with a Hemi Chrysler engine.

Hmm, looks like we both enjoy the purr. Leesa was a hard worker who managed twelve-hour days as the boss at her Keller Williams office. However, I grew anxious as she dropped elegantly into the seat beside me, shivering a little from the cold. Letting the engine warm for a minute, I turned to her.

"Look, Leesa," I said. "We have to discuss something. I don't want you to get the wrong impression about this car because right now my mantra is 'less is more'. . . Can I ask . . . What does that mean to you?"

"Funny you would mention that," she replied easily. "It goes through my head daily. I was a cash girl—and I used it for everything. I've always liked nice things, but as a single mom, I learned to be very frugal and make my children a priority—with one exception. When I began making really good money, my gift to myself was to drive a really nice car," she said, pointing to her Charger, "for my years of hard work. After all, my office is on the road, and clients often judge your competence and success based on what you drive."

"Well, you're obviously a very competent woman," I joked.

She looked pointedly around at the interior of the Porsche, and her eyebrow raised. "I sell houses that cost as much as this car, Gary. When I was a single mom, my entire family and I could have lived for three years on what you paid for this. Many of my clients could too."

"I understand," I said, but only a little sheepishly. "It's about all I have left of everything I built for so long. Everything else is out of my hands— house, studio, land, horses, truck. I have been hesitant to give this up."

She paused for a moment, appraising. Then she responded, "I think I'm like you. We both enjoy nice things but in due time."

Suddenly I felt the prick of tears in my eyes. *Wow, she gets it,* I thought, and loved how she'd said, "in due time."

Well, if she has any doubts about my spending, she won't anymore, I thought as I pulled up to my tiny studio and looked at the worn exterior. *Might be a true dealbreaker this time, more than pajama pants and slippers.* I was nervous as I got out and opened her door, ushering her into the warmth inside.

My small studio was littered with clay forms in progress everywhere. Up the wooden stairs, a little loft held the small bed where I slept. I was nearly back to my humble beginnings as a sculptor, although the studio was mine.

My new friend looked around, seemingly confused, and perhaps even aghast at what she saw before her. I could tell she didn't understand the works of clay in progress. I didn't bother to tell her I had bronzes all over the world now. Without seeing my work in upscale galleries, showrooms, homes, and offices, she just saw my little Mapleton studio with its simple corrugated metal, cement, clay, and tiny upstairs loft.

What I didn't know at that moment was that for Leesa, this *was* almost a dealbreaker. She had been on the treadmill: she had put herself through school; raised a fine brood of educated, creative children all on her own; and built a reputation as a consummate professional in her industry. After her history, she was not about to lean on a man financially—or have him lean on her.

I felt her draw back as she bit her lip. Still, to her credit, she stayed and began asking me many questions. My world was totally new to her. She admitted certain concepts went over her head, although only at first. I could tell right away that Leesa was a quick study. In answering her questions, I found myself a bit distracted by her brilliance, along with her physical presence. She was an alluring beauty—stunning, unique, and original, but how I enjoyed her brilliant mind. Every time she asked me a pointed question, I found myself more fascinated by her.

Feeling a little shy, I showed her some of my recent works as well as some earlier pieces still in clay form. I enjoyed telling her the stories behind the more elaborate pieces, some from my imagination and some commissioned. She noted the lighter themes of children, imagination, flight, storytelling, and the serious busts of great contributors like Abraham Lincoln.

As I walked around the studio, I purposely avoided the clasped hands in three different renditions of the Statue of Responsibility, even though the thirteen-foot one stood front and center. It had become such a painful subject to me, I didn't bring it up. When Leesa asked about it, I answered flatly, "Uh, I don't want to talk about it," and I moved on to show her other works. After all this time, the SOR project was still going nowhere.

As I brushed past those pieces and stirred up a completely different topic of conversation, I shared with her the processes the clay went through once it left my hands. Leesa's eyes widened at the significant processes necessary to turn something like this formed clay into a work of art that could last for centuries.

Grinning, I showed her a few of my favorite finished pieces that I kept in the studio to inspire me.

Leesa stopped still in front of *The Ascent.*

As I looked into her misty eyes, I was overcome with a feeling I'd never had. I didn't know how to explain it, and I thought about it long after I took her to her car and long into the night after that. I felt like I *knew* her. It was bizarre and wonderful. The way she witnessed that piece, I felt like she knew me.

Amorphous to Metamorphosis

"So how does it happen, great love?
Nobody knows . . . but what I can tell you is
that it happens in the blink of an eye.
One moment you're enjoying your life,
and the next you're wondering how you ever lived."
—*Hitch*

I couldn't wait any longer. After enjoying an extended dinner together the next night, I reached for Leesa's hand. I already felt a deep mental and emotional connection with this woman. Nervously, I took Leesa's fingers, enjoying the warmth of her hand in mine. "Whoa, that's weird," I said, looking down. Our hands were molded beautifully together, our pinkie fingers naturally interlocking.

Leesa looked up at me in equal wonder. "It's like I've found my slippers," she whispered, her eyes bright with moisture.

A little electric charge passed between us, and I gulped when in that gaze our souls connected as comfortably as our fingers. I was hit with the same overwhelming feeling I'd had the night before, the feeling that we had spent *lifetimes* together. Was it only days ago I was 1,000 percent convinced I would never step foot into another relationship? Now my life was turned upside down and backward.

As I looked into her beautiful brown eyes, I found it all confusing and at the same time exquisitely miraculous. *Upside down and backward might be okay, after all.*

Leesa and I started seeing each other more frequently. I began to anticipate that feeling of joy whenever our hearts and eyes met. I had new fire in my studio. My friends and colleagues couldn't help but notice that something was happening.

"Gary, you got more work done in one day than you have for a couple of weeks at a time prior to this!" they exclaimed. "What's going on? Why the new spark?"

I just smiled and shook my head. Leesa and I were keeping our new feelings between the two of us. Our relationship was new, and already the emotions ran so deep. Everything was happening more quickly than either of us anticipated.

In addition to separate careers where we kept our personal lives private, we each had children to protect. In addition, I had no desire to flaunt her in front of the kids or their mother, as Leesa was neither a trophy nor a vendetta. Instead, Leesa was a ray of golden sunshine in what had been a very dreary world. In one moment, her beauty and self-confidence took my breath away, then suddenly she would surprise me with something equally soft and tender.

I woke one morning to realize that Leesa was like breath to me. I hadn't told her yet. Now I just had to be brave enough to express it.

The next time we were together, I looked her in the eyes. "I have fallen in love with you, Leesa," I whispered. "I knew it the minute our hands fit together so perfectly."

Her eyes welled up with tears of joy. "I knew from the moment our hands interlocked as well," she admitted, taking a breath. "It's too magical to ignore . . . and I won't resist the miracle of it anymore."

My heart sang. I couldn't believe it! We had each other in this exquisite, extraordinary clasp, and like me, she didn't want to let it go.

Days passed all the brighter, just in the possibility of being together. Still, we found we could not keep our budding romance quiet. It had been four months since Jeff had given me Leesa's number. We were so very happy together, and we lived in a very small town, after all. We were trying to determine a safe time to declare our love to our kids in a way that wouldn't hurt them. We wanted them to hear it from us, not through rumor and innuendo. Neither of us was sure exactly how to break the news.

I tiptoed around the subject with my five boys. Leesa had two boys and two girls: Justin, Jeddadiah, Lynsie, and Leslee. Unfortunately, when her kids found out, Leesa's world exploded. Her four children even staged an intervention of sorts, and she called me, emotionally broken up.

"My kids are at issue with the fact that you are still married, even though you and Lanea have not been a couple for quite some time," she explained over the phone. "They're equally offended that I forced them into this "box of beliefs" that I am no longer willing to live by twenty-five years later. Plus, they think you're a rebel, a starving artist, with your butterfly tattoo and your one ear pierced. They're afraid I'll be taken advantage of, as I have been before."

I was silent, taking it all in. The tattoo and earring were both new for me, symbols of the expression of my own choices. Leesa's children were her world, as mine were to me. I could never ask her to choose me over them. A knot formed in my throat, and the tears welled up in my eyes. This might be the end of something beautiful that had just begun.

In her Leesa way, she wrote her kids a letter explaining that for twenty-five years, especially since their father died, they had all come first, every day, often every moment of every day. "I understand that I forced you into the Mormon box, but I have always supported you in many decisions—and now it's your turn to support me." She then expressed that it was time to do this one thing for herself. "I'm right here for you as soon as you need me, but I'm not going to stop seeing this guy."

My heart skipped a beat as it did whenever Leesa spoke of her feelings for me. This letter was a big risk for her and shocking to her kids. I, too, had witnessed how she *always* put her kids first. Now that they were young people with blossoming adult lives and choices before them, it was a huge deal for her to claim that she had a right to be happy.

I prayed to God with everything in me that her children and my children would come to understand what this—the growing of something greater—meant for each of us.

In the meantime, I had my own boys to work with. They were shocked by the news. Fortunately, they were also very respectful to Leesa, which made me adore them all the more. Leesa's particular skill set for nurturing relationships was needed as we experienced growing pains in bringing together her children and mine. Every Sunday, we invited them all over to Leesa's no matter where in the world they were. As the months passed and winter melted into spring, a thaw in the hearts of our children began to take place, one day at a time, and sometimes one person at a time.

One late-spring afternoon, Leesa was asked to watch her two little grandchildren, Elle and Talan. Their parents were going on a date, and it had been ages since Leesa had seen them. Her son Justin and daughter-in-law Cécile had just gotten back into town from working in New York for quite some time, but the truth was, their relationship with Leesa was still strained over her dating me.

Thrilled to see her kids and grandkids, Leesa let them know I was going to be there that evening to help her. Justin relented, if only because his brother, Jeddadiah, and his sisters said that he ought to at least give me a chance.

It was a balmy summer afternoon, and the lush scent of the grass from the golf-course fairway behind Leesa's townhome was in the air. The smell was intoxicating as it mixed with the perfume of the gorgeous flowerbeds swaying in the light breeze near hole number ten. Leesa and I took the little ones on a pleasant stroll down the fairway.

We had so much fun giggling and laughing. I thought how easily children could renew my faith in humankind and the promise of our future. No wonder I loved sculpting children and the animals they adored so much! And these two? They were the best! I kept chuckling because each was such a character, so determined to conquer cartwheels in the grass. They had me laughing as much as Leesa was.

After an hour of play, the four of us made our way back down the fairway. What we didn't know was that Justin and Cécile had ended up behind us in their car near the straightaway. Leesa had forgotten something and turned around to grab it. I kept walking with the kiddos, blissfully unaware that three pairs of eyes watched me.

I was having a blast, enjoying the children's chatter, their observations on nature, and their cajoling each other. As we walked, they both reached for my hands. I laughed, playing keep-a-way, but they grabbed them again anyway. My heart surged with love for them as they toddled and skipped and laughed beside me. Leesa, who had grabbed the club, caught up with us and was beaming at me. Painted on her countenance was how she loved these kids more than life.

When a tear slipped down her cheek, I raised a brow in question. "They're usually shy without me," she explained, "yet these two loved on you and grabbed your hands. I think they know an awesome grandpa when they see one."

Later, Justin took his mom aside. "Mom, our kids don't trust just anybody . . . but if Elle and Talan trust and love him this much, then I guess we'd better figure this out."

Later as Leesa shared Justin's insight with me, I burst into sobs. I even had to wait for my tears to clear before I could drive home. This tenderness matched what I'd witnessed as Leesa welcomed each of my sons with open and loving arms. One by one, under the intensity of her contagious affection, they melted just as I had, and accepted her maternal affection.

Finally, the meshing of the children became almost effortless. Once they accepted us as a couple, each of our kids enjoyed each other immensely. I loved watching that happen, overwhelmed by the power love had.

Now it was time to get the divorce handled so life could move on for everyone.

"Mr. Price," the mediator began, looking down at his notes, then back up at me. Suddenly he asked me a question that stopped me in my tracks. "Do you want to get back together with Lanea?"

His question—which was really Lanea's question—blew me away, and for several minutes, I sat in a quandary. My attorney silently let me grapple with this new twist, and the mediator left to give us time to think about it. Finally, after what seemed like forever, I lifted my head, opened my bloodshot eyes, and asked my attorney for advice.

"Gary, I've been thinking about this as seriously as you have the past few minutes." He hesitated at my tenderness and then spoke bluntly. "I've seen this tactic before. Based on how this divorce has gone down and having seen this innumerable times, I sincerely believe we will be right back here at this table in less than three months."

That thought was heart-wrenching. I didn't know if the offer from Lanea was sincere or a trick. It broke my heart that I couldn't tell. Sending back my answer was one of the hardest things I'd ever done. My answer was no.

The divorce would finally be complete.

That evening, I drove to Leesa's house to talk it over with her. On the drive over, I contemplated how this woman had become my absolute best friend. I'd shared everything with her. I didn't know how to share this news, but the friendship that had evolved between us was deeper and more lasting than words could describe. I would not keep this from her.

"Lanea asked me through counsel if I wanted to try to work things out with her," I said, carefully watching Leesa's face. "She said she wanted to get back together with me."

"Gary," said Leesa softly, "if there was any way my kids could be with their dad, I would give that to them. You and Lanea had twenty-five really good years together. If you can go back, if you can fix this . . . well, then, you should do that."

I looked at her incredulously, even though my answer was still no.

"I will be fine," she assured me, although her eyes brimmed with tears. She swallowed and continued. "I want you to have that if you can do that. If your kids can have you both, happy and healthy, then that's what I want—what's best for you and your boys. I want you to take the actions that are in all of your very best interests."

I threw my arms around her. I had never known anyone to love this way before, without jealousy or agenda. I sobbed in her arms. I had never dreamed of divorcing Lanea in the first place, and a year or two before, I would have done anything to get back together with her. I would have walked through fire. I would still have refused to go to those blasted trainings, but I would have jumped the Grand Canyon for her. That night, however, I had a different perspective. I had now experienced unconditional love. I had experienced Leesa's kind of love. I had no need to go back.

Despite all the crazy, Leesa openly expressed to me her desire to have a healthy, loving relationship with all our kids—*and* with Lanea. I marveled at that and knew if anyone could do it, it would be her. Leesa had remained good friends through the years with everyone she had dated—and their families. Like me, she didn't believe that breakups had to be ugly, and she took relationships much further than I ever had in terms of forgiveness, reconstruction, and renewal. She was a fantastic example and had a much bigger, long-term vision of what family meant. Her example taught me how to see it as well.

A few days before the house and ten acres were sold to cover the debt, I drove over and looked out on the space that had once received the community's Beautiful Yard Award. All that work with my boys and all of those years of connection came back to me. Happy memories filled my eyes, the good times far outweighing any bad times.

In the warmth of the sun, I sat on a rock overlooking the former estate with Raphy and Justin, rehashing old and delightful memories. Not one ounce of life here had been wasted. Love lived in our hearts, and it was vibrant and alive and beautiful. This is what I would choose to remember.

I glanced down at my first tattoo. Despite tattoos holding a lot of negative firepower and being judged as a no-no at the time, especially for a grown man, my tattoo was the vision of a butterfly about to burst from the chrysalis sketched upon my skin. The bittersweet past was the past. Specifically, I had the artist create a tiger swallowtail butterfly with vibrant yellow-and-black stripes—like the kind I used to chase in Craig's sister's front yard when I was little, symbolizing adventure and the hope of freedom. It meant metamorphosis.

I had learned that once a caterpillar spins its cocoon, it essentially digests itself, releasing enzymes to dissolve all its tissues. It becomes formless, shapeless soup until it lets its imaginal discs prepare its DNA for reformulation.

For a time, I had let my guilt and shame eat me alive, but now I'd pushed my head out of the chrysalis and flexed my baby wings. Today I was becoming renewed and prepared for a whole new journey.

Momentous Ties

"Where there is great love there are always miracles."
—*Willa Cather*

The timing couldn't have been more nerve-wracking.

I had been looking forward to seeing Leesa all day, but when she popped into my Mapleton studio earlier than expected, my heart began pounding in my chest. We had been dating for close to a year now. While her presence still had the power to move me like this, today there was more to it.

Leesa and I had planned to enjoy dinner together at my studio. Arriving early, she happened to catch me in the middle of an informal tour. I was showing two corporate clients around, as these two gentlemen in formal business attire had commissioned a fine new piece. I was excited to help them understand how I worked and answer any questions they might have.

As she slipped in, she gave me a loving, encouraging look, then stole quietly over to the leather couch in the studio so as not to intrude. Blessing her professional patience, I continued with the tour. Keeping her back partially to us, she was staying unobtrusive, checking work emails on her phone. That's when one of my clients pointed to the tall renditions of the Statue of Responsibility.

"What are these, Gary?" the tallest man asked, his voice reverent as he pointed to the largest of the two monuments. The oil-based clay was as good as the day I'd finished sculpting it.

I'm sure all the color drained from my face.

I glanced nervously at Leesa, remembering her natural curiosity about this powerful symbol when we first met. She had honored the fact that I hadn't wanted to talk about it and hadn't asked about them for an entire year now.

I gulped, knowing I couldn't exactly ignore my client's question. I also couldn't help but notice how Leesa's ears perked up as I began to tell the story.

I wasn't afraid of her knowing anything about my business, but my face turned red. I had taken on an odd shame with the SOR project, as it had such a dramatic beginning, yet nothing had moved forward. Because of its deep significance to me, there was also deep pain. It wasn't only Lanea and her attorneys but the fact that so many incredible leaders had come aboard passionately, only to let the flame of inspiration die inside them.

I took a deep breath and continued the story, now with the details of Vienna and Viktor Frankl's family. Both clients' eyes widened in wonder.

Out of the corner of my eye, I also saw movement on the couch.

Was Leesa crying?

I finished up the story and was relieved when the gentlemen noticed the late hour. As I was walking them out, we turned so I could introduce them to Leesa. I watched her shrug her shoulders and straighten her back, clearing her throat before she turned around to stand and meet them before wishing them well on their way out. As soon as they exited the building, Leesa rounded on me.

"Gary," she began, her eyes full of tears and her voice full of throaty emotion. "I . . . have been sitting on that couch trying with every ounce of my being not to sob! Why have you never told me your story?" Then she put her arms around me and looked me in the eye. "This is your legacy; you are meant to do this! You can't deny this. You can't bury this any deeper. Oh, my gosh, Gary, it's got to happen!"

I found myself trembling from head to toe, but not in fear. How had she just grasped what I knew to my core? Yet how in the world could I explain all that had gone awry? Not just on the outside but all of the twisting it had done to me on the inside?

Finally, I sighed in surrender. "Let's prepare the salmon, but I'll start with a glass of wine."

Leesa nodded and then softly smiled at me in a way that let me know I was the luckiest man in the world. I warmed up the barbecue grill outside the studio and prepared the fish with spices. Finally, over dinner,

I poured out the monument's story from the beginning, filling in a myriad of wondrous details beyond the basic story I had told my clients. From *The Ascent,* I spoke of Viktor Frankl's dream and of meeting Dr. Elly Frankl and family and went deep with Leesa into the personal meaning it all had for me.

Her mouth was wide open, and she'd hardly touched her dinner. By this time, the light outside had completely faded into dark. Still she hung on my every word, listening, taking it in, clearly moved by it all.

"Leesa," I began solemnly. "Something has kept me stuck in this project. It goes beyond boards, teams, finances, political bullshit, and nonexistent commissions. On that visit to Vienna, I made a promise to Elly. I would get this monument going. I would help build something of lasting value that sanctified her husband's suffering. I would help create a permanent vision of Viktor's dream so that America—and the world—could have a more profound and visceral understanding of responsibility, because that was who Viktor was."

My voice suddenly broke. "I haven't been able to keep that promise," I said, full of emotion. "I haven't been able to build this monument. Secretly, it has haunted me every day since."

There was a long pause as Leesa gazed at me, her eyes still wide and her mouth open. "Gary," she said finally, "this is phenomenal. I *felt* everything you just told me. Every single bit. This is historic! This is the symbol our great nation needs and deserves. I cannot help but think that with all of the challenges you've had to face from the beginning, it's all the more reason to get this launched!" she cried with sudden intensity. "No, really," she said in reaction to my startled look. "I mean *now.*"

I didn't know what to say.

At her words, "truth bumps" cascaded all up and down my spine. I had already experienced how when Leesa was passionate about something, she put her whole heart, mind, and strength into it. The passion, compassion, and conviction in her voice reignited something in me that hadn't been stirred to life for a long time. Our eyes locked for several long moments. She was right. I couldn't let this go.

Then my heart fell again, knowing I couldn't face what was coming.

"I . . . I don't know if I can move forward with it," I admitted, color creeping into my cheeks and hot tears threatening to cascade down my face. "The legal and monetary fights over it—they just . . . they twist me up inside. It reminds me too much of my childhood, and I become undone. I . . . I can't handle conflict."

A pregnant pause hung in the air, but only for a millisecond.

"Well, you're in luck. I'm *great* at conflict!" she cried with a surprising fire and determination in her voice. "Gary, you can't be a woman real estate broker in Utah County and not be able to handle conflict! I got you covered, babe."

When I looked into her eyes, I realized she meant it.

That night, our conversation continued on the deep lines of vulnerability. Leesa shared with me how her late husband had passed. After suffering deep depression and multiple hospitalizations beginning with an injured knee, the combination of pain pills and antidepressants became his Molotov cocktail. Unfortunately, it was a time when no one recognized the implications of multiple prescriptions, and the effect was disastrous on Leesa and her little family. All the responsibility was suddenly placed squarely on her shoulders.

In March of the year he left her a widow, Leesa and her four babies, all under age six, lived in a one-hundred-year-old uninsulated home heated solely by coal and wood. Her baby was only six months old, and all of them were reeling from the recent loss.

On a night when the second coldest temp in Utah was recorded at *minus* sixty-nine degrees, Leesa awoke to discover they had already burned through her entire supply of coal and wood, which normally would have lasted into the late morning. She would have to brave the below-freezing temperatures to secure the fuel stored away from her house.

"My parents' house was across the way, and for some reason, Dad awakened in the middle of the night too. He got up feeling something was wrong when he saw my back porch. *Why is Leesa's light flipped on?* he asked himself before he saw me swaddled up in my nightgown, coat and boots beginning to push the wheelbarrow through the deep, deep snow in the freezing dark toward the shed hundreds of feet away."

Immediately, her father threw on his clothes and boots, grabbed his coat, and ran toward the door to help collect the fuel and push it back for her. "My Dad knew that in weather like that, frostbite could occur in just ten minutes, maybe faster. He knew the wheelbarrow I pushed was as heavy as sin even before it was loaded. And he knew I still wasn't myself since my youngest was born, especially after the suicide of my husband. He *knew*.

"Yet, in that instant, Gary, a still, small voice stopped him short, right there in the dark. '*Do not do this for her,*' the voice said. '*She must do it herself. It will make her strong. She is going to* need *to be strong.*'

Her dad sobbed as he stood in the doorway, boots and coat half on, watching her struggle out to the granary and back once fully loaded. "He didn't tell me that story for years, but when he did, he sobbed like a baby. 'It *has* made you strong, sweetheart,' he cried. And he was right. It did. It really did. I gathered coal for the rest of that winter myself, plus did everything else that had to be done. That's why I became fearless. That's why there is no storm that will stop me."

I just stared at her. I believed her.

"My love," she said, now more softly. "I want to bring you back to what started this conversation. This statue…it is more than just your legacy. I felt it throughout my body with such awe and wonder as you shared this whole story. This monument is your *destiny.*"

Upon her emphasis of that last word, something shifted.

I literally felt magic in the air, and as the days progressed, this whirling energy of movement renewed my passion for the statue. Within a month of hearing my story, as the real go-getter she was, Leesa came to the table with a bold vision for the project, and every day when we woke up, she had another brilliant idea. She would act immediately on each idea and important contact.

My friend and attorney for the Statue, Bill Fillmore, was impressed by Leesa's zeal. Early on, he told me, "Leesa is an amazing woman. She enables you to be uniquely you, Gary. This woman matches your vision, but she has the tenacity to step in where you cannot." Before I could feel slighted, he winked and added, "There used to be a mantra practiced by Ronald Reagan's staff: 'Let Reagan be Reagan.' Well, with Leesa by your side, Gary gets to be Gary. You get to be artistic and a great visionary. I've never seen you happier or more fulfilled in this project."

Over the next eighteen months, profound things happened. First, something Daniel Bolz had set in motion years before came to fruition. In 2010, the Utah Legislature passed a recurring bill recognizing Utah as "the birthplace of the Statue of Responsibility."

My three-foot stainless-steel version was unveiled in both the house and senate chambers of the Utah Legislature, receiving a standing ovation in both. A long time coming, it was beautiful to see the statue finally begin to show its potential for a much bigger role—a symbol so much greater in magnitude than any single person and one that buoyed all souls involved.

Leesa cried with me, and I felt all that earlier shame about not finishing the project diminish. The principles behind the statue resonated within me as I now observed the results of the unconditional love Leesa embodied. In addition to her passion about this project was her mission to get closer to my children as I got closer to hers. As we shared more companionable Sunday family dinners, we began to wonder whose kids were hers and whose were mine? It didn't matter. They were *our* kids.

Then one Sunday, it was precisely all those children of ours who staged a reverse intervention.

"We've all talked," Justin said, "and we want to introduce you as 'Mom and her husband' instead of 'Mom and her boyfriend' as well as 'Dad and his wife' instead of 'Dad and his girlfriend.' We want all of our children to be able to call you Grandma and Grandpa." The same man who was once so enraged he wouldn't attend a family get-together now looked pointedly at us while everyone else smirked and nodded. "So when are you two getting married?" Justin asked bluntly, and they all broke out in grins, nearly choking on their laughter.

Leesa and I both gave each other a deer-in-the-headlights look. After experiencing so much heartache in our previous relationships and such tremendous joy in our present one, a marriage certificate was just a piece of paper to us. That paper couldn't encompass the deep, abiding love we felt for one another. Yet suddenly it did mean something.

If it means that much to them, it means everything to us!

Blushing and grinning, we cried "Yes!" in unison. Although it wasn't the way either of us would have proposed to the other, it was perfect. From what once was our deepest shared pain came our deepest joy. And the kids? Well, they were so thrilled at our agreement that they planned our wedding!

After a month of rain, it snowed on the morning of May 1, 2011, at Harvest Park Pavilion in Mapleton. The snow made everything white, fresh, and new until the sun melted it into a truly glorious new beginning.

Leesa and I took each other as husband and wife in front of eighty of our closest friends and family, including Leesa's parents, who couldn't have been happier for us. As they joined us in our celebration, I stopped for a moment. I felt a rush of indescribable energy and suddenly knew that my stepdad, my dad, my mother, and my stepmom were all there with us, too, unseen. I breathed in the rich joy of sensing their presence.

As I looked around at the reception now, the joy of our children was palpable—and should have been since this was all their idea! They had even secured the color pallet. Knowing Leesa's favorite color was "princess purple" and mine lime green, our kids made sure the flowers and ribbons complemented the theme.

Someone had even printed colored wristbands for each guest. The purple ones marked L meant "Leesa and Love." The green ones said G, for "Gary and Gratitude." Our home would forever be named "The Home of Love and Gratitude."

During the celebration, each of the children shared stories, laughter, and so much tenderness. Both of us were roasted dry with the teasing, but my heart burst wide open when Talan and Elle, a little older now, came up and hugged me, calling out, "We love you, Grandpa!"

I glanced over at Leesa's son Justin, who grinned, and then at his mom, who gave me a knowing wink, now seeing only the blessings. Divine Turbulence. We had come full circle from anger to love, and that sweet miracle was not lost on me.

The Promise

People need inspiring stories and empowering symbols. By this time, I had sculpted thousands of works of art, each with its own vital story. However, none included such national and international significance as the Statue of Responsibility. As we moved our epic project forward, I decided we needed a larger rendition of the monument to inspire the same sense of awe *The Ascent had.* I was about to start a larger rendition in my studio.

A few nights later, Leesa read in the paper that Utah Valley University (UVU) in Orem now enjoyed the largest student enrollment of all Utah universities—far above BYU or even the University of Utah. We were both surprised. This was a change in the student landscape and obviously the university's leader, President Holland, and his team had been working hard to meet student needs.

After an inspired dream, Leesa woke me in the morning, her eyes wide. "I think you should consider doing the larger rendition of the Statue of Responsibility at UVU. I think you should create it *live* on campus! Think of the students you could touch and encourage through this symbol— and its story." Her voice was low but held an uncontainable excitement.

For a second, I was silent. I had just told Leesa that week that I couldn't wait to work on it in my studio. A moment later, I realized just how inspired her suggestion was. UVU was close enough that I could work on it a few days a week, live, on campus.

How powerful! I thought as I considered it further. Students could witness in real time much of the actual work it took for something of this magnitude. I felt it in my bones. Especially after my Springville art-project experiences, I knew just how inspiring art could be for the whole community. The thought of the Statue of Responsibility inspiring tens of thousands of students every single semester bowled me over.

"Sure! Why not?"

Leesa immediately set up a meeting, and the two of us visited UVU's campus to meet with then-President Matt Holland. Not only was Holland extremely knowledgeable about Viktor Frankl, Stephen Covey, and *Man's Search for Meaning,* he was intrigued by everything the statue stood for.

"Your statue and stories are representative of UVU's three core values, Gary," Holland explained, "exceptional care, exceptional accountability, and exceptional results. To have these values embodied upon something so significant in mankind's history is exactly what UVU is all about."

Leesa and I looked knowingly at each other, and chills ran up and down my spine. *Oh, heavens, yes!*

At the end of our meeting, President Holland asked Val Hale, UVU's vice president, to tour the campus with us, looking for the perfect spot. Within one hour, we found it! It was just outside the Losee Student Union building.

And so it began.

The next day, Leesa came buzzing into the studio during her lunch break, a notebook clutched in her hand. Her visage was alight with energy, and her voice was full of a powerful reverence. Something had changed inside of her.

"I know you know this, Gary," she said, pointing to the six-foot rendition of the statue in the room. "But this . . . is not just a statue. This is not just a monument. Gary, this is a MOVEMENT!"

I blinked, a bit overcome. Leesa had just put into words what I had been trying to say for such a long time. *Not just a monument but a movement!*

Letting her inspirational words settle into me, I worked with my foundry and UVU to prepare. Usually, it would take time on the part of the university and for us as well, so we were surprised when everything went so smoothly the insurance and logistical pieces only took two and a half weeks. We could begin the work immediately!

That first day I walked into UVU with my sculpting tools, I carried Viktor's dream with me, albeit grumbling a little at the inconvenience of not sculpting in my own studio in my comfortable pajama pants.

Bit by bit, as the scaffolding unfolded to allow access to the different dimensions, however, I was suddenly grateful Leesa hadn't allowed me to hibernate, bear-style, in my studio, pajama pants and all. It became abundantly clear that my wife's idea was truly inspired.

From the very first week, I made some of the most significant and beautiful connections of my life. Crafting the monument right inside the Losee Center turned out to be an absolute delight. Several times a week, you could find me up on my ladder sculpting, with Leesa organizing speeches and presentations for the students, faculty, and public at large. While I worked relentlessly on the symbol, she educated people on Viktor's profound message and vision for this country.

As people would stop to talk, I was intrigued. It astounded me the number who had already read *Man's Search for Meaning*. Many of those even knew of Viktor's reference to erecting such a Statue of Responsibility! What blew me away as well was overhearing the miraculous stories of when this book was given or seemed to appear during a tragic or difficult point in their lives. What Viktor's message gave to person after person was undeniable. I arrived home feeling quite emotional on many of those sculpting days, heartbreak mixed with gratitude for such a powerful message of hope.

That's when the magic of each person's story started to change me. These real-life people, many of them so young, had such extraordinary tales of survival, suffering, and moving beyond. As we shared, I watched the light dawn in each person as they came to watch Viktor's epic idea unfolding for the first time, right on their own college campus. I added their energy to the sculpture.

The students' and staffs' responses stoked my fire, especially now that I was happy to be sculpting it here, among students from around the world. Since the Losee Center was where all campus tours started, I met many of them. It also attracted random strangers who turned out to be *not* so random.

One such visitor was a man with an unforgettable name and personality to match. Woody Woodward walked into the center, mouth agape at what he saw before him. This blond-haired, professionally dressed businessman stopped in his tracks, his piercing-blue eyes wide. Working from above, I quietly watched this guy read over each pamphlet and flyer we had about the project.

I motioned to Leesa, and soon the two were engaged in deep conversation. Leesa told me later that Woody and his wife were originally from Utah. Having left years prior with no desire to move back, both were astonished when they felt an unexpected pull to return. Just for kicks, they put their house on the market. Nine days later, it sold and they were back in Utah. At first, they didn't know why.

Now, Woody was so intrigued he requested a meeting at my studio the next day for an hour. That hour turned into six as Woody shared his life purpose and then asked us penetrating questions. When I shared my story of tragedy and its significance to the statue, Woody cried, "Gary, you need this recorded! People *have* to know about this." When I explained that this was all self-funded and filming was not affordable, Woody paused. Then he asked, "What are you doing Monday? I want to give you a gift."

By the time Woody left that day, Leesa remarked, "If I turn around, and 'POOF!' he's gone, I won't be surprised. I believe an angel just walked into our lives." Woody booked his videographer from out of state and shot a series of segments about the whole story, creating a professional video Leesa and I and our team were able to use immediately. It truly was a gift. He also said he would introduce us to "some people." Well, *that* was an understatement. Through Woody, we met some of the most extraordinary people, *and* he never disappeared. Woody became a lifelong friend.

In the meantime, throughout 2013 and 2014 as I sculpted at UVU, Leesa engaged iconic speakers, like retired professional basketball player Thurl Bailey, who motivated the students to begin living their best lives now. We often had famous entertainers and singers fall in love with our project and support our cause.

As students listened to these talks and music, enjoying dozens of donated Krispy Kreme donuts, they created burgeoning friendships and experienced firsthand how one person could extend a hand to lift another. I loved watching it all unfold.

After several months, I finished up my live sculpting. I had my foundry crew, Alchemy Arts, come to UVU and create the mold live, in front of the student body. After molding, they cast it at the foundry, which took another six months. I was excited to come back and dedicate what I felt had been a huge, community effort.

Even as the UVU project continued into production, Leesa and I searched for a location for the 305-foot statue. We held San Diego in our hearts as the most viable, permanent location. Elly had told us it was her and Viktor's favorite place in all of America and where they would spend time together before traveling back to Austria.

Naturally, Leesa and I felt major efforts should be expended to have the monument built there. Bill Fillmore, who had orchestrated our historic Vienna visit, agreed. The three of us traveled to San Diego, where we met the most extraordinary cast of characters, including Steve Cohen, a well-respected news executive, along with Jack Berkman, a gregarious local public-relations professional who seemed to know everyone in San Diego on a personal or professional basis.

The snowball started rolling, and they passionately introduced us to local civic and business leaders, many equally as committed to higher ideals. As part of my dream come true, I got to meet with the inspiring world-renowned architect Gordon Carrier. Gordon was not only talented at creating marvelous buildings but also stunning opportunities for people to interact with those buildings and grounds. I watched as the vision I'd had in Vienna unfolded inside his creative mind, and we shared additional ideas, artist-to-artist.

Before we left California, the three of us met with Alexander Vesely, Elly and Viktor Frankl's grandson. That was such a pleasure, as we remembered each other from Vienna! In short order, Alex introduced us to Mary Cimiluca, the American representative for the Viktor Frankl Institute. It was an honor to meet her and find out how she and Alex had met. They were assigned booths right next to each other at a conference. Alex simply asked Mary to watch his equipment as he slipped in and out to conduct interviews. She was kind enough to do so, despite not knowing who Alex was. The moment she found out he was Viktor Frankl's grandson, however, Mary froze in astonishment.

Just six months prior to meeting him, Mary's life had crumpled when her very best friend and her friend's husband were murdered in their own home. Mary became so distraught that she sought to take her own life. In the hospital, the doctor would not let her leave until she had read *Man's Search for Meaning*. Viktor's book literally saved her life, and she threw her arms around the young man she just "happened" to meet. Sometime following that meeting, Mary became a producer on a special project Alex was compiling and directing.

I stood in awe as Mary shared with us Alex's special documentary about his grandfather, entitled *Viktor and* I. Alex was a talented storyteller, and he had put together this touching collection of interviews with those personally affected by his own grandfather. Viewing it gave me even more profound respect for Viktor and tremendous insight into things I had never known about him.

On the way home, Leesa and I shook our heads, marveling at the benevolent force that brought such like-hearted people together to produce miraculous results. It was another witness to what was happening all around us.

When the casting on the work I sculpted at UVU was finally finished, I hoped it honored Viktor to the same degree Alex's documentary had. Both were labors of love. I was so grateful to my entire crew, who skillfully created the finished beauty from the raw art. *The energy of so many people was poured into this*! I marveled, experiencing a thrill of anticipation for the unveiling.

Isaiah called me from the road that week on an installation at a corporate office on the East Coast. "Dad, everywhere I go, I keep running into your statues in the least expected places. I ran into a *Journeys of the Imagination* in front of a children's museum today! I'm sending the pic."

"Wonderful," I beamed excitedly, and began looking for it on my phone. Our sculptures were often purchased from our website. Unless installation was requested, they were simply shipped via truck to various parts of the world—and not always to their final destinations—for display. Many pieces were privately donated, too, so it was a unique thrill whenever a team member or a friend or family member came upon one in an unanticipated place. Parks, museums, libraries, and cemeteries were just the beginning, and Isaiah started documenting any known locations in wonder and celebration.

"Yay! Time for another pin on our map! How is the dedication coming? You still nervous?"

Isaiah and others close to me were rather surprised to learn just how momentous this occasion felt to me, particularly when the day arrived, and I wrung my hands a little nervously.

"C'mon, Dad, said Isaiah, "you've got twelve life-size bronzes in Hong Kong in one of the biggest libraries in the world! Your work has been permanently placed at two air-and-space museums, for heaven's sakes! You've crafted thousands of pieces in, what, libraries, multiple churches, and cemeteries worldwide—"

"And botanical gardens, arboretums, galleries, corporate offices, and now airports." Leesa grinned proudly, elbowing Isaiah and me. "I think he's sculpted more monuments than any other sculptor I've ever heard of."

"Yeah," agreed Isaiah sagely. "So why would today's dedication seem so significant?"

"Because," interjected our new friend, Woody, "the Statue of Responsibility is not just his passion project, but he's finally claiming it is, as Leesa says, 'his destiny.'"

The energy overcame me like a thunderbolt. They were right. I was more than nervous. In that moment of awe, I could not help but feel a kinship with Frédéric Bartholdi, a dreamer and sculptor who also understood when a project was massively bigger than himself. His final endeavor to erect the Statue of Liberty, which he had entitled *Liberty Enlightening the World,* was only made possible by 160,000 donors, including young school children, nurses, and even street cleaners! The

BBC later reported that more than three-quarters of the donations for Liberty amounted to less than a dollar.

For our new national monument, we might not have the exact funding needed in place or the exact leadership team it would take to bring it there, but we had a powerful idea whose time had come. Time and again, God showed us he knew the intention of our hearts and saw the bigger picture.

After years of work sculpting live at UVU and the enormous efforts of my team casting the pieces at the foundry, plus all of their meticulous work to weld it together beautifully, the fifteen-foot Statue of Responsibility was unveiled on April 15, 2015, on a grassy courtyard outside the Losee Student Center, beneath overcast skies.

Regardless of the clouds, it turned out to be a gorgeously temperate spring day. I was delighted to see the faces of so many sweet friends and associates in the crowd of several hundred people.

I looked around at the groups of students gathered and realized that some of our nation's emerging leaders were witnessing the unveiling of a powerful symbol. I prayed those same faces would someday see the unveiling of a national monument and be a part of it, maybe bringing their young families to visit.

The dedication was beautiful, and we were honored by UVU's president, media, and our board's own Dr. Nancy O'Reilly. She was a longtime friend, one of the first major supporters of our cause, and an internationally renowned women's leader. Viktor and Elly Frankl's grandson Alex Vesely and many other dignitaries came out to be a part of the ceremony. One of those dignitaries touched my heart beyond words. We didn't even know she was coming, although we had certainly extended an invitation. It was the late Stephen Covey's extraordinary wife, Sandra Covey.

I tried not to cry like a baby when I saw her. Sandra was carrying on their legacy after her husband's death, just as vitally as Elly was carrying on Viktor's. Sandra wasn't in the best of health, and Leesa and our team got choked up to see her arrive with her daughter Catherine Covey Sagers pushing her in a wheelchair. When I realized what it must have taken for Sandra to be part of this monumental occasion, I was overjoyed when she seemed touched by the event and reveled in the mention of her husband's role in helping this portion of Dr. Frankl's dream come true. Her appearance was the epitome of what we all stood for—believing in the ongoing promise of humankind.

As the dedication started, I kept wiping back the tears. As I looked around, I was blown away by the number of people in the crowd who'd made a personal contribution to this monument. Peering into each of their faces, I thought about how each had played a role so significant that this dedication wouldn't have happened without them.

Leesa and I couldn't help it. We were full of emotion on the way home, uplifted in the hope that this was a taste, a promise, of the fruition of our dreams. We spoke of each person in attendance that we knew, with immense gratitude for the many people who had made this day happen.

That gratitude continued until we pulled into our driveway in Mapleton. I turned to her.

"Leesa, you do realize that this day would not have happened if it were not for you?"

She stared at me, blinking, and I went on.

"I thought I had overcome most of the demons in life, but right before you came along, it's like the project was stuck in a quagmire, a swamp of foul emotions and unrealized dreams. Meeting you gave this man a new perspective and a new life," I admitted. "Then, a year later, you resuscitated a dream I thought was too far gone."

My wife looked at me, her eyes full of warmth and understanding. "Hmm," she said in her knowing but kind way, letting me continue to pour out what was on my heart.

"I was embarrassed," I admitted. "I was ashamed the project hadn't taken hold. I felt like it must be all my fault. The design wasn't good enough, my skill set must not be strong enough, or I trusted at times in the wrong people or didn't trust the right ones at all. I'd lost my fire, my self-confidence—which I know was crazy because it was Viktor's story that inspired my deepest healing and meaning in life."

"Right?" agreed Leesa. "With all that you went through beyond facing Craig: especially having to confront your father and his paternity, your grandparents' untrue stories in raising Bill, and the army's police reports, Viktor's story inspired you to let go of all the blame and just accept your own responsibility. That's powerful, Gary."

"True, but it wasn't enough to overcome the voices in my head before you came along." This time I was the one who looked at her pointedly. "Did you know? Did you know that I fell back in love with Viktor's dream the moment you fell in love with the statue the *first* time?"

"Yeah," she acknowledged, clearing her throat. "I'll certainly never forget it. My life's trajectory changed that very moment."

We grinned. That seemed to happen to people all the time when it came to this monument. I would never forget when it first took hold of my soul and became anchored there. Even in my darkest night, I had never let it go. Just like in my studio, I had never let it out of my peripheral vision.

Leesa and I stayed talking in the car for a while, neither of us ready to let go of the energy of the day. It still cascaded over us as if with a force of its own. We sat for a while under the darkened sky, envisioning how many more people it would require to bring the monument into reality in California.

Like Bartholdi's dream, would it take another 160,000?

We didn't know. But together we had the craziest, most beautiful visualization of being around a *huge* table, a feast celebrating the opening of the grand monument. Every single person who had played one role or another in the puzzle of this great destiny was seated there celebrating, even those who had come and gone, honored for every part that was played.

That night, I was on a high and still thinking of Elly Frankl. Oh, how I wished she could have somehow made it to UVU's Statue of Responsibility dedication!

Elly, we started it, I breathed happily that night in my prayers before I slipped into bed. I reached my energy across the chasm of the sky to the little apartment on a cobblestone street in Vienna.

At the thought of her lively face and sparkling eyes, I felt a lump in my throat. But after this day and my talk with Leesa, I wasn't embarrassed or ashamed. I didn't allow myself to wallow in my mistakes or feel not quite big enough for this colossal project. Instead, I just felt gratitude.

We started it Elly—all of us.

Epilogue—The One

"I am only one, but still I am one. I cannot do everything, but
still I can do something; and because I cannot do everything,
I will not refuse to do something that I can do."
—Edward Everett Hale

A lot of authors like to include this thing called an epilogue, meaning a section at the end of a book that serves as "a comment or conclusion to what has happened."

Well, I'm going to set that tradition on its ear. (Artists can do that—just ask Picasso.) I'm ending this book with a challenge and an invitation uniquely meant for you.

First, allow me to share that after the UVU dedication, Leesa and I felt that pull of a purpose much bigger than ourselves. The Statue of Responsibility event had created a beautiful awareness and a grassroots landslide of well-meaning people who saw the vision.

Of course, there were also the challenges that come with any project of such tremendous scope. We had new and influential leaders wanting to be part of the statue. Some members of our new team held events and brought on other influencers. Others went on the road, gaining further attention for the cause in schools across the nation.

Everywhere we turned, it seemed like people were hearing about this amazing project. Leaders were coming out of the woodwork. They were seeing real struggles and challenges in our society and strongly felt SOR represented the higher ideal of personal accountability and responsibility.

Leesa and I were pleasantly surprised when a wonderful powerhouse woman named Jana Babatunde-Bey reached out to us. Jana worked as Chief of Staff for Will and Jada Smith, two famous entertainers and influencers. After Jana first visited our home in Utah to make sure we were the "real deal," she invited us to meet Will Smith in LA the following week for lunch to discuss our project. Of course we said yes!

Upon meeting Will in a cordoned-off section of a restaurant, Leesa and I found the actor and musician to be even more charming than he was on screen, if that was even possible. In our conversation, he was both serious and funny. In his funny moments, he helped us feel at ease. In his serious moments, he spoke of the world needing a movement that inspired people to walk away from entitlement, victimhood, and self-pity. He wanted opportunities for folks to operate with more responsibility, gratitude, and love.

Leesa and I stared at each other, wide-eyed. Did he know we were speaking the same language?

Will then shared with us the wisdom and message of a woman he had ultimate respect for—his grandmother. Her connection to the divine was undeniable, and she'd told him she had a deep inner knowing that he had important work to do in the world. This message had never left him.

During the Ferguson unrest, over four hundred people were arrested in Missouri during protests and riots that began the day after the fatal shooting of Michael Brown by police officer Darren Wilson. Anger, betrayal, and feelings of unfairness were rampant. It was just the beginning of much-needed change.

Will reached out to help friends and family he knew who were personally impacted. In the aftermath, one of his relatives felt alone and bitter.

"I came into town and sat down with him," Will explained. "I listened. Then I gave him a copy of my favorite book . . . *Man's Search for Meaning*."

Chills ran down my spine. I glanced at Leesa, and her eyes were misty as they fixed on Will.

"I always give this book to people who are battling their demons," Will explained. "Then it hit me as clear as a lightning strike. I wrote it on a piece of paper, and the next morning I called my assistant. 'Jana,' I said, 'Somebody's gotta be doing this right now. Find them.'" The sincerity and presence in Will's eyes blew me away. He had an integral understanding of responsibility, magnified by his gift of compassion.

I was still in the middle of writing my new book, but in that moment, I got vulnerable and disclosed some of my past and how Frankl's story had affected me. As I recounted my emotional visit with Elly in Austria, I explained the significance of Viktor's precious wooden statue, *The Suffering Man*. Will seemed as moved by our stories as we were with his. All we knew was we had met another kindred spirit. We were not sure where all this would go, but as we said goodbye, we knew we were looking into the eyes of a soul committed to the ascent, a soul willing to lift others.

Will invited us to attend a premiere of his film *Focus*, released the following month. Excited, Leesa and I dressed up to attend the event at the Grauman Chinese Theater, right on Hollywood and Vine in Beverly Hills. Our cabbie dropped us off in front, and we chuckled as people took *our* picture.

Directly in front of the theatre lay the famous forecourt. Honestly, upon our first visit, we had no clue what that was. Later that night, we would discover that celebrities from the 1920s to the present day were invited to leave "imprints" of fame—their footprints and handprints. Distractedly, Leesa and I made our way across it and onto the red carpet to the exquisitely designed theatre.

The night moved fast, as LA does. After the applause, everyone rose excitedly. Like a herd of cattle, the crowd stepped out of the theatre as one, milling back onto the forecourt. Some of the bigger celebrities were whisked away, but in the midst of the rest of the crowd, Leesa and I made headway with baby steps. We just grinned and took our time. When the crowd finally pushed past us, we paused and gazed up into the beautiful night sky, holding each other tightly. The moment felt magical and perfect.

"Gosh, pinch us!" Leesa giggled.

"Yeah . . . look at us, the realtor from Utah and the sculptor from Podunk, Idaho. We're right here," I said, and I wrapped my arms around her more tightly as I kept my gaze up to admire her face against the sky. "Whether the stars around us or the stars in the sky, we all need each other."

Leesa nodded, her large brown eyes filled with affection and deep understanding. As Frankl taught, life has the meaning you give it.

Finally, and reluctantly, I released my tall, beautiful queen—stunning to me as always in her classic high heels—from my embrace. Glancing down to watch her step on the uneven cement, Leesa gasped.

"Gary, look!" she cried. "You will not believe this. We are standing directly on Will's handprints . . . and his footprints!"

"No way!" I was incredulous. I thought she was teasing me.

I peered down for a closer look, reading the words Will Smith had written in the concrete years prior: "Change the World," it said. I clutched my wife's hand, and we stared at one another, then back down at the ground at our feet.

Magic often seemed to happen when Leesa and I were together, but we weren't sure in this moment if it was our magic or Will's. Maybe it was both.

Our faces shone. "Okay, we get it!" We laughed, honoring the Great Spirit and caught up in the bliss and meaning of the moment.

The whirlwind of the last few years reminded us that miracles would continue to happen when expansive, open-minded, and deep-hearted individuals came together for a higher cause. Just as Dr. Nancy O'Reilly, Woody Woodward, the Smiths, and other leaders realized, the Statue of Responsibility was a project the nation needed because it symbolized lifting together instead of tearing apart. Despite the country seemingly so divided, we kept moving forward, even when the project stuttered from time to time.

Even though the Statue of Responsibility was not yet towering 305 feet tall over the West Coast, there was an orchestra at the ready! Instruments might start and stop, but everyone played a piece, and together it made for something truly glorious.

Not long after, Leesa and I visited Liberty Island in New York, where we stood at the foot of the Statue of Liberty, officially known as *Liberty Enlightening the World*. Together, we had been reading aloud a book called *Liberty's Torch*, in which the sculptor's life came back into full view for me. As we gazed up into Liberty's magnificent face, it was refreshing to be reminded that it had taken Bartholdi two decades from his inspired dinner meeting to the dedication of the monument.

Standing under Liberty's feet in all her magnificent glory, Leesa peered up and said, "Gary, our statue project started in God's hands. It will continue in God's hands—and He keeps bringing extraordinary people together." I grinned at her. We'd just received word from Steve Cohen, the news executive in San Diego. He had been a silent supporter for eight years, but he informed us that day that he was willing to do whatever it took to make the Statue of Responsibility a reality; he believed in it that much! *Thank you, God.*

Despite our dogged persistence to believe in humanity, it seemed that every time we turned around, our world was facing harsh and horrible challenges. Like so many others, I often felt buffeted about by the winds of hateful social media and press.

"Today, if we have no peace," said Mother Teresa, "it is because we have forgotten that we belong to each other."

I tucked away a thread of hope that our symbol could inspire people to remember and awaken to the reality that we truly belonged to each other. I knew symbols had the power to inspire to that degree.

Sculptures and certainly monuments were never something secured on a whim. Most pieces tended to be an emotional, even a spiritual, acquisition. I remembered one of my first collectors was a young couple from Lake Tahoe who purchased a pair of bronze ducks called *Partners*. It was their very first fine-art piece as they started their lives and collection together. For me, that was a great honor.

I was sad to learn that Chuck had recently passed from cancer. Jeanie called my current manager, Isaiah, to see if we had any eagles—two eagles together, to be exact. "Chuck and I felt *Partners* symbolized us in the beginning, loyal and adventurous," she explained, "but over a lifetime together of love and leadership, we evolved into majestic eagles. I want a symbol of that."

Since I had only one eagle entitled *Soaring*, I decided to create a custom sculpture symbolizing the shared love and leadership of Chuck and Jeanie. The new design showcased two eagles soaring in a never-ending circle. Almost speechless, Jeanie ordered a large bronze for the cemetery and then proceeded to order more to share their precious legacy with their children—flying high despite their own divine turbulence.

This was the power of a lasting symbol, and Jeanie knew it. She had lived it. Now it would mark their shared remembrance where Chuck currently rested, and Jeanie was passing on their inspiration.

I poured my dear friend's heartfelt tenderness into my sculpting for weeks, thinking about the thousands of pieces of fine art I had designed, hoping to lift and inspire for centuries. Beyond my career, I too had married my soul mate; we'd created miracles together with our children and worked with extraordinary people from around the world. Freedom was my life's first, greatest dream. The second was to continue to lift the human spirit, and clients like Jeanie reminded me daily of my purpose.

And then a forward-moving energy hit us like a tidal wave, and BAM, Leesa and I felt compelled to move to Arizona. Within a matter of days, we found the perfect place, complete with detached studio and landscape designed to inspire. Easy enough to travel to our foundry and family in Utah to the north, Arizona was only a four-hour drive to San Diego, where we hoped to build the Statue of Responsibility to honor Elly and Viktor's dream.

Our move opened the floodgates to meeting more dynamic leaders. Like us, these folks were seeing tragedies, struggles and challenges within our society. Unparalleled divisions had erupted, the extent of which had not been seen since before the Civil War. Concerned individuals like Leesa and I felt strongly that SOR represented a higher ideal of personal accountability and responsibility at a time when our country desperately needed it.

And so I continued to sculpt through the second most divisive election in my years as an adult and through an isolating, global pandemic as well as horrific events that turned deadly in the streets and soul of our great nation. The whole time, I held the dream in my heart.

One morning, in the thick of the world's chaos, I chose the quiet meditation of my studio. With the world raging outside, I contemplated my book as my stained hands worked the clay. Was it time?

From age six to twelve, I was expected to grovel. Still, I knew there was heaven because I had lived it. I knew there was such a thing as great heights because my mother showed me through an elevated love a way of being that included color and form as well as rich laughter and deep joy. The span of her earthy influence may have been brief, but it was poignantly sweet. She had endowed me with a gift.

I pondered a truth Viktor Frankl had spoken when he said that love is the ultimate and the highest goal to which anyone can aspire. "The salvation of man is through love and in love."

My fingers squeezed the clay in my hands as I thought of my mom, my dad, Leesa, and every person who had ever touched me and affected my life for good with their love. More kept coming. Over and over, scenes flashed before me, filled with such power that I could literally see the ripples in my life. I gasped, then whispered, "Responsibility is an act of creative genius, an act of great love. Possibly it is one of the greatest acts any human can ever choose to do."

From my own often painful and liberating experiences, I knew that as humans, we could not hold on to hate when we aspired to loftier ideals and focused on ways to contribute to something greater than ourselves. It really was time.

In that moment, too, I knew that I wanted to extend a challenge and an invitation to you—but not just any invitation:

First, I invite you to see that the winds that have buffeted you have likely made your muscles, your resolve, and your intentions stronger. I challenge you to look past the betrayal, hurt, and pain to see where these winds have sculpted the gifts inside you.

Second, I will be frank with you. There has never been a time when Liberty needed Responsibility as much as she needs it NOW.

As our planet reels and sputters from a dramatic timeline of chaotic events, may we all take a closer look at our freedoms. May *this* be the window in time that creates the view to a more responsible world—a world where blame has no place. A world where we each take responsibility for our own lives and our own happiness. A world where the message that we are all connected is more powerful than the messages of division that have created this intense pain and suffering. A world where the violations inflicted on Mother Earth are recognized and her life-sustaining gifts appreciated before it is too late. May this be a new beginning for each of us who calls this great planet home.

May Responsibility stand side by side with Liberty as a fellow lighthouse for generations to come. May we have the courage to move into a new reality, one in which we care for ourselves and each other more, where we slow our thoughts enough to think of the heavy consequences we are paying emotionally, spiritually, mentally, financially, and physically. For if left unattended to, these will be the steep price the blood of our next generations will have to pay.

This I know: we can do something, and we can do it now.

If you feel called, I invite you to be a part of the mission of the Statue of Responsibility, envisioning a world where this powerful movement goes "hand in hand" with our rebirth as a planet and people. We know it's a lofty goal, but you are the individual that makes a difference. Join forces with us so that we are the generation who builds a Statue of Responsibility in America to bookend our beautiful Statue of Liberty when America needs it most. In doing so, may we set an example to the world of what coming together for a greater good looks like.

What does this invitation mean? We're giving this to you.

This is no longer "Our Statue."

It is now "Your Statue."

We strongly and sincerely invite you to be part of the solution the entire world desperately needs. Join us. Bring your energy and your passion, your neighborhoods and your volunteer projects, your ideas to educate school children and others to heal the broken and downtrodden. This is not just a monument; it is a movement. Bring us your brilliant concepts of growth and collaboration, that our children and children's children will come to recognize this historic, defining moment in time.

Let us take hands in joy.

Gary Lee Price StatueOfResponsibility.org

Remember, they rise highest who lift as they go.

Acknowledgements

I believe in Angels, both seen and unseen! The longer I live, the more I realize that we are not alone and that we are all intrinsically, beautifully connected. This "Divine Orchestration" of all of our lives results in masterful creations. Although I cannot begin to name all the earthly and heavenly Angels who have shown up in my life (or we would have three more volumes) that consequently resulted in this book, you know who you are. I could not have even possibly imagined doing it alone! I'm eternally indebted and massively grateful to each and every one of you.

With that said, I must at minimum recognize a few who without them we would not be here, reading this book. First and foremost, I wish to acknowledge and thank my best friend, confidant, and sweetheart Leesa for her big brain and even bigger heart! She supports me in all my crazy endeavors in countless ways not to mention countless hours. To Bridget Cook Burch, thank you for being such a gentle soul who has delicately handled my heart and my ego with such beautiful balance. You have taken the darkest part of my life and with Hannah Lyon, given it light. Beautiful light! Thank you Rebecca Hall Gruyter (and all of your teams) for your gifts of pure talent, hard work, peacefulness and especially laughter and giggles (that's you, Rebecca). What a journey!

And finally, I thank all our family and dear friends whose inspiration and continuous encouragement and support I've grown to count on and depend on.

LIFE IS BEAUTIFUL. YOU ARE BEAUTIFUL and DIVINE.

I LOVE YOU - I LOVE YOU - I LOVE YOU. THANK YOU!

About the Author

Ralph Waldo Emerson said, "The spirit of man is what makes him unique above all of God's creations." Gary Lee Price bronzes come as close to capturing this spirit as is humanly possible: sculpture with meaning, sculpture to inspire and lift the human spirit.

Gary began his art career young, selling paintings in his region of Idaho as early as high school. Continuing his studies at the University of Utah, he earned his Bachelor of Fine Arts in 1981 while working for renowned sculptor Stan Johnson, who introduced him to clay. Gary discovered he had a gift to take the visions in his mind and create them three-dimensionally. Later, he would be inspired by his children to create permanent, touchable art for children, benefiting entire communities.

Gary's ability to create symbols of great power and meaning merited him growing acclaim in galleries and corporate offices, gardens and arboretums, museums and cemeteries. One of the largest libraries in the world, the Hong Kong Central Library, standing a proud twelve stories high and boasting three hundred thousand square feet, features twelve of Gary Lee Price's life-size bronze sculptures. This impressive display includes bronzes of young readers and happy children releasing doves, playing with shells in water, and soaring through the air as if weightless. Additionally, two twenty-two-inch-round frogs, *Puffed Up Princes*, stand sentinel at the entrance of the children's section of the library.

Gary's eleven-foot *Celebration!* featuring joyous children soaring around a globe celebrating life was first unveiled in Surrey, England, at the American Community Schools with the most recent being dedicated in Decatur, Georgia, by former First Lady Rosalyn Carter. A twenty-two-foot version of the same sculpture is located at the entrance of the ten-story corporate headquarters of NuSkin International in Provo, Utah.

Literally thousands of Gary Lee Price sculptures are showcased in public and private collections throughout the world. His twelve-foot angel *Messenger* monument in Iceland honors four hundred early immigrants to the United States. Gary completed the sculpture *Communion* as a fifteen-foot-high monument of grasping hands for the United Methodist Church of Brentwood, Tennessee. The handclasp has been an important aspect of his work, as reflected in such pieces as *Synergy, Helping Hand, The Ascent,* and *Circle of Peace.* Uplifting others, helping others, and joining hands in brotherhood and sisterhood are essential parts of both Gary's life and work.

Gary was commissioned to create the 305-foot Statue of Responsibility—Viktor Frankl's vision from his book, "Man's Search for Meaning" and meant to be the bookend to the Statue of Liberty; only this one is to be built on the West Coast. This monument and movement are currently underway, and the organization is in the process of procuring land.

"My passion for art and belief that art empowers and lifts the human spirit have only grown stronger throughout my life. I have been blessed with many generous and selfless mentors, and my dream is to pass those gifts on to others."

Gary is a perpetual student who finds travel and research an important part of his life. He spent two years in Germany, six months in Israel, one month in Egypt, one month touring the jungles and ruins of Mexico and Guatemala, and has explored art in eleven European countries.

In 1991, Gary was elected a member of the National Sculpture Society and was recently elected by his peers as a Fellow of this prestigious organization, earning FNSS designation. He loves to teach workshops to individuals, groups, and corporations on the aspects of creation and manifestation and is an acclaimed international keynote and workshop speaker.

Additional works of Gary Lee Price can be found in public and private collections throughout the world, just a few of which include the Culver Military Academy, Culver, Indiana; American Community Schools, Surrey, England; Westside Preparatory School, Chicago, Illinois; Helen DeVos

Children's Hospital, Grand Rapids, Michigan; the Dallas Arboretum in Texas; Birmingham Botanical Gardens, Alabama; Children's Scottish Rite Hospital, Dallas, Texas; the Gladney Center for Adoption, Fort Worth, Texas; the Galería Paseos Mall, Puerto Rico; Blue Grass Airport, Lexington, Kentucky; Neverland Ranch, Los Olivos, California; the Indianapolis Children's Museum in Indiana; The Church of Jesus Christ of Latter-day Saints Conference Center, Salt Lake City, Utah; the Museum of Church History and Art, Salt Lake County permanent art collection, Salt Lake City, Utah; and the Springville Museum of Art, Springville, Utah.

Pieces have been commissioned and donated to remarkable facilities around the world, including air-and-space museums. The sculptures of Gary Lee Price are displayed with a select group of fifteen galleries throughout the United States.

When Gary began his research for a sculpture featuring Amelia Earhart, he was shocked to discover that fewer than two hundred statues, or less than 4 percent of 5,575 outdoor sculpture portraits nationwide, portrayed historical female figures! He decided to accelerate change. He finished *Amelia* and went on to sculpt *Mother Teresa, Joan* (d'Arc), and *Harriet* (Tubman).

"I hope I can assist the world in visualizing a place where fences and boundaries, both real and imagined, are nonexistent," says Gary, "a place where bias and prejudice are long forgotten. And finally, a place where acts of kindness, mutual respect, and love are everyday happenings."

Gary resides in Buckeye, Arizona, with his beautiful wife, Leesa Clark Price. Together they are the proud parents of nine remarkable children and sixteen very energetic grandchildren.

View Gary's work at www.GaryLeePrice.com. Also visit www.Statueof Responsibility.com.

Bridget Cook-Burch is a *New York Times* and *Wall Street Journal* best-selling author, best known for her riveting tales of transformation. She firmly believes in the power of story to change the world.

Her unique books have been showcased on *Oprah, Dateline, CNN, Good Morning America, 20/20, Dr. Phil, The History Channel, NPR,* and in *People Magazine,* among many others.

Bridget's national and international best-sellers include:

The Witness Wore Red: The 19th Wife Who Brought Polygamous Cult Leaders to Justice with Rebecca Musser

Shattered Silence: The Untold Story of a Serial Killer's Daughter with Melissa Moore

Skinhead Confessions: From Hate to Hope with TJ Leyden

Leading Women: 20 Influential Women Share Their Secrets to Leadership, Business, and Life with Dr. Nancy O'Reilly

Living Proof: Celebrating the Gifts That Came Wrapped in Sandpaper with Lisa Nichols from "The Secret"

CEO and founder of Your Inspired Story, Bridget mentors emerging authors and leaders to write deep legacy books that create movements. She hosts intimate Inspired Writers Retreats in breathtaking natural settings in Utah and Ireland, and leadership retreats in Italy. She teaches online courses, is renowned for her keynote speeches, and still manages to write . . . some days.

As a passionate leader, storyteller, trainer, and humanitarian, Bridget has been a strong advocate on initiatives to end violence against women, abolish human trafficking, and honor the veterans and first-responders who serve our nation every day. She cofounded Sheroes United, a non-profit organization, serving as executive director for several years. Author of the acclaimed *Inside-Out Leadership Training,* Bridget and her teams have served women refugees from Congo, in the Utah State prison system, and victims of human trafficking wherever they are found.

When Bridget was very young, she read the *Diary of Anne Frank, Uncle Tom's Cabin,* and *To Kill a Mockingbird.* She dreamed of quietly making a difference in the world and being a writer in the mountains with her beloved husband, amazing children, rambunctious grandchildren, and "puppy-bear" Saki.

Well, five out of six ain't bad.

Visit www.YourInspiredStory.com, and www.InspiredWritersRetreat.com. Also visit www.SheroesUnited.org.

Reviews

"The captivating account of an extraordinary life full of darkness, light and love. Gary's book is a reminder that no matter the circumstances, we can always choose how we respond. As Viktor Frankl said, 'Every deed is its own monument.'"

–**Alexander Vesely**, MA, grandson of Viktor Frankl, Producer, Award-winning Documentary Director, Head of the Viktor Frankl Media Archives in Vienna, Co-founder of the Viktor Frankl Institute of America

"This is a story that must be told. It will bring tears of joy and hope to all that read this book. Gary is a world-class sculptor and artist who has made this journey for the good of us all. *Divine Turbulence* represents the passion and purpose we need in this world."

–**Dr. Nancy O'Reilly**, Psy D., Founder and CEO of Women Connect4Good

"Gary lays himself out vulnerably, in a life that transforms pain into promise, and heartache into heartfelt inspiration. You will find his life and career so extraordinarily meaningful, it will touch your life in ways beyond your imagination–as one who comes out victorious and as an advocate for all the bounty life holds."

–**Jay Abraham**, Founder & CEO of The Abraham Group, Inc, Marketing & Revenue Strategist, Business Innovator

"I became completely mesmerized by Gary's honest and revealing story that brought him to the final realization that any price paid is worth a gift to the world. This book bridges the chasm between the East Coast and the West Coast, bringing life to the dream of a man destined to breathe character into the very thinking of mankind. Viktor Frankl had the dream, Gary Lee Price had the answer. Their two visions are brought together by an earnest desire to achieve a moment of clarity for people of all ages, faiths, races and nationalities."

–**Gerald R. Molen**, Film Producer, Academy Award Winner/Best Picture for *Schindler's List*

"Despite horrific events in his early life, Gary Lee grew up to create magnificent and inspiring works of art. His beautifully told story will leave you speechless, teary-eyed, and in awe of how his spirit could not be broken. I highly recommend this well-written memoir, which is worthy of the big screen."

–**Dr. Connie Mariano**, Rear Admiral, Former White House Doctor, Author, Radio Showhost, Concierge Physician

"What perfect timing for this book! It will inspire, uplift and give hope for humanity in dark times. It illustrates the liberating power of responsibility and choice even when confronted with the worst that life has to offer. Gary's personal story of beating impossible odds–to eventually lead a movement on par in significance with the Statue of Liberty–will move you to play bigger in life."

–**Brett Harward**, Author, The 5 Laws That Determine All of Life's Outcomes, Speaker, Trainer

"*Divine Turbulence* is a deeply cleaved testimony of the grace and evolution of the human spirit–a journey as innovative and precise in its artistic splendor and intimacy as his stunning art pieces. This memoir carries its reader through the crucifixion of innocence to the soul's ascension; from extraordinary childhood violence, trauma, and abuse, to the medicine of divine human compassion, hope, forgiveness and the call to social justice."

–**Piper Dellums**, Director, Filmmaker, Writer and Victims Advocate

"I was spellbound by this book and at times, could not put it down, nor forget its impact on my heart, nor get it out of my mind for hours. This is not a story you read very often, as its messages and inspiration transform you with every page you turn . . . and live."

–**Jack Berkman**, CEO and President of Berkman Strategic Communications

"Through reading such travails as Viktor and Gary experienced in their lives, our own personal searches for meaning are propelled into the realm of action—and in my case—a commitment to see the Statue of Responsibility become a reality."

–**Ted Field**, American Media Mogul, Entrepreneur, Film Producer

"More than an autobiography. Master Sculptor Gary Lee Price maps—or more accurately "sculpts"—a path to meaning in Divine Turbulence that can inspire and guide readers to answer life's call no matter what their personal circumstances."

–**Alex Pattakos**, Ph.D., coauthor, *Prisoners of Our Thoughts: Viktor Frankl's Principles for Discovering Meaning in Life and Work (3rd edition)*; cofounder, Global Meaning Institute

240d2f84-1d1b-4430-a42e-85bb7c01dc78R01